SPIES, PATRIOTS, AND TRAITORS

SPIES, PATRIOTS, AND TRAITORS

American Intelligence in the Revolutionary War

KENNETH A. DAIGLER

GEORGETOWN UNIVERSITY PRESS

WASHINGTON, DC

Library of Congress Cataloging-in-Publication Data

Daigler, Kenneth A.

Spies, patriots, and traitors : American intelligence in the Revolutionary War / Kenneth A. Daigler.

pages cm

Includes bioliographical references and index.

ISBN 978-1-62616-050-7 (hardcover : alk. paper)

1. United States—History—Revolution, 1775–1783—Secret service. 2. United States—History—Revolution, 1775–1783—Military intelligence. 3. Military intelligence—United States—History—18th century. 4. Espionage—United States—History—18th century. 5. Spies—United States—History—18th century. I. Title.

E279.D35 2014

973.3'85—dc23

2013026131

15 14   9 8 7 6 5 4 3 2   First printing

Printed in the United States of America

To Zach and Quinn,

in the hope that you will read history and learn from it.

THESIS

major ideas

focus: · command-and-control
· tactical organization
· logistics

culper ring
↳ Benjamin Tallmadge
- organized by washington
Aim: relay info re: British
intelligence in New
York City
ⓐ 1778-1783

CONTENTS

ILLUSTRATIONS

ACKNOWLEDGMENTS

Completion of a study this broad would have been impossible without the assistance of researchers and librarians at numerous facilities across the country. I was constantly amazed at the interest and initiative taken by these people, including at local historical societies where volunteers handled my research inquiries. Noting all these facilities and organizations would involve several additional pages, so I shall name only a few of the most heavily involved as representational of the rest: the National Archives, the Library of Congress, the Massachusetts Historical Society, the New York Historical Society, the Rhode Island Historical Society, the Central Intelligence Agency's Historical Collection, the Fred W. Smith National Library for the Study of George Washington at Mount Vernon, the Boston Public Library, the Minuteman Library Network (especially the libraries in Needham and Wellesley, Massachusetts), the District of Columbia Public Library, the Minute Man National Historic Park, and the National Park Service.

There were also several friends who assisted by reviewing the text and providing suggestions to improve its content and flow: Margaret Martin, Carol Herwig, and Bob Lavery. Two others, both authors themselves, provided support by their encouragement and knowledge of manuscript creation: retired US ambassador Edward Marks and Bob Stephan. Special thanks for encouragement and support is also due Donald Jacobs at Georgetown University Press. Finally, my wife Gerry, who had a strong belief in the value of the book from its inception, deserves special thanks for surviving my occasional emotional outbursts, usually early in the morning when I did much of my writing.

Of course, regardless of the assistance and support of those mentioned above, the content of this book is my responsibility alone.

PREFACE

W hile I was a senior case officer in the Clandestine Service of the Central Intelligence Agency (CIA), one of my managerial responsibilities during a headquarters assignment was to create a suite of conference rooms for use with foreign intelligence liaison visitors to the headquarters complex. In assessing the requirements for this effort, I learned that many foreign intelligence services, especially those having been in existence for centuries in one form or another, often looked upon the agency as being new to the game. While they recognized our skills in the use of cutting-edge technology and respected our other resources, there seemed to be doubts about our experience level and practical understanding of how intelligence activities were conducted.

Having a graduate degree in history, I was aware that as a country, the United States does have more than two hundred years of intelligence experience, including activities during the era of the American Revolution at home and abroad, with successes in all three of the traditional intelligence disciplines: foreign intelligence collection, counterintelligence, and covert action. I decided to name each of the three separate conference rooms after a Revolutionary War figure who had demonstrated success in one of those disciplines. To educate foreign liaison personnel regarding our history in intelligence, I also authored a pamphlet explaining the reasons for the rooms' names and providing a brief description of each of the three individuals' intelligence activities. George Washington represented foreign intelligence collection, John Jay represented counterintelligence, and Benjamin Franklin represented covert action.

Copies of this pamphlet, *The Founding Fathers of American Intelligence*, were provided to our foreign liaison visitors, and the positive impression it conveyed caused the agency to make the pamphlet available to the public on its website. This was in 1999, and it has remained a popular download publication ever since. Its content, though quite general compared to the information in this book, has also been used as source material by authors and educators.

This book expands the objective of that pamphlet to educate the general public on the role intelligence activities played in the American Revolution. Covering the period from 1765 to 1783—from the organization of the Sons of Liberty to the British withdrawal from New York City—it discusses how intelligence techniques, operations, and individuals contributed to the cause of American independence.

Much of the book describes intelligence-collection activities against the British by various American agents during the war. Individual chapters describe intelligence efforts in British-occupied Boston, Philadelphia, and New York, and in areas of Pennsylvania and New Jersey. Particular attention is given to the Culper Ring, the best-documented American intelligence network of the war, which operated in and about New York City. However, the book also provides details of George Washington's background in intelligence, which started prior to the French and Indian War and gave him the mindset and experience to organize and direct intelligence activities while commander of the Continental Army. Also, in an area of the Revolutionary War not well covered previously from the intelligence perspective, Gen. Nathanael Greene's intelligence activities, especially as commander of the Southern Army, are discussed and analyzed.

Counterintelligence operations, both running and detecting enemy spies, are covered in several chapters, including separate ones devoted to in-depth analysis of the tradecraft, or lack thereof, of the two most famous Revolutionary War spies: Nathan Hale and Benedict Arnold. Another chapter deals with John Jay's efforts, at least for a few months, to develop a responsible counterintelligence program above New York City in the Hudson Valley. American counterintelligence failures are noted, with a chapter on how the British successfully penetrated the inner circles of the American Commission in Paris, the country's first diplomatic mission abroad.

Covert action of all types, including paramilitary, political action, and propaganda, is described as conducted in the American colonies and overseas. In this vein the Sons of Liberty's activities are reviewed from the perspective of the political-action role the organization played, under the direction of its radical leaders, in moving colonial public opinion from financial independence to political independence from Britain. Various propaganda efforts are highlighted, and paramilitary actions conducted at American direction in Europe and elsewhere are described, including John Paul Jones's attack on seaports in England and Scotland.

I have also included a chapter on the role that African Americans played in Revolution-era American intelligence activities. Documentation on their role is not plentiful, and local folklore has created some longstanding myths that cannot be verified. However, many African Americans undertook dangerous missions and played useful roles, and they deserve more recognition for their efforts. I have concluded the book with a few brief thoughts on the significance of intelligence in the Revolution, Washington's role as the senior intelligence officer, and how intelligence activities of the period may have some applicable lessons for today. I have attempted to make this book a comprehensive overview of American intelligence activities in America and abroad in support of independence—a "one-stop source" for significant American intelligence activities during the period.

In many areas of Revolutionary War intelligence history, excellent research has been conducted and published. Noted scholars such as Morton Pennypacker, John Bakeless, and Carl Van Doren have comprehensively analyzed papers from American and British participants to identify "sources and methods" on such topics as the Culper Ring, the plotting between Benedict Arnold and British major John André, and American intelligence agents' activities in the New York, New Jersey, and Philadelphia areas. The noted diplomatic historian Samuel Flagg Bemis researched and published material on the activities of the British intelligence establishment against the American Commission in Paris. Consequently, in some areas I have traveled a research road well worn. In those areas where previously scholars have published research from primary sources that produced facts and context matching my own work, I have sourced this material to them rather than to the primary sources that they have cited in their publications. In those cases where I have concluded a different context or found other information useful, I have cited the primary source.

In addition to the usual archives, papers, and documents related to this subject, I have also benefited from my previous access to material in the CIA's Historic Intelligence Collection and copies of notes and research from the collection's original director. This collection contains books, articles, and copies of primary documents and correspondence focused on intelligence activities during the era of the Revolution. And local historical societies, some with rather disorganized collections but very enthusiastic researchers, have provided additional information on lesser-known figures involved in intelligence activities.

Every profession has its unique vocabulary, and I have had to remind my computer's dictionary of this on a vast number of occasions during the writing of this book. These tradecraft terms do not always have the same exact meaning within the US intelligence community, with the civilian and military services often having significant different definitions. But I am a creature of my background and experience and use these terms as I was taught them within the CIA. However, other intelligence professionals may find my usage different from their own.

While the basic elements of clandestine tradecraft have been known since biblical times, the words used to describe them have changed as these techniques were modified to fit more modern environments. For this reason I have included a brief glossary of the common tradecraft terms used in the book, as I believe they were applied during the era of the Revolution. In eighteenth-century intelligence activities, the general meaning of the tradecraft techniques would have been the same, but the terminology identifying them was sometimes different. For example, in the eighteenth century the word "intelligence" had a much broader meaning and referred to any new information or news received, whereas today, the word usually refers to information of value regarding an adversary, often obtained in a nonpublic manner.

In the twenty-first century the public tends to think of intelligence collection, and increasingly semicovert paramilitary actions, by their technical means: drones, internet monitoring, website manipulation, and satellite collection of worldwide communications. In fact, clandestine human collection represents an extremely small percentage of total intelligence information gathering. But as a HUMINT (human intelligence) case officer during the last phase of the Cold War, I can attest from personal experience that the reporting of an agent with access to a country's national-level plans and intentions can represent the best intelligence available. This type of reporting can tell you what the country's leaders intend to do and how they plan to do it before it happens. It gives policymakers the opportunity to take actions to stop a course of action, as opposed to reacting to that action.

In the eighteenth century, HUMINT was the major source of intelligence, from agents with access to either senior government officials or to the documents describing the plans and intentions of the government. While the structure and organization of British intelligence during the Revolutionary period was less sophisticated than now and much more decentralized in its collection efforts, it was effective and productive in France and the colonies. Intelligence collection and analysis responsibilities were divided among several government elements: offices within the Foreign Ministry, offices within the Admiralty, individuals within British Army commands, individuals in British diplomatic installations, and even an office in the British postal service.

In the ranks of the Foreign Ministry and the military establishment, some individuals with the appropriate skills and interest spent much of their careers involved in the collection and analysis of intelligence. While little formal training was offered, mentoring by others involved and experience gained from hands-on activities did produce individuals readily capable of recruiting foreign agents, observing and reporting on political, economic, and military issues in a foreign country, and similar activities now conducted by professional intelligence officers. In British diplomatic missions of the period, there existed no separation of diplomats and intelligence officers; those diplomats with the required talents handled clandestine activities along with their more traditional diplomatic responsibilities. In Paris, Lord Stormont, the British minister, was the senior government representative to the French court for intergovernmental relations. He also directed the recruitment of British agents against that government, directed networks of agents monitoring activities at French ports, and interjected several agents into the Paris Commission. He reported back to William Eden, later called Lord Auckland, who was an undersecretary of state in the Northern Department of the Foreign Ministry and had intelligence responsibilities for France.

The Admiralty was responsible for collection of intelligence on naval issues, and actual collection responsibilities fell to the senior officers of the various fleets. A similar chain of collection responsibility existed in the various British military commands. The commanding general had staff officers responsible for directing recruitment of agents and coordinating their reporting for the general's use. Maj. John André served in this role for Gen. Henry Clinton until his capture. The performance and achievements of these army and navy officers varied, based upon their personal capabilities and actual hands-on intelligence experience. However, specifically in France, there existed numerous agent networks in place from before and during the Seven Years' War (called the French and Indian War in the colonies) that had well-established capabilities and tradecraft procedures.

Finally, the British government had developed, over centuries of political and military rivalries with other nations, excellent capabilities within its customs and postal facilities to monitor and covertly open and copy correspondence, both private and official, as it entered or left the country. This capability, along with research on encoding and secret writing techniques, provided details on foreign intelligence activities in Britain, as well as identified individuals reporting on British issues.

Thus, while their intelligence organization was not comparable to modern ones, the British did have a functioning, if not well coordinated and trained, intelligence capability in place as war in the colonies broke out.

CHAPTER 1

George Washington Learns the Intelligence Trade

To identify George Washington as the founding father of American intelligence collection was an easy task.[1] There can be no question that he functioned as the senior intelligence officer for the Continental Army, as well as being its prime intelligence consumer. With both these responsibilities, he was able to direct his collection efforts on what he wanted and needed to know, rather than what could readily be collected. This focus enabled him to direct the collection of strategic intelligence, while also receiving and using tactical intelligence obtained from his subordinate commanders. In addition, his personal management style fit well into these responsibilities. As one biographer described him, Washington "worked with almost superhuman stamina, organizational ability, and regard for detail. He was a micromanager in the best sense of the word."[2] Equally important was that Washington had previous experience, both good and bad, in military intelligence collection and, as was his character, he had learned from his experiences.

Washington's introduction to intelligence collection came from his experiences during the period of the French and Indian War. Many of these experiences provided valuable lessons based upon intelligence failures, while others demonstrated that Washington possessed a mind and nature oriented toward the intelligence discipline. By July 3, 1775, when he assumed command of the army surrounding Boston, Washington possessed at least a basic knowledge of how to integrate intelligence activities into military planning. However, his

immediate priority was to create some structure and discipline among ragtag
colonial militia units that composed the army of observation around Boston
and to turn them into the Continental Army. His priority had to be in the areas
of command-and-control, logistics, and tactical organization. That said, he did
instigate some basic collection activities and moved to create communication
channels for intelligence information collected by subordinate commanders
to reach his headquarters. But a more focused and disciplined approach to
his intelligence activities would have to wait until he got his army somewhat
organized.

Washington's first exposure to intelligence collection came in 1753 when
the royal governor of Virginia, Robert Dinwiddie, dispatched him to the
Ohio Territory to deliver a letter to the French commander there and return
with a response. Washington was at this time a major in the Virginia militia. Dinwiddie, as well as the royal governors of Pennsylvania, New York,
and South Carolina, was concerned, with good reason, that the French were
encroaching on British territory. The Ohio Territory—generally the Ohio
River Valley area and populated mostly by Indians—was seen by both the
British and the French as the next area for economic exploitation within
North America. Dinwiddie wanted to build a series of forts to protect this
British frontier, but he was unable to obtain adequate funds from the colonial
legislature, the House of Burgesses. Finally, he took his concerns directly to
King George II, and the king supported his views. In addition to his official
concerns regarding French expansion into what he considered English terri-
tory, Dinwiddie was also a stockholder in the Ohio Company of Virginia.
The British government had granted this land company about 350,000 acres
on the Ohio River for sale to new settlers.

To what degree his personal interests affected his aggressiveness in desiring
to secure the territory remains speculative. In those days as today, the public
and private interests of government officials seem to have a way of interrelating
in a personally beneficial manner. However, in the greater geopolitical, worldwide rivalry between England and France, protecting English interests in the
territory was a major concern for the British government.[3]

Dinwiddie was directed to obtain funding from the colonial legislature,
purchase armaments, and build the forts. King George noted that as he had
reports that "a number of Europeans not our subjects are appearing in a hostile
manner in the area, you are instructed to inquire into the truth of the report.
If you shall find that any number of persons shall presume to erect any fort
or forts within the limits of our Province of Virginia, you are first to require

[margin annotation: desired by both sides]

of them peaceably to depart."[4] In reality, it is highly doubtful that the British government had any accurate concept of what portions of the Ohio Valley were within the domain of the colony of Virginia. However, Governor Dinwiddie's views on the issue would become, de facto, the British position.[5] With royal support Dinwiddie began publicizing the French threat in the Ohio Territory, and the House of Burgesses endorsed his concerns. Subsequently, the governor selected Washington to carry the formal letter of complaint to the French commander in the territory.

Washington received the governor's letter on October 31, 1753. It was a polite and diplomatic note, stating that the Ohio Territory was well known to be the property of Great Britain and making a formal complaint regarding French efforts to build military fortifications there. He requested justifications for the French actions, if there were any, and under whose authority these actions had been taken. Dinwiddie concluded the letter by asking for a peaceful French departure from the area and that Major Washington be treated in a polite and candid manner.[6] Washington was also tasked to observe and report on French military forces and facilities in the Ohio, as well as attempt to ascertain France's plans and intentions there.[7] It was a dangerous mission because the French had already taken British subjects as prisoners, and the local Indians represented an equally dangerous adversary in the territory, if not more so.

Washington was always disciplined about record keeping, and his journal of the mission was published in Williamsburg in 1754.[8] He obtained his first intelligence on the French on November 25, 1753, by debriefing four French deserters who had traveled with about a hundred others from New Orleans to join with French forces from along Lake Erie. They said the French had constructed four small forts along the Mississippi River. He also learned from a local Indian chief that the French had a fort on Lake Erie and another on French Creek, connected by a road. He obtained drawings of both forts.[9] Three days later, another chief told him the French were planning for war against England and intended to move more soldiers down the rivers into the Ohio Territory in the spring.[10]

On December 4, Washington reached an old Indian town called Venango, at the entrance of French Creek into the Allegheny River. There he saw a house with a French flag flying and met three French officers, one of whom, Captain Joncaire, claimed to be the French commander of the Ohio. However, Joncaire said that there was a French general officer nearby to whom Washington could present his letter. As was the custom among European military officers,

Washington was invited to dine with the French officers. In his description of the meal, Washington makes it clear that the wine flowed freely and the French officers spoke openly about French intentions in the Ohio.[11] This is the first specific mention made by Washington of his elicitation skills and, perhaps more important, his personal discipline in the face of heavy drinking and an atmosphere of friendly conversation.

Elicitation is an important intelligence skill that is often aided by food and drink. It must also involve what appears to be a natural and mutual exchange of conversation. The challenge for the intelligence officer is to keep the conversation flowing without providing too much information, while using various techniques to steer it toward topics of collection interest. Being able to hold one's alcohol in these situations is paramount, as the secret to a successful elicitation is to stimulate the conversation in the direction desired without actually saying all that much. More than a few intelligence officers have ended up giving their adversaries more information than they obtained because of a lack of personal and professional discipline. Practicing successful elicitation was a skill that Washington understood and used effectively.

The technique Washington exhibited in this elicitation was not based upon specific intelligence training. Rather, not unlike a great deal of what is called tradecraft, it was a disciplined and focused pattern of behavior based upon a set of rules. In Washington's case his social education had established many of these rules early in his life. These rules came from a book titled *Young Man's Companion*, which comprised 110 rules guiding an individual's personal conduct. Several of the rules have direct application to elicitation:

Rule 6. Show respect while others are speaking by paying careful attention.

Rule 19. Have a pleasant manner.

Rule 33. Show proper respect to others.

Rule 41. Avoid being arrogant.

Rule 62. Keep the conversation on positive things and use wisdom in sharing your thoughts.

Rule 69. If others argue, try to make peace.

Rule 73. Be a thoughtful, clear and careful speaker.

Rule 86. In a dispute, don't overwhelm your opponent so they cannot clearly state their position.

Rule 99. Don't drink too slowly or too quickly.

Rule 105. Avoid showing anger.[12]

Following these rules allowed Washington to create a gentlemanly, and seemingly open, social environment that encouraged the French officers to state their opinions freely while he carefully weighted his responses to stimulate additional details and clarification of French plans.

As the dinner progressed, the French officers became quite open in discussing their intention to take control of the Ohio Territory. They claimed this right based upon the exploration of the area by René-Robert Cavelier, sieur de La Salle, a French explorer of the seventeenth century who explored the Great Lakes, the Mississippi River, and the Gulf of Mexico.[13] He did most of his exploration in the Ohio Territory in the period 1672 to 1682. The validity of this claim, as indeed that of the English claim, was legally questionable because the Ohio Territory was a vast wilderness of no set boundaries beyond references to geographical features. However, Washington did not engage the officers in a debate over the issue. Rather, he allowed them to educate him on their position and, more important from an intelligence perspective, their plans and intentions.

Based upon the dinner conversation, Washington subsequently gave Dinwiddie valuable military information. He reported that the outpost at Venango was to prevent English settlers from entering the area. He estimated the French had six hundred to seven hundred troops holding four forts. One was located by a small lake near French Creek, about sixty miles north-northwest of Venango. A second on Lake Erie was about fifteen miles from the first fort, a third was at the Lake Erie falls (Niagara Falls) and was used to store supplies sent from Montreal, and the fourth was on Lake Ontario, about twenty miles from the falls. He also learned that between Montreal and the third fort, three outposts were established to guard the supply route.[14]

About a week later, a French Army escort arrived to take Washington to Fort Le Boeuf, where he would present the royal governor's letter to the fort's commander. On December 12, Washington met Jacques Legardeur de Saint-Pierre and Captain Repentigny, another fort commander, and formally presented the letter. While the French met to discuss its contents, Washington took advantage of the time to scout Fort Le Boeuf and its armament. He noted it was almost fully surrounded by water, being at a fork of French Creek. He described the fort as having log walls, pointed at the top and about twelve feet high. The walls had portholes for cannon and others for small-arms use. There were eight 6-pound cannon—two on each side of the fort—and a 4-pound cannon at the gate. Platforms on the interior walls were used to mount the cannon and for soldiers to fire from. The fort consisted of a guardhouse, a chapel, a doctor's office, and the commander's private store. Outside the fort were barracks made of logs and other buildings, including ones for horses and blacksmiths. He estimated the fort was garrisoned by a hundred men plus officers. Using his companions to scout the number of canoes available to the garrison, Washington reported 50 made of birch, 170 of pine, and several more under construction.[15]

On December 15, Washington received the French reply. After a somewhat hazardous journey back to Williamsburg, he presented it to Governor Dinwiddie on January 16, 1754. The reply, typical of diplomatic correspondence to this day, was polite in rejecting any illegal or incorrect actions, while obfuscating any issue of blame or accountability.[16] This set the scene for Washington's first combat command. This experience would be painful but one from which he would learn valuable practical lessons. It would also provide the opportunity for more practice of his intelligence-collection skills.

Based upon the French reply, Dinwiddie issued a call for troops and promoted Washington to lieutenant colonel to command them. On April 2, 1754, he and about a 150 Virginia troops left Alexandria, Virginia, for the Ohio Territory. By late May, Washington had reached an area known as Great Meadows and began construction of a small defensive stockade he called Fort Necessity. Based upon a report from Indians he had sent to scout the French, on May 27 he led his troops from the fort on a night march to attack a small party of French soldiers some ten miles away. He was successful, killing a third of the French force including its commanding officer, Ensign Jumonville. His journal entry of that date notes that he was able to confirm from the prisoners that their mission was to make a reconnaissance of his position and the terrain surrounding it.[17] While the French party had claimed to be on a diplomatic mission rather than a military one, its real purpose was collection of military intelligence. Washington also learned that the information regarding his location and strength had already been sent back by messenger to the French commander, with the understanding that he would act upon it. Based upon this knowledge, he then returned to the fort and prepared to defend it. In early June, Washington received some reinforcements. With these additional troops, he had about four hundred soldiers under his command.

During this period, Washington kept Indian scouts active screening his fort and searching for French scouting parties. On June 12, he sent a small force to collect nine French deserters previously identified by those scouts. In addition to debriefing the deserters, he decided to try to influence other French soldiers. He created a propaganda story in the form of a letter from them to their former fellow soldiers describing the benefits of deserting to the British side.[18] The letter represents yet another indication of Washington's recognition of the potential military benefits of a broad approach to military intelligence activities.

A second example comes from his late June meetings with representatives of the Indian tribes in the region. His primary objective for these meetings was to seek their loyalty and cooperation against the French, but he also used them to make statements directed at influencing French actions. Demonstrating what would professionally be called a counterintelligence situational awareness, Washington recognized that the French had sent some Indians to the meeting who were in their pay, to both identify his military resources and learn his plans and intentions. Recognizing this as an opportunity to spread some disinformation, he included in his speeches to the Indians information he wished the French to believe. His journal entry of June 21 states that at the conclusion of the council, the Indians "who had been sent by the French to act as spies, returned, though not without some stories prepared to amuse the French, which may be of service to make our own designs succeed."[19] Both of these offensive intelligence tactics—propaganda use of prisoners to induce enemy defection and spreading disinformation for transmission to the enemy—would become a standard part of Washington's overall intelligence strategy during the Revolutionary War.

However, despite his best efforts to collect intelligence on French plans and activities, Washington remained mostly ignorant of enemy actions. Apparently, he had not planned to utilize Fort Necessity as his base but rather, with the reinforcements and promises of additional support, intended to move forward and attack the major French fort at Duquesne. In any event, his military actions during this period demonstrated poor leadership of his forces and that his grasp of military tactics and strategy was inadequate. They led to a military disaster. However, from the perspective of his developing intelligence skills, it taught him an important lesson that he would not forget regarding the necessity of knowing the enemy's strength and plans as key to any military action.

Washington's attempted advance toward Fort Duquesne, plagued from the start by poor logistical conditions and his inability to muster significant Indian support, failed, and upon his return to Fort Necessity on July 1, Washington's forces were exhausted. Also, Indian scouts working for him reported that a strong French force was rapidly approaching. Created in response to Washington's May 27 defeat of the French, it was led by Capt. Louis Coulon de Villiers, the older brother of the French officer killed at that battle. His men included

French regulars, Canadian militiamen, and perhaps a hundred Indian allies. They attacked about midday on July 3. Coulon, an officer experienced in wilderness tactics, used the terrain to his advantage, as Washington had poorly situated the fort in a valley surrounded by wooded hillsides. A combination of French fire into the fort and problems with his troops' weapons caused by recent heavy rains reduced Washington's defense capability to almost nil.[20] By evening his command was disintegrating.

The French, recognizing the situation of the English, made an offer of negotiation. If Washington would sign articles outlining the terms of the surrender, his troops would be allowed to depart safely. Among the terms were statements of responsibility for the May 27 action and the surrender of two of Washington's officers as hostages to guarantee adherence to the surrender terms. The terms were, of course, written in French and included a statement that Washington bore responsibility for the assassination of Coulon's brother.[21] How this statement was missed by Washington when he signed the articles has never been clarified fully. Various reasons have been put forth for this mistake, including poor French reading proficiency, the document being rain-soaked, and inadequate reading light.[22] However, when the French later published the articles, this statement would prove a serious blow to Washington's ego and personal honor.

Two of Washington's company commanders volunteered to become hostages, captains Jacob Van Braam and Robert Stobo. The latter would prove to have learned the importance of intelligence collection while serving under Washington and would contribute significantly to British knowledge of French facilities in the future. As Washington's force slowly marched back into Virginia, the French destroyed Fort Necessity and by mid-July had destroyed the few remaining sites of English occupation in the Ohio Territory. Upon their return to Fort Duquesne, Captain Coulon and his men were greeted as heroes.

Washington delivered his report to Governor Dinwiddie in Williamsburg on July 17, 1754. Anticipating a rebuke, he was surprised when the House of Burgesses voted him its thanks. The governor was also supportive of Washington's action in his conversation with him but less so in his private communications with London.[23] It was noted that Washington had suffered from poor logistical support and that the quality and training of the soldiers under his command had been poor to begin with. Dinwiddie at first hoped to organize another military expedition from colonial forces to reengage the French in the Ohio but by fall recognized he did not have the resources necessary for the job. He would have to await the arrival of regular British Army units. As he disbanded the Virginia Regiment into garrison companies, Dinwiddie offered Washington a reduced role with the rank of captain in a new Virginia force. Washington, quite conscious of his status in Virginia society, resigned his commission after unsuccessfully attempting to negotiate a better rank.[24]

However, Washington's taste for leadership and military action quickly renewed itself when British forces arrived under Maj. Gen. Edward Braddock. Dinwiddie had duly reported the military situation to London, putting as good a face as possible on the events but clearly warning that the French presence in the Ohio Territory was a grave threat to all the British colonies in North America. He also made it clear Virginia lacked the capabilities to counter the threat—that Great Britain must provide the means. King George II's government quickly agreed that the French intrusion in the Ohio Territory could not be tolerated, and a plan of attack was developed. While lesser military campaigns were to focus on Nova Scotia and French forts on Lake Ontario and at Crown Point on Lake Champlain, Fort Duquesne would be the major objective. Braddock was appointed commander in chief of all British forces in North America and dispatched with two regiments to Virginia in early January 1755. He also brought along a large and cumbersome artillery train, which would prove difficult to move through the North American forest. When he arrived in Virginia in mid-February, he found a colony totally unprepared to support his military plan.[25]

Braddock's first priority was to develop a plan of approach to attack Fort Duquesne. By this time, Captain Stobo, resident there in a hostage status, had been able to draw a map of the fort, which had been smuggled back to Virginia authorities by a trusted Indian.[26] However, Braddock's entire military experience had been in European combat, and he was totally ignorant of the geographical area he was about to enter.[27] While this fact did not seem to bother Braddock, he was willing to accept the assistance of someone with knowledge and experience in the Ohio Territory.

Washington had sent Braddock a note of congratulation upon his arrival in Virginia, and he was still somewhat of a favorite of Governor Dinwiddie's. Also, Braddock was well aware that Washington had firsthand experience with conditions on the route that he would want to take. However, issues of military rank and personal status had to be addressed before Washington would join the campaign. British military regulations stated that a colonial officer within a British unit must be lower in command status than a British officer by at least one and possibly two grades. For example, were Washington to again be ranked as a Virginia colonel, he would effectively be ranked below a British

major or even a captain.[28] This was an important status issue for Washington
and within the social structure and culture of the time quite understandable.
But it meant that he would not serve under Braddock as a colonial officer. After
discussion, Braddock and Dinwiddie agreed that they could not approve rank-
ing Washington above a captain. Negotiations continued through one of Braddock's aides until a solution was found. Washington would join Braddock's
staff as an aide-de-camp, outside the regular chain of command. Washington
accepted the proposal, satisfied that it would give him both appropriate status
and authority within the military expedition. As he explained to his younger
brother John Augustine Washington in a mid-May letter, "I am thereby freed
from all command but [Braddock's], and give Order's to all, which must be
implicitly obey'd."[29]

While the issue of rank and status were of great importance to Washington
based upon his position in Virginia society, he also recognized that serving in
the British expedition would be a significant educational and professional opportunity. He was well aware of the military mistakes he had made, and one of
his great strengths of character was his ability to recognize such mistakes and
learn from them. As he wrote to Braddock's aide upon accepting the aide-de-
camp position, "I wish for nothing more earnestly than to attain a small degree
of knowledge in the Military Art."[30] Thus Washington became an adviser to
Braddock for the expedition. However, his advisory role, based upon the military and social culture of the times, was quite different and far less interactive
than one would assume today.

Braddock had been selected as the commander in chief of British forces
in North America based upon his political loyalty and his disciplined administrative skills. He was a man of direct words and actions. His actual military
skills, both strategic and tactical, were not his strongest talents.[31] He arrived
determined to conduct a rapid and successful campaign against the French and
immediately moved to force the colonial legislatures to provide what he needed
in terms of resources: both men and supplies. In addition to interpersonal skills
that did not create the most productive relations with the local legislatures and
governors, an equally significant failing was of an intelligence nature.

To be successful, every military commander needs basic information regarding the enemy and the conditions related to the environment in which
the combat will occur. The vast majority of military intelligence of any nation
is focused upon ensuring that its military is well aware of the strengths and
weaknesses of any enemy it faces, as well as the details of any geographical area
where it might fight.

Braddock apparently did not feel the need to understand either.[32] As to the enemy, most of the French combatants would be Canadian militiamen and Indians, who did not fight like regular French troops or for the same reasons. The militiamen felt comfortable in dense forest environments and fighting in a style that eschewed European combat formations, based on their experience against their usual enemies, the Indians. The Indians had their own style of combat. But equally important, the Indians' reasons for fighting were quite different than those of the Europeans. The Indians would seldom fight to hold a specific location. Based on their martial spiritual beliefs, they fought for trophies such as scalps, which demonstrated publicly their valor, or for economic benefits such as supplies or captives.[33] In his initial dealings with potential Indian allies, Braddock seemed totally incapable of treating them as anything other than servants of the king who were to obey his orders.[34] He lacked any cultural understanding of them and made no effort to acquire such knowledge.

Braddock was equally ignorant of the realities of the ground upon which he would fight. While London had general maps of the area indicating geographical features such as mountains, valleys, rivers and streams, and settlements, the actual condition of the route to be taken was misunderstood.[35] It was hilly, if not mountainous in locations, heavily wooded and overgrown, and often marshy—clearly not suited for a European-style military supply train with heavy artillery, nonessential baggage, and camp followers. This lack of basic ground-truth intelligence was to beset Braddock's campaign from the start. And Washington was not in a position to educate Braddock regarding his limitations in this knowledge. Within the military command structure of the time, and as often has carried over in modern times, a commander's aide's role was not to offer suggestions unless asked. Braddock's personality indicated that he seldom felt he needed military advice from junior officers or unofficial aides.

On May 29, 1755, Braddock departed Fort Cumberland with about two thousand men but only a few Indians willing to act as his scouts. Within the first week of the march, he realized the difficulty of the terrain and decided to separate his forces into two elements: a lead element that could move faster through the wilderness and a support column containing most of the heavy artillery and baggage. By the first week in July, his forces were approaching Fort Duquesne.

Popular history often states that Braddock's poor march security was a major factor in his defeat, but this is a dubious point. He had established a point element of Indian scouts, followed by a three-hundred-man advance guard composed of light infantry and grenadiers under the command of Lt.

Col. Thomas Gage—later to become commander of all British forces in the colonies, and the military governor of Massachusetts. He also deployed flanking patrols shadowing the column on both sides. In fact, in early July, flanker units had been in contact with Indian scouts aligned with the French and had driven them off. The main body of troops followed, including Washington, who was suffering severely from dysentery and from hemorrhoid pain, making it necessary for him to ride with a cushion covering his saddle. The last element of his column comprised Virginia troops. Thus Braddock had taken adequate precautions to protect his forces on the march.[36]

On July 9, as Braddock approached within ten miles of Fort Duquesne, the French attacked with a force of French Army regulars, some Canadian colonial regulars, Canadian militiamen, and Indian allies—well over half of the total French force. A scout party ahead of Gage's guard observed them while they were still a couple of hundred yards away. As the French halted to form themselves, Gage's guard advanced and fired into them, killing their commander. While the French and Canadians were momentarily confused, the Indians immediately moved into the forest brush and took whatever natural cover was available, firing into Gage's unit. Both sides then engaged using the tactics common to their training, the British forming company lines and firing company volleys and the Indians shooting at specific enemy targets from positions of cover and concealment. British officers, easily identified by their uniforms as well as their leadership efforts at the front of their men, were prime targets for the Indians. As the officers became incapacitated, command and control began to break down.

Braddock, often with Washington near him, made heroic efforts to maintain discipline, with several horses shot out from under him before he too was shot. Effective British resistance to the French ended within the first half hour of the battle, which became known as the Battle of the Monongahela, yet the fighting continued for about three hours. British units fired meaningless volleys into trees, and on some occasions the fog of war even had British units firing on other British or Virginia units. The conditioning of the British soldier was such that regardless of the realities of the circumstances, ranks would close as men dropped, muskets were reloaded, and volleys were fired without specific targets. Some American units fought well, taking natural cover and returning fire, while others panicked and fled, adding to the overall confusion.[37] The chaotic scene, with Indian war cries, bloody dead and wounded British, the wooded setting floating in a cloud of gunpowder smoke, and the emotionally charged voices of British officers trying to rally their troops had a lifetime impact on Washington.

An 1834 illustration imagining Col. George Washington on horseback at the Battle of the Monongahela during the French and Indian War, 1755. In the foreground in a red coat, British general Edward Braddock lies mortally wounded. After Braddock was wounded, Washington helped maintain order as the combined British and Virginia forces retreated. *Library of Congress*

As the various British and colonial units broke and fled, the Indians moved in to take scalps from the dead and wounded and whatever other valuables were available, rather than pursuing the fleeing enemy. Once out of the killing zone where the attack had occurred, the remaining officers and sergeants began to reestablish some order among the units. However, it took nearly two days for the survivors of the advance column to reach the support column. Washington's role once Braddock was wounded was, at Braddock's instruction, to go to the support column, advise its commander of the battle's results, and return with additional forces. Riding through the retreating force all that night, Washington did not reach the support column until the next day.

The British had suffered a devastating defeat, losing about seventy percent of the advance column as well as their commander for North America. But Washington had learned a military lesson of value. While unwilling to criticize Braddock's tactics, he felt that the lack of military training specific to combat conditions in North America, particularly the wilderness areas, and his troops' rote behavior were the reasons for the defeat.[38] These issues became Washington's focus as he commanded Virginia troops during the remainder of the French and Indian War. And when appointed to head the new Virginia Regiment, he made every attempt to ensure that his forces were well disciplined and trained.[39] Also, Washington carried away from Braddock's defeat recognition of the importance of intelligence as a vital element in military planning. He well understood that the greatest British failure in the French and Indian War had been that of poor basic intelligence.[40]

For the remainder of the French and Indian War, Washington saw little action, primarily guarding the Virginia frontier from French and Indian raids. He played a small role as the Virginia commander during the poorly executed but eventually successful British campaign led by Gen. John Forbes that forced the French to destroy Fort Duquesne in 1758 and drove them out of the Ohio for good. By the end of the war Washington could boast, and did so, that his regiment was the finest in the colonies.[41] And as he moved into the political scene as a member of the House of Burgesses in late 1758, his name became well known throughout the colonies based upon his military exploits during the war.[42]

In terms of Washington's growth as a military and political figure in the colonies, this period was the springboard for him to become commander in chief of the Continental Army over such rivals as John Hancock, Artemas Ward, and Charles Lee (the latter later proving to be of dubious loyalty to the colonies when he was a prisoner of war during the Revolution). Washington's appointment was assured by the actions of John Adams of the Massachusetts delegation. Adams, through his association with various patriot organizations, watched Washington's commitment to the cause of independence grow as British measures upset more and more of the colonial population. Adams was well aware of Washington's military experience, and his political instincts told him a man known throughout the colonies must be the choice if all the colonies were to contribute to the army. The other rivals were men with regional, mostly New England, reputations. Also, as the southern center of patriot political activities, Virginia was important in its own right, and having a Virginian military commander would significantly assist in uniting the colonial efforts.

The period of the French and Indian War was the foundation of Washington's knowledge and experience in intelligence activities and would serve him well as he leveraged these skills against British numerical superiority on the battlefield. By the war's conclusion, Washington had demonstrated a solid understanding of intelligence collection beyond the traditional military activities of scouting and reconnaissance. He had demonstrated skills in elicitation, propaganda, deception, and the use of collection agents. His recognition of the importance of intelligence, gained from his experiences during this period, was clear. Several years later, but well prior to the start of the Revolution, Washington wrote to a friend, "There is nothing more necessary than good intelligence to frustrate a designing enemy, & nothing that requires greater pains to obtain."[43]

CHAPTER 2

THE UNITED FRONT CAMPAIGN THAT LED TO THE AMERICAN REVOLUTION

T o many students of the American Revolution, the Sons of Liberty are best caricatured in the image of a drunken mob gathered around a liberty tree, with a tarred and feathered British customs official in the background. There is some accuracy to this. However, lost in this scene is the reality that the organization was the eighteenth-century equivalent of a united front used by radical Founding Fathers for their successful political action campaign against the British authorities in the American colonies.

This united front campaign, at first loosely directed but well-coordinated in later years, was conducted by radical politicians in the larger population centers of the colonies. It could be argued that even the most skillful practitioners of united fronts, such as the communist parties of the former Soviet Union, the People's Republic of China, and Castro's Cuba, never engineered a greater success than what Samuel Adams and others accomplished between 1765 and 1775. While its success did benefit significantly from the unwitting assistance of inept British government policies and actions, its activities enabled a small group of radical individuals to bring the American colonial political structure into armed conflict with the world's greatest military power.

A united front organization is a principle tool for political and social organization. The term first came into use after the Bolshevik Revolution, but the general principles behind it are much older. It espouses a broad and somewhat general objective to a large number of groups and individuals willing to claim some connection to it. But its leadership usually has a more specific set of objectives—often more radical than the general membership realizes. Within this context, it can also be an effective operational tool for political action, one of the intelligence disciplines of covert action in the intelligence discipline. The Sons of Liberty's objective was to create a mass movement that first opposed specific British policies and then promoted political independence. While current national security emphasis on counterterrorism focuses on the paramilitary aspect of covert action, the other two basic elements—propaganda and political action—have a long tradition of use within the American intelligence community.

The first requirement for a united front campaign is a broad political objective, one that has current popular appeal and can also be described in flexible terms in order to engage as large an audience as possible. In the colonies this objective started to take shape in the political, social, and professional organizations in the major cities in the mid-eighteenth century. For example, in Boston such groups included Masonic lodges, fire companies, charitable organizations, and clubs based on professional disciplines.[1] While some of these organizations were extensions of the traditional British clubs that focused on the debate of philosophical and political doctrines, in the colonies their membership had a broader base. There the social system, at least among white males, was more flexible: Tradespeople, farmers, and merchants, as well as wealthy and politically influential individuals, made up the memberships of these organizations.

In the American colonies the economic and intellectual interests of these individuals were closely entwined, and the physical distance from Britain gave them a highly localized perspective on trade and government. While in the mid-1700s some radical colonial politicians, such as Samuel Adams, spoke early on in terms of political independence from Britain, most Americans favored freedom in the sense of the ability to pursue their economic enterprises without interference from the British government.[2] Thus the radicals used the concept of economic freedom to appeal to the general population as they moved the political debate, and political confrontation with British authorities, forward.

With this broad popular objective, a group was needed both to organize political activities and to demonstrate in the streets against British policy. The Sons of Liberty became this group. And the guiding hand behind this organization was a failed businessman with a last name well known in America but who, like most involved in behind-the-scenes activities, has seldom received the public recognition he deserved. Samuel Adams, cousin of Founding Father

Samuel Adams was a key leader in Boston of the Sons of Liberty and
one of the earliest proponents of political independence from England.
Library of Congress

John Adams, is best associated today with a Boston brewery that produces
hoppy beers and ales. However, in real life he failed as a brewer but found his
true calling as the head of the political-action campaign seeking independence
from Britain. One prominent Revolutionary period historian has referred to
Samuel Adams as "the Lenin of the American Revolution."[3]

While radicals in other colonial population centers were active and important leaders in this campaign, Adams was a key organizer who gave it direction and orchestrated its momentum. His ability to take the lead resulted to a great degree from his physical location. Boston was a well-developed society, both politically and economically. Its royal governor was weak and had little in the way of force to back up British authority. The British military commander, Gen. Thomas Gage, resided in New York City with several British regiments. Thus in Boston, Adams was able to orchestrate activities and maintain pressure on British authorities through the ten-year period leading to the armed conflict. His skillful use of propaganda, street action, and political action in the colonial legislature enabled him to assume a key leadership position in the radicals' program for independence.

As with most political-action operations, some luck and mistakes on the part of the opposition are necessary to bring success. In the British government of the period, Adams found an excellent ally in this regard. As nations seem to have to relearn periodically, attempting to govern a country with a different social or cultural structure is a most difficult task. The British power structure was the product of a class system that did not export well to the American colonies. Different living conditions, radically different views of social and religious structures, and simply the great distance between the two land masses created a broadly different view of how one was supposed to live in relationship to a central government. Even after the Revolution succeeded, it took many years to settle the major issues regarding states' rights and central government authority, and such issues continue today. The government in London did not recognize the degree to which this difference in perspective existed, although minorities of British politicians were more perceptive. The Crown's arrogance and ineptitude, as well as its poor timing of responses to colonial actions, was a major contributor to Adams's successes. As one historian has noted, "the American Revolution was eminently avoidable."[4]

The Sons of Liberty was formed in 1765 in response to the Stamp Act. This law instituted a tax intended to fund the British troops stationed in the American colonies as a result of the French and Indian War. The organization's name originated from a phrase used in a speech by Isaac Barré in a parliamentary debate opposing the tax. When another member, Charles Townshend, who as chancellor of the Exchequer would later inadvertently play a key role in encouraging the Sons of Liberty's activities, described the colonists in terms of being "dependent" upon England's care, Barré responded by describing Americans as "the sons of liberty."[5]

At its inception the Sons of Liberty was meant to be a semiclandestine organization with a fluid membership depending upon the specific issue and event. Its leadership, while not concealed, was not publicly acknowledged.[6] Its first activities were against imposition of the Stamp Act. Both New York City and Boston seem to have organized groups under this name at about the same time, with chapters developing from New Hampshire to South Carolina by the end of 1765. During the ten years between the Stamp Act protests and the armed conflict at Lexington and Concord, the Sons of Liberty evolved into a powerful and effective organization directing political action throughout the colonies. Its leaders formed the political and military leadership cadre of the Revolutionary era. By the time the minutemen responded to the British march to Lexington, they could well be described, as they were by a Concord man, as "a united family of the Sons of Liberty."[7]

The Stamp Act particularly affected the merchant and tradesmen classes, requiring a stamp for most legal and commercial transactions. These individuals were the core members of the Sons of Liberty leadership. In Boston, Samuel Adams and James Otis Jr. were the senior leaders and planners of the group. Their roles were initially hidden from public view. Instead, a group known as the "Loyal Nine" was discreetly recognized as the Sons of Liberty leadership. This group consisted of well-known merchants and tradesmen. It included the publisher Benjamin Edes of the *Boston Gazette*, which became a key propaganda outlet for Adams and other radicals.

Early on, the radical leaders saw the value of city newspapers as propaganda vehicles and recruited their publishers into the Sons of Liberty. These included William Goddard of the *Providence Journal*, Samuel Hall of the *Newport Mercury*, William Bradford of the *Pennsylvania Journal*, John Holt of the *New York Journal*, and Isaiah Thomas of the *Massachusetts Spy*. Another well-known individual, Paul Revere, also served effectively as a propagandist and then as an intelligence agent for the organization. Within the Boston branch of the Sons of Liberty, members exchanged cryptic signals and passwords and wore special insignia for recognition: silver medals picturing a liberty tree and the words "Sons of Liberty."[8] By the summer of 1765, the Sons of Liberty was a powerful force both in the streets and in political circles in Boston and other major American cities.

At this early stage of development, the Sons of Liberty leadership had little control over the street mobs that protested violently against the Stamp Act. Rather, Adams and other radicals focused their activities on spreading information among the loosely connected chapters and attempting to form a united political position against the British authorities. And the street mobs had personal agendas as well. While the radical leadership preferred peaceful mass demonstrations, press articles, pamphlets, and public speeches attacking the act, the street leaders preferred riots, looting, physical destruction of the stamps, and assaults on British stamp agents. In Boston, rival neighborhood-based gang leaders such as Samuel Swift and Ebenezer MacIntosh both associated their organizations with the Sons of Liberty.[9] Similar associations developed in other colonial cities as street gangs and criminal organizations saw the benefit of sheltering their activities under the guise of popular resistance to British authority.

While street violence was originally not part of the plan, the radicals soon discovered that it was an effective way to intimidate local British officials. In Boston on August 14, 1765, an effigy of Andrew Oliver, the stamp distributor, was hanged in the South End, the city's area under MacIntosh's control. That evening, at the direction of the Loyal Nine, he led a mob that destroyed Oliver's residence. Oliver wisely resigned the following day. Less than two weeks later, MacIntosh led a mob attacking the residence of the British lieutenant governor, Thomas Hutchinson. The mob looted the residence down to the bare walls and floor. In Newport on August 27, effigies were hanged of the stamp distributor and two other pro-British figures. The distributor, Augustus Johnston, immediately resigned. In New York City, four days after the looting of Hutchinson's home, the stamp distributor also resigned. And in Annapolis a mob burned the warehouse where stamps were to be stored and drove the distributor out of the colony. Similar events took place throughout the colonies.

While Adams and others involved in directing the activities publicly disassociated themselves from the violence, they were well aware of the plans for such actions.[10] As one historian put it, the dirty work was left to the mob while the Sons of Liberty provided the direction.[11] These intimidation tactics were so effective throughout the colonies that by November 1765, when the Stamp Act was to take effect, the British had just about no one willing to implement it.

While hiding its role in the street violence, the leaders of the Sons of Liberty were more visible in colonial politics. In newspapers, pamphlets, and speeches, they warned the British government of the mistake it was making and of the consequences that would follow. For example, on May 29, 1765, Sons of Liberty member Patrick Henry made a speech in the Virginia House of Burgesses warning King George of the dangers of implementing the Stamp Act. Similar voices were heard in the other colonial legislatures.

Within a year the British government repealed the Stamp Act. The Sons of Liberty leaders rightly viewed this as a significant victory, and it encouraged them to maintain political tension with British officials. Communication channels among the various chapters were improved, and radical leaders began regular correspondence to plan and coordinate future political moves. Efforts were also made to get better control over the street gangs so that political objectives were not harmed by unnecessary or poorly timed violence. Another benefit was the change in political thinking that repeal brought to many moderate colonial politicians and businessmen. Previously, their emphasis had been on noninterference with colonial commerce, but the British government's repeal of the act stimulated them to think that more political self-government, albeit within the framework of the British government, was possible.

The period from 1766 to 1770 was one of consolidation of political forces and planning by the radicals to move the colonial political agenda toward less British control. Moderate colonial politicians such as John Adams began discussions with the radicals, which would eventually create the political coalition that led the Revolution.[12] This was also a time of maturation for the Sons of Liberty. Key radical leaders made their political orientation public. In Boston, Samuel Adams, Otis, John Hancock, Dr. Joseph Warren, and William Molineux were recognized leaders. In Philadelphia, Samuel Simpson, James Cannon, Thomas Young, Charles Thomson, John Bayard, William Bradford, and John Leacock led the Sons of Liberty. In Connecticut, future general Israel Putnam led. And in New York City, John Lamb, Gershom Mott, Isaac Sears, Thomas Robin, William Wiley, Joseph Allicoke, John Hobart, Edward Laight, Francis Lewis, William Livingston, Alexander McDougall, John Scott, and Jacobus van Zandt were publicly recognized leaders. In Providence, John and Moses Brown, of the wealthy and politically influential Brown family, also became involved as Sons of Liberty.

These years prior to the Boston Massacre saw intensive debate and political as well as physical confrontation over the future of British administration of the colonies. And with nearly perfect timing, Charles Townshend brought his ignorance of colonial sensitivities and British class arrogance to the aid of the radicals' liberties. Just as the Stamp Act was revoked, he proposed a new series of laws known as the Townshend Acts. In 1766, Townshend took the lead policy role regarding how the government would pay its debt covering the cost of the Seven Years' War (known in the colonies as the French and Indian War). He decided that taxing the colonies' imports was the proper approach because they had benefited from the removal of the French threat along the western frontier. While recognition of the colonial attitude toward Parliament's levying of taxes was well known after the Stamp Act fiasco, Townshend had neither concern nor interest in how the colonies felt. His only concern was with financing the British government.

He could hardly have chosen more provocative provisions for his legislation. They focused directly on the issues most sensitive, both politically and economically, to the radicals' target audience. The acts' two most abhorrent provisions were taxes on glass, lead, paint, paper, tea, and other necessary imports, and reaffirmation of the Writ of Assistance—a blanket type of search warrant that permitted British customs officials to search as they determined necessary for smuggled goods.

Here it is necessary to note that a significant part of New England's economy—perhaps even most of it—and indeed the wealth of its political and business leadership was built on what must be described as a rather lax enforcement of official British trade policy. The British government had a long-established practice of regulating colonial trade with the objective of financially benefiting the Crown. However, America's extensive coastline and the limited customs resources available to the British colonial government made enforcement difficult. A de facto situation evolved wherein local importers avoided taxes whenever possible, and when circumstances forced them to pay, they often understated their cargoes' values. This created an economic environment for the colonial population that they were loath to give up.[13] Because these business practices had been tolerated, if not actually encouraged, by local British authorities for decades, the obvious conflict that was to develop should have been apparent.

By 1767, the Sons of Liberty was a political force to be reckoned with in the local politics of the Northern colonies from New York City to Boston. In smaller towns such as Providence, the Sons of Liberty constituted a significant part of the local political machine.[14] But it was in the Boston area where the organization best demonstrated its capability to conduct large-scale political and street actions. Propaganda to build further public support into a united front political structure was the next step. The first major step in this direction was accomplished on December 21, 1767, when Philadelphia lawyer John Dickinson's first installment of his *Letters from a Farmer in Pennsylvania* was published in the *Boston Chronicle*. Dickinson's twelve essays in the *Letters* series developed a moderate and logical argument that the British government was disregarding the political rights of the colonists as Englishmen. His argument made clear that a united and coordinated effort by the colonies would be required to redress this situation.

While Dickinson was neither a member of the Sons of Liberty nor a supporter of the radicals, his argument supported their position that united colonial action was needed. The Sons of Liberty leadership publicly supported the *Letters* and helped publicize its message. Samuel Adams then took the next step by orchestrating the passage of a call for colonial unity against the acts in the Massachusetts colonial legislature in February 1768. His first attempt failed. However, his second attempt did not. Aware that he did not have majority support for his position, Adams had his legislative allies drag out the session until most of the members had departed. He then rose and called for a motion, which subsequently became known as the Massachusetts Circular Letter, requesting all the other colonial legislatures to join in a petition to the king requesting the repeal of the Townshend Acts. His allies, who now constituted a majority, passed the motion.[15] To celebrate and to publicize the legislature's action, the Sons of Liberty commissioned a member, Paul Revere, to create a large punch bowl in honor of the issuance of the Massachusetts Circular Letter.

Throughout the winter of 1767–68, the radicals in Boston kept up a constant campaign of harassment against British customs officials. Verbal threats of personal injury and actual damage to the residences and property of the officials were common occurrences in the city. By spring the Massachusetts royal governor requested a military show of support for his administration, and General Gage dispatched a British naval detachment to Boston. On May 17, the HMS *Romney*, carrying fifty guns, accompanied by the schooner HMS *St. Lawrence*, anchored in Boston harbor.

The ships' appearance created little concern among the Sons of Liberty's leaders, as they knew that a ship in the harbor had no effect on who controlled the streets of Boston. The actions of *Romney*'s commander, Capt. John Corner, to impress local sailors into his crew assisted in keeping Bostonians' emotions high.[16]

By mid-June, one of the Sons of Liberty's senior leaders, John Hancock, found an issue that motivated him both politically and personally. One of his ships, the *Liberty*, had arrived in port in early May carrying a shipment of wine, and, as was the common practice, Hancock had underdeclared the quantity in order to reduce the import duty. However, on June 10, with the assistance of the *Romney*'s commander, customs agents seized the ship based upon a tip regarding its cargo's undervaluation. A mob quickly gathered and began throwing stones at the officials. As the officials left the scene and the *Liberty* was moved next to the *Romney*, the mob followed the officials to their residences. This action, now referred to as the "*Liberty* Riot," resulted in the commissioners fleeing to the safety of the *Romney* and then taking up residence at Castle William, a

British fort located on an island in the harbor. It took three boatloads of British marines and sailors from the *Romney* to evacuate the commissioners. Thus by June 11, 1768, only one British customs commissioner remained in Boston to enforce the import taxes, and he was quite friendly to the radical cause.[17]

Meanwhile, the royal governor attempted to have the Massachusetts legislature rescind the Circular Letter. When the members refused, he dissolved that body. As a result, the Sons of Liberty could accurately publicize that as of the 31st of June, the colony had no representative government.

These incidents encouraged the radicals to further actions. On July 5, a Boston mob went to the Roxbury home of one of the departed commissioners and destroyed its grounds. A few days later, a mob boarded a schooner that had been seized for nonpayment of customs duties and hauled away its cargo. On the political front, Adams and the Sons of Liberty encouraged the merchants of Boston to sign agreements not to import British goods covered by the duties. This encouragement was, as appropriate, mixed with threats of actions against those not complying. Similar nonimportation agreements were enacted by other Sons of Liberty chapters in the colonies.

In the same time frame, Sons of Liberty mobs were equally active in other colonial cities. For example, in Newport, Rhode Island, mobs publicly beat any individuals suspected of supporting the import taxes or acting as informants to assist the customs officials. In New York City merchants attempting to import items covered by the acts were convincingly threatened by the Sons of Liberty.

By late summer, Massachusetts royal governor Francis Bernard was well aware the Crown had lost control of Boston. He noted, "So we are not without a Government, only it is in the hands of the people of the Town."[18] On July 27, the British cabinet decided to send two regiments of troops to Boston to demonstrate British authority over the colony. In New York City, General Gage began steps to move troops into Boston. On August 31, he sent one of his aides to Boston, under pretense of private business, to confer with the governor regarding the number and placement of the troops. By early September, arrangements between the civilian and military authorities had been made, though the governor intended to remain publicly ignorant of the plans.[19]

Word, however, did get out, and Boston political leaders asked the governor to call a session of the legislature. He refused. The radical leadership then called for a convention to meet at Faneuil Hall and elected Thomas Cushing as its chairman and Samuel Adams as its clerk. From his position as clerk, Adams controlled the agenda and activities of the group's committees that would soon be responding to the presence of British regulars in the town. As the convention met at the hall, also present were four hundred muskets, which the town aldermen had previously moved there under the guise of maintaining them properly. To the radicals their purpose was clear and publicly stated at a committee meeting by James Otis: They were to be used by the people to oppose any troops sent to enforce unconstitutional laws.[20] The convention subsequently voted to defend their British liberties and urged the Bostonians to ensure they were prepared with weapons and ammunition.

On October 1, 1768, elements of four British regiments began landing in Boston. Gage had moved quickly and with significant force to reestablish British authority. Pronouncements notwithstanding, the local political leadership was not prepared for armed resistance. However, the Sons of Liberty was preparing for other actions against the troops. To regain control of the streets, the British authorities had agreed that troops must be quartered in the city. Units from the Twenty-Ninth Regiment were sent to Boston Common and elements of the Fourteenth Regiment took over Faneuil Hall, in the process seizing control of the town's supply of muskets. The Sons of Liberty denounced the troop landings in their propaganda organ, the *Boston Gazette*, which described the action as a British measure to "dragoon us into passive obedience."[21] The propaganda campaign continued to build, and by mid-October the troops were the target of civilian taunts and provocations on a daily basis.

On October 15, General Gage arrived in Boston for a personal view of the situation. He insisted that the royal governor quarter the troops in private homes. However, the radicals and their street forces were able to prevent this from actually happening. As Gage noted regarding British control in Boston, "in Truth [there was] very little at present."[22] On October 17, an article in the *Gazette* by Adams provided a carefully reasoned argument that the military presence would create an overreaction to civil protests sanctioned by British law. He warned that the safety of the public was in jeopardy.[23] This article set the opening scene for the public violence that he knew would result from the military occupation of Boston.

By mid-November, two additional regiments, the Sixty-Fourth and Sixty-Fifth, had arrived. Believing that adequate royal forces were now on hand to control the population, Gage returned to New York City. He was confident that tranquility would prevail even if firm control of the city was not yet restored to the British civilian authorities.

The radicals were biding their time, waiting to determine the willingness of the British civil authorities to use the troops in the streets. Rather than encouraging large-scale protests, the radicals continued their propaganda campaign and orchestrated constant harassment of the troops by civilians. British soldiers were insulted and even physically abused. In addition, legal suits were filed with sympathetic local magistrates over issues, from payment of bills to property damage. Numerous British officers were forced to spend considerable time and money on these harassment suits. In mid-October, the Sons of Liberty also used a journal, in the model of a daily report of events, to spread stories regarding the poor behavior of British troops in Boston. This journal appeared in newspapers in Boston and New York and as far south as Georgia.[24]

By the spring of 1769, there had been no major disturbances in Boston since the troops arrived. However, Gage was well aware of the continued weakness of the civilian authority there. The population's hostility had made the lives of the soldiers very difficult, and their officers were seeking orders to withdraw some units. Placed in a difficult position, Gage sought to obtain a formal request from the British civilian authorities in Boston that the current troop presence was necessary. However, local authorities were too intimidated to make such a statement. Privately the officials expressed their concerns, but this provided little political cover for Gage.[25]

Based upon the quiet winter, he decided to withdraw two regiments. The Sons of Liberty recognized this action as both a statement of weakness by the local British authorities and an opportunity to increase the pressure on the civil administration. Its first step was to seek out conservative and moderate political leaders to chart a common strategy. On August 14, a large meeting of the Sons of Liberty was held in Dorchester, then just outside of Boston, at the Sign of the Liberty Tree inn. This meeting featured numerous speakers and apparently an abundance of alcohol, as some forty-five formal toasts were drunk by the participants. As John Adams noted, such gatherings "tinge the Minds of the People, they impregnate them with the sentiments of Liberty. They render the People fond of their Leaders in the Cause, and averse and bitter against all opposers."[26]

That summer British authorities faced a direct confrontation in Newport. A British warship, the HMS *Liberty*, was assigned to the area to enforce the import duties. After several encounters with ships suspected of smuggling, the ship opened fire on a vessel. The following day, the *Liberty*'s captain came ashore at Newport and was surrounded by a mob, which forced him to order his crew off the ship. A group of local leaders then boarded the vessel, scuttled it, and a few days later burned it.[27] This act, the physical destruction of a Royal Navy craft, was dramatic evidence of the degree to which radical colonial leaders were willing to go to demonstrate their control of the local environment.

That British local authorities were unable to punish those involved provided more encouragement to the radicals.

By the fall in Boston, tempers on both sides flared up again. On September 5, James Otis, one of the most outspoken radical leaders, was physically assaulted in a coffeehouse by a group of loyalists that included some British officers. Although Otis had provoked the incident by going to the Tory hangout and insulting a royal official, he widely publicized the incident as an attempt to assassinate him. A little over a month later, John Mein, the Tory editor of the *Boston Chronicle*, and a companion were surrounded and attacked by a group of Sons of Liberty led by Molineux. They were barely able to reach a British guard post for protection. However, by this time, the mob had swollen to several thousand, and the British sentries became the focus of their anger. Stones were thrown and had the British officers not responded with calm and discipline, massive bloodshed would have occurred. Years later, Governor Hutchinson wrote that this attack "was the first trial of a mob since the troops had been in town, and having triumphed in defiance of them, a mob became more formidable than ever."[28]

The radicals continued to focus their attention on the boycott on imported goods and punishing those who continued to import such items. Street mobs harassed these merchants and damaged their commercial facilities on a routine basis. Before long, one of these demonstrations developed into a deadly confrontation, which the Sons of Liberty exploited to its fullest.

On February 22, 1770, Ebenezer Richardson, a well-known loyalist, visited a merchant who was the target of a large protest. Upon leaving the man's shop, he attempted to destroy a sign condemning the merchant. Members of the mob stopped him and then followed him home throwing sticks and stones. Local leaders of the Sons of Liberty joined in and threatened him as he hid in his home. The situation escalated with the mob throwing rocks and wood through his windows. His wife was struck with a rock, and his two daughters were also in danger. Richardson and a friend then poked muskets out the broken windows to frighten the mob. This had only a momentary effect, and the hail of missiles continued. Finally, Richardson fired into the crowd, wounding several people, including an eleven-year-old boy named Christopher Seider. The mob pushed forward, and Richardson's life was spared only when Molineux stepped forward to calm the crowd. Richardson was then taken to a justice of the peace and placed in jail until a trial could be arranged. That evening, young Seider died of his wounds.

Adams immediately saw the propaganda value in the youth's death and on

February 26 staged a grand funeral for Seider. It began at the Liberty Tree and was led by hundreds of schoolboys carrying signs in Latin referring to the murdered innocent. Six youths carried Seider's body, followed by his family, friends, relatives, and some two thousand other mourners. Lt. Governor Hutchinson subsequently wrote that if the Sons of Liberty had been able to save the youth, they "would not have done it, but would have chosen the grand funeral."[29]

By March relations between the Boston population and the British troops were reaching the flash point. General Gage descried the situation as "the People were as Lawless and Licentious after the Troops arrived, as they were before."[30] Tense environments also existed in other cities with sizeable troop presences. In New York City for the past year, a contest had existed between the local British garrison and the Sons of Liberty. A liberty pole would be erected on Golden Hill, and the troops would march out and cut it down. Finally, on January 19, Sons of Liberty led by John Lamb and Alexander McDougall decided to confront the British. The resultant riot, subsequently called the Battle of Golden Hill by the radicals, reportedly left several on both sides wounded and one civilian dead, although reports of the casualties and the size of the conflict may have been more propaganda than fact.[31]

Meanwhile in Boston, building on the propaganda value of Seider's death, the radicals began planning how to orchestrate a conflict with the troops that could clearly be blamed on the British authorities. The issue was how to create such an incident without having it get out of control. It called for a delicate balance in that too much violence would offend the moderate colonial politicians being courted by the radicals, and too mild a demonstration would not advance their political objective of forcing the removal of the troops from the city.[32]

The conflict, which became known as the Boston Massacre, began in a manner that had been repeated numerous times before. On March 2, an off-duty soldier of the Twenty-Ninth Regiment sought casual work from a Boston rope and cable maker.[33] He was rebuffed and insulted by the owner. He returned with several comrades seeking satisfaction. The resultant brawl sent the soldiers back to their barracks physically and emotionally beaten. The following day, other members of the same regiment engaged in a fight with some town laborers. That evening, a sergeant failed to show up for a roll call, and false rumors spread that he had been killed. At the same time, rumors in town were spreading that a large-scale brawl with the troops was being planned.

The flash point was reached on the evening of March 5. The Twenty-Ninth Regiment had earlier that day taken over responsibility for the sentry posts in the town. About eight o'clock in the evening, a young wigmaker, Edward Garrick,

John Lamb addressing the Sons of Liberty at the New York City
Hall on December 17, 1773, about the landing of British tea at New
York Harbor. *Library of Congress*

harassed a sentry near the customhouse, shouting insults about the character of
an officer and of the regiment. The sentry responded by striking the lad with his
musket. As the boy cried out in pain, a mob gathered, and the sentry became
agitated. As snowballs joined verbal insults and threats, the sentry moved to the
steps of the customhouse, loaded his musket, and fixed his bayonet.

Meanwhile, another confrontation was starting a few blocks away near the
barracks. Some unknown issue had evolved regarding a soldier's treatment of
some citizens, and a crowd had gathered to protest. Snowballs were thrown and
tempers flared on both sides. Then a third conflict broke out at nearby Dock
Square. A crowd of several hundred were addressed by an unidentified man who
had cloaked his features. After the speech, the crowd moved toward the noise
coming from the customhouse. Also drawn by the noise were people from the
barracks area. Church bells were ringing and cries of "fire" were heard.

By this time, word had reached the main guard that the sentry was in difficulty, and a relief party was ordered out to assist him. Cpl. William Wemms
and six privates composed this corporal's guard. Capt. Thomas Preston led
these men to the customhouse. Upon arrival, the muskets were loaded. Preston
ordered the sentry to join his formation and attempted to march back to the

barracks. However, the crowd refused to let them pass. Threats were directed at the troops as they formed a single line with their backs to the customhouse. Preston called upon the mob to disperse but was met with more curses, threats, and snowballs. The mob pressed forward to the tips of the soldiers' bayonets, daring them to fire. Vastly outnumbered, the soldiers were described as "shaking," probably out of both fear and anger.

Then a club was thrown, knocking down one of the soldiers, Hugh Montgomery. Rising to his feet, he fired his musket into the crowd. Other soldiers followed suit. No one heard Preston give an order to fire, nor was he heard to order a cease-fire. However, when the troops reloaded and took position to deliver a second round of fire, he halted them. The shock of the shooting had taken the spirit out of the crowd, which began to disperse. Preston was able to march his soldiers back to the main guard post. Rumors reached him that four to five thousand people were preparing to storm it. Throughout the city, church bells were ringing, drums were beating, and cries of "to arms" could be heard. Preston sounded the general alarm for the entire Boston garrison. The stage was set for an armed conflict wherein a real massacre might occur.

However, reacting quickly, the Sons of Liberty urged restraint on the population. Leaders such as Thomas Young, who had moved from Philadelphia to Boston to be closer to the political action, worked the streets to calm the people. Meanwhile, Adams and Molineux worked behind the scene with local officials to have the soldiers arrested for their actions. Their plan was to use British law against the troops and prove publicly that the citizens had been attacked without cause, even if it took false depositions from various "eyewitnesses" to make the case.

Over the next several days, the radicals held public gatherings to demand "justice," used the same theme in printed articles, and then on March 8, Adams staged a funeral for the victims that made Seider's event pale by comparison. He organized a procession of some twelve thousand people, led by the coffins of the dead, which circled the Liberty Tree before marching to the burial ground. Two days later, the radicals' objective was achieved. The Twenty-Ninth Regiment was sent to Castle William, with Molineux walking beside its formation to provide "protection" from the town's population. The next day, the final remaining regiment, the Fourteenth, also moved to the castle.

Now that British civil authority in Boston ceased to have any real protection, the radicals continued to build their pressure for a trial for the soldiers involved in the Boston Massacre. The propaganda campaign moved forward aggressively, with more public meetings, more dramatic newspaper

A depiction of the Boston Massacre, March 5, 1770, in which British troops fired into a crowd, killing five people. *Library of Congress*

condemnations, and a focusing of responsibility on Captain Preston, the officer in charge. A local artist, Henry Pelham, drew a dramatically inaccurate depiction of the incident, and Paul Revere quickly distributed copies of it vividly colored to highlight the blood of the victims and the uniforms of the soldiers.

However, the radicals were also working a parallel approach to the trial. Because the maximum propaganda objective was conviction of the soldiers in a court of law, the Sons of Liberty needed to create as fair a trial as possible, while still ensuring that the responsibility for the deaths would clearly be placed on the British authorities. To this end, Samuel Adams enlisted the support of John Adams and Josiah Quincy, both political moderates and respected lawyers, to defend the soldiers. Both had been involved with the Sons of Liberty but had never associated themselves with the group's street actions. This did not quite work out the way the radicals had hoped. The British authorities found several reasons to keep postponing the trial.

Finally, on September 7, Captain Preston, the soldiers, and four loyalist civilians whom the Sons of Liberty had dragged into the case under less than honest evidence were arraigned. All pled not guilty. A lengthy period of judicial inactivity then occurred, as both sides developed their legal positions. The jury was also selected for Preston's trial, which was held separately because it dealt with the issue of whether or not he had given the order to fire on civilians. Here fate seriously hurt the radicals' purpose. For reasons unknown, Samuel Adams was absent from the courtroom when the final jurors were selected, and John Adams failed to challenge several prospective jurors who were loyalist in nature. Under Massachusetts practice, a unanimous jury was required for conviction, and this did not now seem possible. As the trial proceeded, the defense was able to paint a picture of great confusion and identify conflicts in the testimony of various witnesses. On October 30, the jury delivered a verdict of not guilty. Upset by the verdict, the Sons of Liberty attempted to get those who had been wounded to file civil suits against Captain Preston. However, he quickly retired to Castle William, out of the reach of any process servers.

The soldiers' trial was scheduled for November 20 and moved somewhat quicker, but again the radicals' objectives were not met, although some minor satisfaction was gained. John Adams did a masterful job of convincing the jury that the soldiers had acted in their own defense under circumstances that legally absolved them of murder charges. On December 5, the jury found five of the soldiers not guilty and two guilty not of murder but manslaughter. These two were subsequently granted clemency, known in this case as the "benefit of clergy," which involved branding their right thumbs and voided any sentence. With this act, in the legal sense, the Boston Massacre became history.

While Samuel Adams had lost the legal battle to establish public blame on the British authorities for the deaths, he was determined to win the battle for the public and subsequently the historic perception of responsibility. Writing in the *Boston Gazette*, he blandly misrepresented the facts in the case, unfairly criticized the judicial process, and misstated testimony on record.[34] Of course, it worked. He further pressed the propaganda campaign by arranging to have the fifth day of March set aside each year as an annual day of mourning, replete with appropriate speeches, memorial ceremonies, and publications. Speaking in retrospect, John Adams stated that the foundation of American independence was laid on the night of March 5, 1770.[35]

With the end of the trials, a political weariness seemed to descend on Boston. The streets quieted down without the presence of British soldiers, and the nonimportation agreement was working. All and all, 1771 was a relatively quiet year but with political maneuvering on both sides. In September, writing in the *Boston Gazette*, Adams began the first of a series of articles that focused on the growth of colonial freedom within the context of its disputes with British rule. A second set of articles discussed British concepts of individual rights and the separation of powers, further building the political and intellectual argument for greater self-government in the colonies. These articles were reprinted throughout the colonies and created a groundswell of support for the people's "natural rights" that Parliament was violating.

However, 1772 was not going to be quiet. This time the conflict would occur in Rhode Island rather than Massachusetts. Early in the year, the HMS *Gaspée*, a Royal Navy schooner commanded by Lt. William Dudingston, sailed into Narragansett Bay to assist local royal officials with the smuggling problem. Dudingston, somewhat characteristically of British naval officers, held the colonials in contempt and did little to mask his feelings. Smuggling in Rhode Island was a long-established business and pretty much considered a right. However, Dudingston had a different view. He quickly developed a reputation for harassing all shipping in the bay. On February 17, he seized the *Fortune*, a sloop owned by Nathanael Greene & Company of Rhode Island and captained by Rufus Greene, a cousin of Nathanael's. After the boarding party insulted and threatened the captain, Dudingston took the ship and its cargo of rum and sugar to Boston, via Providence, for action by an admiralty court, in direct violation of local colonial laws.[36]

This action had two long-term effects: It demonstrated Dudingston's determination and arrogance regarding colonial rights, let alone sensibilities, and caused Nathanael Greene, previously nonpolitical, to move down the road toward active participation in the fight for freedom from Britain. In Dudingston's case the Rhode Islanders' revenge on him would be quick and painful. As to Greene's politicization, by the 1780s during the war's southern campaign, the British would be very sorry they had so motivated General Greene, commander of the Southern Army. He proved to be a master of mobile warfare, effectively degrading a larger British force and forcing it to seek resupply at Yorktown. As they say, the rest is history.

At the time, Greene stayed within the law and filed a suit against Dudingston. But before a legal remedy could be adjudicated, Dudingston's aggressiveness led to his downfall. On June 9, he chased the packet sloop *Hannah* sailing from Newport to Providence, believing it was carrying smuggled goods. The *Hannah* deliberately lured the *Gaspée* into shallow waters, where she ran aground. Upon arriving in Providence, the *Hannah*'s captain reported to his owner, John Brown. Brown immediately saw a situation where personal financial interests coincided with political views. Well aware of Dudingston's infamy among the local population, he summoned a crowd to a local tavern to discuss the situation. Later that night, eight longboats filled with patriots boarded the *Gaspée*, took its crew prisoner, and then set it afire, resulting in the explosion of the powder magazine. Dudingston was shot in the groin during the attack; it is unknown if the shooter's aim was intended or accidental. Brown proudly led the attack.[37] Subsequently, in the best Rhode Island tradition of colonial justice, British colonial authorities could find no credible witnesses capable of identifying his involvement.

This incident fitted nicely into Samuel Adams's strategy. In correspondence with Rhode Island's deputy governor, Darius Sessions, he wrote: "I have long feared this unhappy contest between Great Britain and would end in rivers of blood." He concluded that "America, I think, may wash her hands in innocence."[38] Throughout the colonies, newspapers played up the attack and followed British efforts to identify and punish those responsible. This incident also produced one of the most widely published pamphlets of the pre-Revolutionary era, *An Oration on the Beauties of Liberty* by the Rev. John Allen of Boston. While often overlooked as a major contribution to Revolutionary literature, at that time its effect could be compared to later works by the propagandist Thomas Paine. This spirited defense of the rights of Americans, widely read and debated throughout the colonies, was another element in support of

Adams's call for committees of correspondence between various colonial governmental bodies.

While Adams had had some success implementing such committees within the colony of Massachusetts, it took the impact of the British government's reaction to the *Gaspée* incident to develop a consensus among the colonies' politicians that a method for the comprehensive and timely dissemination of information regarding British actions and colonial responses was necessary. That many of these committees would be under the control of Sons of Liberty leaders meant that the information communicated might not be completely objective.

By the fall of 1772, the British commission of inquiry on the *Gaspée* affair grew increasingly frustrated with its inability to punish those responsible for the attack. The king granted the commission the authority to send those suspected of the crime to England for trial rather than having them tried in the colonies. This meant that a defense for the accused would be more difficult, as witnesses for them would seldom be available, and it was believed that an English court would be prejudiced against them. This logic was no doubt based on the fact that the traditionally independent colonial courts tended to side with its people in most legal proceedings against British authorities. However, regardless of the king's wishes, there was no American-based British official interested in such a course of action. Peter Oliver, a commission member and the chief justice of the Massachusetts colony, noted that fear of violence by the colonists meant that no one would take any such action.[39]

In an exchange of correspondence between Adams and radicals in Rhode Island early in 1773, Adams suggested that they send letters to the other colonial legislatures requesting support in opposing such a measure.[40] On this specific request for support, most of the colonial legislatures responded positively. This encouraged Adams, who decided the time was right to establish committees of correspondence between all the colonial legislatures. He orchestrated his plan through his Sons of Liberty contacts in Virginia, particularly Richard Henry Lee, believing that if this large southern colony sponsored the concept, the other southern colonies would be more inclined to support it. On March 12, 1773, the House of Burgesses created its committee and invited the rest of the colonies to join in communication regarding common issues. By the summer Rhode Island, Connecticut, New Hampshire, and South Carolina had formed committees. The channel was now established for local political leaders throughout the colonies to coordinate their actions, even when local royal governors chose to officially close down colonial legislatures, as would increasingly become the case.

Late in 1771, while this was occurring, Benjamin Franklin, then the Boston commercial representative in London, had obtained several private and official letters written by Governor Hutchinson, his lieutenant governor Andrew Oliver, and Boston customs officials calling for the use of British troops to reduce the liberties being exercised by the colony's population. A British official had secretly provided Franklin the letters, which were meant only for the British government leaders. Recognizing their significance, Franklin sent them to Thomas Cushing, the speaker of the Massachusetts legislature. Samuel Adams, Hancock, and other radicals were shown the letters just as Hutchinson had decided to address publicly the issues of what rights and freedoms the colonials could expect.

In early January 1773, Hutchinson spoke to the legislature at length, espousing an argument that the colony's charter did not provide for liberties or rights besides those of all subjects of the British Empire. He concluded firmly that the rule of Parliament was supreme and the colony's grievances should be forgotten. Adams drafted the legislature's response, citing British history's progression of increasing the rights of the individual and their constitutional basis. His arguments were well received as logical and sound, bringing more political moderates into the radical fold. Also, he chose this time to use the secret letters to their maximum effect.

In late May, at a closed session of the legislature, Adams read the letters aloud, dramatically emphasizing the portions regarding deployment of troops and the reduction of liberty. However, he advised that he was unable to provide the actual letters or allow them to be copied at that time. As anticipated, the delegates exploded with emotion, called for Hutchison's resignation, and passed a resolution that he was attempting to subvert the rights of the colony. In early June, Adams agreed to publish the letters but only after he published an article casting the letters in the appropriate darkest and harshest light.[41]

Adams felt the time was right a few months later to issue a call for a colonial congress to represent the American colonists as an independent state. Hutchinson had long advised London that Adams was guilty of treason and was the most dangerous man in Boston, and his call for independence further brought home that point. But the British government was unsure how to handle him. One group hoped that Adams might be bribed by a government appointment. Hutchinson responded that he doubted Adams would accept any government post and also that such an appointment would place dangerous powers in his hands.[42]

While Adams's call for a congress enraged the British authorities, favorable reaction among the colonial legislatures was not forthcoming, except among his Sons of Liberty colleagues. But once again, British actions worked to his advantage. News of the Tea Act arrived in Boston in October 1773. This was an attempt by the British government to assist the financially faltering East India Company and at the same time create an incentive to break the colonial tea boycott, thus reducing the radicals' political power. The Tea Act placed a duty on imported tea but permitted the East India Company to sell directly to the colonies, eliminating the middlemen and thus making the overall cost to the colonial consumer significantly cheaper—even cheaper than smuggled tea.

The radicals were ready this time. The committees of correspondence were established, and both news and coordination of efforts spread rapidly. Newspaper articles throughout the colonies carried the same anti–Tea Act theme, and reports circulated of efforts in New York and Philadelphia to force the tea importers to cancel their shipments. Once again, Boston became the focal point. With British troops on Castle William Island and the British North American fleet now headquartered in Boston, Adams planned carefully and secretly, relying on the compartmentation and discipline of the Sons of Liberty.

Early in the morning of November 2, two men knocked on the door of Richard Clark, a Boston agent for the East India Company. They left with him a written demand that he and other tea shipment consignees meet at the Liberty Tree the following day and resign their positions. Notices of this event were posted around the town. The day of the meeting, Adams, Hancock, and several hundred citizens waited at the Tree but no one showed up. The next day, Adams held a town meeting that voted to support Philadelphia's efforts to force its tea agents to resign. A few nights later, Clark was revisited by a mob that threatened him and his family.

The situation came to a head in mid-December, when a ship with a cargo of tea faced a customs deadline to land its goods and pay the required duty. The radicals refused to allow the tea to be landed, the ship's owner was refused permission to sail out of the harbor, and the tea consignees volunteered to warehouse the tea and not place it on sale. Adams organized a meeting for the evening of December 17, attended by several thousand people. At the meeting Hutchinson refused any compromise. Adams closed the meeting, stating for the public record that this gathering could do no more.

This was the signal for a group of Sons of Liberty, led by Paul Revere and

Dr. Warren, to move to the wharf where the three vessels carrying tea were moored: the *Dartmouth*, the *Beaver*, and the *Eleanor*. These men were dressed as Mohawk Indians to symbolize American freedom and perhaps also to hide their true identities. As planned during a secret meeting on November 29, the group split into three sections, boarded the ships, and tossed 342 chests of tea into the harbor. The British authorities were paralyzed. The fleet could not open fire without destroying the ships, their cargoes, and the crowd of by-standers watching from the wharf. As to the troops, there was too little time to organize and transport them to the city.

By coincidence, perhaps, in New York City at about the same time Alexander McDougall organized a group of Sons of Liberty, also dressed as Mohawks, who boarded a ship there and dumped its cargo of tea into the harbor.[43]

In Boston, Hutchinson believed that military force was the only solution to regain British control of the colony. Parliament reacted to the tea destruction by passing the Boston Port Bill on March 31, 1774. This law prohibited all commercial shipping activities at the port of Boston, with the exception of food imports required to feed the city. It immediately put thousands of people out of work. The bill was to remain in effect until Massachusetts provided restitution for the loss of the tea. Shortly after news of the bill reached Boston, General Gage assumed the role of royal governor. He announced that four regiments would soon arrive and that the Massachusetts legislature would be closed until June, clearly indicating that his orders were not focused on negotiation.

About the same time, trusted members of the Sons of Liberty formed the Mechanics, today recognized as America's first intelligence organization.[44] One of its first leaders was Paul Revere, who reported to Adams, Hancock, Warren, and Dr. Benjamin Church. Its purpose was to gain intelligence on the activities and movements of the British troops in Boston. In addition to this observation of troop activities, its members developed informants within the British administration.

Creation of an intelligence-collection capability is a key element in any mature political action campaign, and members of united front organizations are often used as intelligence agents. Their previous efforts in the organization would have demonstrated their loyalty and commitment to the cause. Without an intelligence-collection capability, the leadership loses its ability to take the initiative, only being able to react to its opponents' actions.

The Sons of Liberty offered the opportunity over time to identify and recruit its most committed members into more selective and secret activities. Dr. Warren used some of these individuals in his Massachusetts Committee of

Safety, which did some overt observation of British activities but focused primarily upon defensive measures to protect colonial military supplies from British seizure, by organizing and training local militia forces. However, during the Revolution other organization members became intelligence agents operating behind British lines.[45] Hercules Mulligan of the Culper spy ring in New York City was one such former Sons of Liberty member.[46]

With the implementation of the Port Bill, Adams renewed his call for a colonial congress. This time he received widespread support. Cities, towns, and colonial legislatures responded positively as his call moved southward: Providence supported the call on May 17, Philadelphia on May 21, and New York City on May 23. The congress was to be held in Philadelphia, and while it was organized by radicals, political moderates also wished to attend, as a united voice might yet avoid a direct confrontation with Britain.

However, the British government continued its plan to force the colonies back into a disciplined relationship. On June 2, Parliament extended the Quartering Act of 1765 to all the colonies, with particular aim at Boston. This allowed Gage to quarter his troops within the city of Boston in taverns, public buildings, and even private residences. British troops were now back on the street, interacting daily with the people.

As the Massachusetts legislature was about to reconvene in June, Samuel Adams faced a serious issue: how to get it to officially designate a delegation to the Philadelphia congress without Gage dissolving the body. Lacking official standing, the Massachusetts representatives, and Adams himself, would have little ostensible authority to represent the colony. To develop a plan of action, he met secretly with other Sons of Liberty members of the legislature and crafted a scheme, which he put into action on June 17. As Adams rose to address the body, he ordered the doors locked and the windows closed. His colleagues took up positions by the doors. He then proposed that he, John Adams, and three other members be designated as the Massachusetts delegation to the congress. Using a prearranged political strategy manipulating the parliamentary procedures of the legislature, Adams was able to mute the opposition and get his proposal passed. While a loyalist member of the legislature had been able to get word to Gage of Adams's motion, by the time Gage was able to send a representative to close the session the official was unable to enter the building.[47]

Gage, well aware that Adams must be dealt with, made one last noncoercive effort to negotiate with him. He sent a senior British officer to offer Adams a bribe, which included both a significant amount of cash and a royal appointment within the colony.[48] Adams declined, apparently politely.

With the legislature closed down, Adams and his colleagues moved to create a colonial body with its allegiance to the Continental Congress being organized in Philadelphia. He and Warren drew up proposals that effectively rendered the royal governor's institutions powerless, denying them legal authority and withholding tax revenues that enabled them to function.

On August 10, Samuel Adams went to Philadelphia, leaving Warren to move the proposals through the newly created colonial convention. Upon arrival, he and his fellow delegates were well received. But radical members in other delegations warned that many representatives were concerned about his political positions. He took careful note of these concerns and modified his rhetoric. He also ensured that John Adams, with his more moderate representation, became the public face of the delegation. However, behind the scenes Samuel Adams played the role of power broker. Working with other Sons of Liberty in the Virginia delegation, especially Richard Henry Lee, he obtained that delegation's support for the Massachusetts agenda. In return Adams negotiated a deal to have Peyton Randolph of Virginia elected chairman of the Congress.

Rumors of British actions in Boston soon played into Adams's hands. Initial reports were alarming, claiming that the city had been bombarded by the British fleet. The truth was less dramatic but still troubling. On September 1, Gage had his troops seize weapons and gunpowder from a Sons of Liberty arsenal in Charlestown. This use of the British military to seize private property struck a sensitive nerve within the Congress and increased support for Adams's agenda.

In early September, the resolutions drafted by Adams and Warren were passed by the Massachusetts convention, and this news was carried to Philadelphia by Paul Revere. These Suffolk Resolves, as they came to be known, were read to the Congress on September 17. Gage's seizure of private property, as well as his fortification of the entrance to Boston, created a favorable political atmosphere for Adams's proposal that the Congress support the resolutions. It did so, and its endorsement was publicized in newspapers throughout the colonies.

As the result of these actions in Philadelphia, British administration throughout the colonies began to collapse. British legal authorities were challenged on every front, and without tax revenue their capabilities to enforce and administer civil authority withered. Leaders of the committees of correspondence began taking control of local government responsibilities and organizing local militia to support their efforts. In a report to London, John Murray, Earl of Dunmore and the royal governor of Virginia, stated that as of the end of 1774, companies of militia were forming throughout the colony to protect the committee and he no longer controlled the colonial government.[49]

By December 1774, the Mechanics had established some sources within Gage's administration in Boston. They received information that he was about to send reinforcements to a fort at Portsmouth Harbor in New Hampshire, and they were able to warn John Sullivan, a radical leader in the colony, early enough to allow Sons of Liberty to seize the fort and strip it of cannon and gunpowder before it could be reinforced.[50] In a similar action in Newport, militiamen seized forty-four cannon from a local fort and sent them to Providence for future militia use. Removal of weapons and gunpowder from British and colonial facilities and military installations occurred throughout the colonies during the fall and winter of 1774–75.

As the fifth anniversary of the Boston Massacre drew near, Adams and his fellow radicals had growing concerns for their physical safety. A group of British soldiers, apparently without formal British government approval, developed a plan to create a confrontation at the commemoration service and use the resultant confusion to assassinate Adams, Warren, and Hancock. Hundreds of soldiers agreed to participate. However, the signal to start the confrontation was to be an egg thrown at the ceremony. As fate would have it, the soldier responsible broke his egg prior to its intended use, and the plot did not take place.[51] Between learning of the plot and obtaining information through the Mechanics that Gage was preparing to take action against them, Adams and his colleagues decided it was time to move out of Boston to Lexington. Gage, through his own intelligence capabilities, soon learned of their whereabouts, and the scene was set for the "shot heard 'round the world."

With the commencement of armed conflict, the radicals' political-action campaign had succeeded. They had motivated and manipulated a significant number of colonists to equate their future with independence from Britain-based rule. As the armed conflict grew, emotions reinforced radical views in many more and complete political independence became an accepted objective. Now all the colonists had to do was defeat the best army in Europe—or, more accurately, not allow their meager army to be defeated.

And of course, intelligence activities would play a significant role in the outcome. But before the shooting started in earnest and the political-action campaign gave way to armed revolution, the Sons of Liberty intelligence group had a last role to play. As events led up to the British march on Lexington and Concord on April 19, 1775, Gage was confident that his intelligence regarding the location of radical leaders and military supplies was accurate. The Sons of Liberty believed they had obtained accurate intelligence on Gage's plan and could thwart it. Both sides believed their sources in the enemy's camp had provided accurate intelligence. Both sides were correct.

CHAPTER 3

THE INTELLIGENCE
WAR BEGINS

The military refers to it as "prepping the battlefield." Civilian intelligence professionals often refer to it as "putting in the plumbing." Both phrases refer to establishing a basic intelligence framework for collection of information. In 1775 Boston, both the American colonial leaders and the British civilian and military leaders knew that armed conflict was not far away. And they had each begun to establish the basic infrastructure necessary to collect on the plans, intentions, and capabilities of their anticipated enemy.

When Gen. Thomas Gage assumed command in Boston in May of 1774 as military governor of the Province of Massachusetts Bay, he was well acquainted with the political realities of the situation. He had first arrived in the North American colonies in 1755 when his regiment was assigned to General Braddock's troops, seeking to oust French forces from "the Ohio Country." It was there that he first met George Washington, the commander of Virginia troops, in the expedition. After the conclusion of the French and Indian War, he was made military governor of Montreal. In 1764, after a year in an acting capacity, he was appointed commander in chief of all North American British forces, which were based in New York City. There he watched the activities of the colonial rebels become more aggressive in response to increasingly harsh British legislation. His view of the rebels' activities was clearly stated in his letter of November 12, 1770, to William Barrington, the British secretary at war: "America is a mere bully, from one end to the other, and the Bostonians by far the greatest bullies."[1]

Within five years' time, he would find that these "bullies" had some substance to them.

In 1773, he briefly returned to England but with Massachusetts's Gov. Thomas Hutchinson unable to control the colony, he was sent back to stabilize the political and military situation there. By the fall of 1775, he was well aware that the Massachusetts provincial congress had ordered various supplies, including military equipment and provisions, to be collected and stored at Concord and Worcester. He was also well aware that militia units surrounding Boston were actively drilling and organizing for conflict. Though he and his troops were stationed in Boston, individuals loyal to the king living in the surrounding towns and villages made sure he was knowledgeable of these events. In fact, he had at least one paid informant placed in the center of the patriots' political-action and intelligence-collection leadership.

On February 26, 1775, an incident occurred that would have changed an important date in American history, partially as the result of poor intelligence on the part of the British. In an effort to demonstrate to the colonialists that he would not permit their stockpiling of weapons, Gage ordered Lt. Col. Alexander Leslie, commanding the Sixty-Fourth Regiment, to seize cannon and other military weapons and supplies reported to be at the forge in Salem, outside of Boston. This raid, known locally in the Salem-Marblehead area of Massachusetts as "Leslie's Retreat," could easily have become the "shot heard 'round the world" two months earlier than it eventually took place. Based upon apparently faulty intelligence, which may have come from a Salem Tory named John Sargent, Gage believed the rebels had twenty cannon at the forge. As with much of the narratives describing this incident, facts differ on whether these were old iron cannon or newer, French-made, brass cannon. Regardless, Gage wished to make a strong statement to a town that had previously demonstrated strong support for the patriot cause.

Leslie placed his regiment on a British transport ship under cover of darkness from his base at Castle William the evening of the 25th and arrived off Marblehead Bay the next morning, a Sunday. He planned a rapid march into Salem while the population, good churchgoers, was at services. However, Marblehead residents, who perhaps were not quite as religious as their neighbors, were not all in church and quickly spotted his landing. Messengers were sent to Salem, and the Marblehead militia was called out. When Leslie arrived at Salem, he found his way blocked by a raised drawbridge over the North River, the only approach from Marblehead, and a few angry townsfolk. At this point the British and colonial versions of the story differ significantly. The British version, officially reported to London by Gage, was that Leslie found the cannon to be only eight, old, iron pieces, accomplished his mission, and departed. The colonial version is that Leslie found himself in a difficult position, with rebel militiamen gathering from the surrounding countryside, and made a face-saving deal. It was agreed that the drawbridge would be lowered and Leslie would march his men into the town of Salem, thus fulfilling his orders, and then turn them around and march back to the ship.[2]

As the event played out, the colonial version seems more accurate. It has been documented that several cannon, rather old iron types, were at the forge and poorly concealed. Leslie did not seize them, and he marched back to Marblehead Harbor and departed for Boston without any further conflict with the locals. In any event, bloodshed was avoided for another two months, and Lexington and Concord became the sites of the first combat between British and American forces.

About the same time as the Salem raid, Gage instructed two of his officers to conduct a reconnaissance of the roads between Boston and Worcester. His instructions to Capt. William Brown of the Fifty-Second Regiment and Ens. Henry de Berniere of the Tenth Regiment made it clear that he wanted details to plan a raid against Worcester. In an effort to be discreet, both officers dressed in the country style of brown coats and reddish neckerchiefs. However, both officers were well known in Boston. The fact that they were going through areas where families had lived as neighbors for generations made them obvious as outsiders. That evening, they stopped at a tavern for dinner, and an African American serving woman recognized Brown and quickly deduced their mission. For the remainder of their trip, they seemed to be monitored by local patriots even though they stayed in the taverns of local Tories on several nights.[3]

On March 20, a few weeks after their return to Boston, Gage sent them on a similar mission to Concord, with instructions to ascertain what military supplies were stored there. Apparently traveling in similar country dress, they took a circuitous route to bypass areas of their previous trip. Their contact in Concord was a known Tory, Daniel Bliss. While attempting to locate his residence, they once again came to the attention of the local patriot leaders. However, the officers were able to obtain details of the stored supplies, most likely from Bliss, and learn that field guns and mortars were also in the village. Bliss, fearing for his safety, joined the officers in their return to Boston. Gage was pleased with their report, and Ensign de Berniere was subsequently chosen to guide the British forces on their march to Lexington and Concord on April 19.[4]

Thus, while the British reconnaissance had been successful in the tactical sense of having collected the required information, from an overall intelligence perspective it was a failure. The patriots were now aware, at the local level, that routes to both Worcester and Concord had been studied for future use. This knowledge allowed local leaders to refine their planning for mobilization of forces, as well as consider where to deploy them against a raiding force. This was a classic example of why a reconnaissance mission that does not give proper importance to its counterintelligence protection can lead to disaster. While this example regards a military mission, in intelligence activities it holds true for any intelligence target. Whether it is a foreign government office or a private-sector location suspected of intelligence connections, approaching it to gather such basic information as physical location, entrances, floor plans, specific office locations, and so forth requires a carefully constructed plan that does not raise the counterintelligence alertness at that facility or in the area. A professional casing of a target can take months and involve numerous one-time specific data-collection missions.

Military historians have long known that the British experience at the Battle of Bunker (or Breed's) Hill, charging in formation uphill against fortified American positions, affected their aggressiveness and strategy throughout the war.[5] This was especially true during the British campaign in the Long Island–Manhattan area, where their hesitation to attack certain American positions on the high ground resulted ultimately in allowing Washington to evacuate the majority of his army safely to New Jersey.

A similar lesson was learned from the experience of the American militiamen using nontraditional tactics against the British troops retreating from Concord. These tactics proved a very effective way for militiamen to engage British troop formations, and this lesson was not lost on British and American commanders.

British troops, both officers and soldiers, did not hold the colonial militias in high regard during most of the war. Certain political officials in the British colonial service knowledgeable about American militia skills from the French and Indian War were more realistic. On April 19, 1775, the British were not prepared for the type of resistance they would encounter once the militiamen had arrived and their march back to Boston from Concord began. Militia use of small-unit tactics, firing from cover within the woods, and then moving ahead of the road-bound British column to engage them once again were effective in producing significant casualties. More important strategically, these tactics were of grave concern to an army trained to move and fight in heavy formations with but slight flexibility to counter such tactics.

American militia success against British formations in this initial engagement made an impact on the British Army leadership. These tactics created a frustrating insurgency type of war of attrition that hurt British morale because the American militias would not fight like civilized Europeans. Most important, it caused the British to concentrate their forces in large garrisons, leaving most of the countryside open to the rebels. It also forced the British to employ larger numbers when moving into contested areas. And it caused the British to prefer sea routes to transport their troops rather than land marches, because the Royal Navy could control the coastal waters better than the army could control the countryside. This was particularly true in the western frontier areas and the South, as well as in areas in Pennsylvania and New Jersey.

Comparing the American militias to the Taliban or Viet Cong guerrillas in terms of the tactics used and the result thus imposed upon the British occupying force has some validity. In this regard, while not displaying the greatest discipline and trustworthiness in set-piece battles—perhaps with the exception of the battles at Cowpens and Saratoga—the militias posed a significant military threat to British forces when engaged in small-unit tactics protecting their countryside.

In the constant back-and-forth game of intelligence collection and counter-intelligence that was being played in Boston at this time, the patriot leadership was well aware of the British interest in identifying where weapons and provisions were being stored. Because the British lived surrounded by a hostile population in the city, there were endless opportunities to learn what the British knew and how they planned to act. By late 1774, the Mechanics had learned of planned British actions in New Hampshire and early in 1775 of plans to seize military supplies from Salem.[6] The Mechanics were organized and led by some of the most talented and influential individuals in the Massachusetts patriots' leadership. However, their security procedures were based more on their belief in the honorableness of their cause than sound operational security. Their vetting procedure to ensure secrecy at their meetings apparently consisted of all present swearing on the Bible to keep secret their activities.[7] As Boston was a relatively small town, and the many members of the Mechanics had known each other throughout the past ten-plus years of political conflict, little thought was given to the possibility that the British had penetrated the group. They had. One of its senior members was a paid spy for General Gage.

The word "traitor," even more so than "spy," has a decidedly emotional and pejorative sense to it. Also, considering that at the time all the colonists were subjects of the British king, placing that label on an individual should be a carefully considered act. Had the war ended differently—and there were many times during the conflict that such an outcome seemed imminent—there is no doubt that we would be describing the patriot leadership as traitors. So a great deal of value judgment, primarily in the area of the person's intent, is involved when I describe Dr. Benjamin Church as the first American traitor and arguably the first real British spy, as opposed to British loyalists who maintained their allegiance to the Crown by reporting on the rebels' efforts to overthrow the legitimate royal colonial government.

An example of the latter was Benjamin Thompson. He used invisible writing to send messages to Gage regarding the Continental Congress's efforts to raise forces for the army, as well as reported rebel military activities in the Boston area. He was a discreet intelligence collector whose political loyalties were not hidden. As late as early November 1775, after Sir William Howe succeeded Gage in Boston, he was still reporting information on rebel activities. However, when the British evacuated Boston on March 17, 1776, he went with them to England. So it would be unfair to even label him a spy, let alone a traitor. While his political loyalties were clear, his personal loyalties were more complicated. When he left with the British, he did not bring his wife and their young daughter along or even mention to her that he was leaving.[8] Residing eventually in Europe and using the name Count Rumford, he became a highly respected scientist.

And the day of his, and the British, departure from Boston remains a significant local holiday within the city. In fact, until a few years ago the day was a paid holiday for Boston city employees to allow them to celebrate the departure of the hated British "redcoats" or "lobster backs." The fact that March 17 is also Saint Patrick's Day is, apparently, a coincidence—or a consequence of the luck of the Boston Irish.

As to the first traitor, Church was born in Newport on August 24, 1734.[9] Coming from an educated and relatively prosperous family, he attended Harvard and graduated in 1754. It would be an understatement to say he came from solid British stock, as his great grandfather, also named Benjamin Church, was an effective officer for the Crown in several of the minor wars fought in the late seventeenth and early eighteenth centuries in North America with the French and various Indian tribes, including King Philip's War, King William's War, and Queen Anne's War. In fact, if one wished to really push the question of who was the leader of the first North American ranger-style unit, Church's great granddad has a well-documented claim to that honor.[10] He adopted Indian-style fighting tactics for his unit, which were, to a degree, subsequently copied by Roger's Rangers and various other colonial units, as well as a few units of the British regular army stationed in North America.

After graduation from Harvard, Church studied medicine and eventually moved to London to further his studies. He returned to the Boston area in 1771 with an English wife and established a respectable medical practice that provided a moderate standard of living. He became involved in radical political activities soon after his return, joining the Sons of Liberty and speaking publicly in support of political independence from Britain. His involvement with the patriot leadership in Massachusetts soon propelled him into leadership positions in the Massachusetts Provincial Congress, the Massachusetts Committee of Safety, and finally the Mechanics. However, just as his political life was expanding, his personal life was undergoing some significant changes.

Exactly when Church began spying remains a matter of some discussion. At least one researcher, citing a letter to a London newspaper, suspects he could have started his reporting to Governor Hutchinson prior to Gage's governorship.[11] However, that he was doing so by late 1774 is quite well established. His lifestyle changes from 1772 onward give solid clues as to his motivation for assisting the British: money. Within a year of his return from London, Church took up with an expensive mistress. She must have been quite beautiful and talented, because history demonstrates she was not all that bright. He built an expensive home, more costly than justified by his income at the time. He also developed a personal relationship with a British officer in Boston who was retired on half pay, Captain Price. Through him, he met and socialized with other government officials, such as Commissioner Robinson and local Tories. All the while, he was also rising in the patriots' ranks and leadership.

These changes should have signaled some reasons for concern if even a rudimentary counterintelligence effort existed. But no such organization existed in the patriots' political or intelligence structure. In fact, with the exception of a few months early in the war, the American side in the war never had a counterintelligence service or centralized approach to identifying and neutralizing enemy spies.

An intelligence agent, in this case a penetration agent because Church was inside the leadership of the patriots' organization, is recruited and directed through the use of personal motivators. In a general sense, these tend to be the same motivators that drive most people in life: ego, money, political ideology, and so forth. However, understanding the priority of the agent's motivations, and the deeper psychological implications of why they exist in that individual, is the key to effective utilization of the agent. Thus it would be most interesting to know why Church cooperated with Gage and was willing to take the risks he did to report. It is well documented that Church received financial compensation from Gage, and most studies of him tend to see that as the reason for his cooperation. Because he also reported to General Howe after Gage departed, he did accept a new operational manager, so his personal relationship with Gage would not appear to be a significant factor in the espionage relationship. Based upon analysis of his writings, one student of Church believed that upon the arrival of British reinforcements, Church became unsure of the patriots' capabilities, and in a pragmatic attempt to protect himself regardless of the outcome agreed to assist Gage.[12] This makes sense, as Church's ability to seemingly demonstrate loyalty to two opposing factions is a characteristic of a nonideologically motivated agent—one whose real loyalty is only to himself.

Then why did Church decide to spy for the British? He left no record of his motivations, so one can only speculate. However, other information of record seems to indicate that traditional intelligence-recruiting tradecraft may also have been involved. It is likely that individuals who befriended him may have helped him decide to work for the British. It was quite common for British officers on half pay to supplement their incomes by working for local intelligence officials, and Captain Price could well have fallen into this category. He would have traveled in the same social circles in Boston as Church based upon his professional rank. He could have identified Church to his intelligence superiors as a rebel leader with certain proclivities for an expensive lifestyle. Or he could have been directed to develop a social relationship based upon Church's position within the rebel structure. In that case, Price could have then orchestrated a seemingly innocent meeting and begun a social relationship based on Church's interests and habits. He could have learned that Church was motivated by money or needed money because of his desired lifestyle and could have spoken in support of any doubts Church might have regarding who would win in a conflict with the British military. Commissioner Robinson could also have played a similar or supporting role in assessing and supporting Church's desire to protect himself regardless of the outcome of events. Either or both of these individuals could have identified Church to Gage as a potential agent. The basic framework for assessing, developing, and recruiting a target is pretty standard and used by virtually every intelligence service worldwide. This procedure is as old as spying itself. While there is no documentation to support the above scenario specifically, it probably happened very much like that.

Church's reason, or cover for action, in frequent meetings with Robinson and eventually Gage was that he was using his social interactions to obtain information of value to the rebels from British officials. This story was acceptable because Church was trusted by the rebel leadership as "one of us." Throughout history, regardless of the inner leadership circle's culture and political ideology, it is seldom willing to believe that one of its own would betray it. Current examples of this abound, as will future examples. It is a human reaction to trust someone espousing similar values and loyalties, even in the face of suspect behavior. Paul Revere's letter of January 1, 1798, to Jeremy Belknap, the founder and president of the Massachusetts Historical Society, discussed Church and makes this point:

> He appeared to be a high son of Liberty. He frequented all the places where they met, Was incouraged by all the leaders of the Sons of Liberty, and it appeared he was respected by them, though I knew that Dr. Warren had not the greatest affection for him. . . . I was a constant and critical observer of him, and I must say that I never thought him a man of Principle; and I doubted much in my own mind whether he was a real Whig. I knew that he kept company with a Captain Price, a half-pay British officer, and that he frequently dined with him and Robinson, one of the Commissioners. . . . The day after the battle of Lexington, I met him in Cambridge, when he shew me some blood on his stocking, which he said spirted on him from a man who was killed near him, as he was urging the militia on. I well remember, that I argued with myself, if a man will risk his life in a cause, he must be a friend to that cause; and I never suspected him after, till he was charged with being a Traytor.[13]

Church's treason was finally discovered due to a change of his usual method of getting information to Gage. This is the historic "double-edged sword" of creating a strong security presence around an area to protect it: Just as it becomes more difficult to get information *out*, it becomes equally difficult for agents outside to get information *in* to their superiors. As Gage felt the need to better secure the city of Boston from its surrounding areas, he created a denied area in terms of restricting the free flow of individuals and therefore information. At that time, Boston was almost an island, with only a narrow strip of land called the Boston Neck connecting it to the mainland of the colony. His logic was sound from his perspective: Shielding one's forces from observation by the enemy is a traditional military tactic and objective. However, this also forced his collection agents outside of Boston to find new methods of reporting their information to him. No longer could they easily make a journey into Boston under the guise of professional, commercial, or social business to report directly. Or if they did, questions could be asked as to why they were allowed to enter Boston.

Church's downfall began in the summer of 1775 as Boston became a besieged city. Previously, when he was in the area, he had been able to personally deliver his messages to Gage in Boston. In fact, on one occasion after Lexington and Concord, he was observed at Gage's residence there in a friendly conversation with the general. A patriot sympathizer noted the incident and reported it to the Mechanics. Subsequently, Church was able to explain his meeting with Gage by stating he had been arrested while attempting to enter the city to obtain information and that after being taken to Gage for questioning, he was able to talk his way out of the arrest.[14]

With his normal method of reporting restricted, Church decided to try an alternative communication channel. How he decided to accomplish this was a serious mistake, predicated upon poor judgment on several levels. Once again, we have a case of catching a spy because he or she does something dumb. Church decided to send a letter, with the text openly encrypted, to a British officer of Gage's staff. For his courier, he picked his mistress, a woman who lacked the ingenuity or common sense for such a sensitive mission. She traveled to Newport and contacted a former lover, Godfrey Wenwood, who ran a bakery on Bannister's Wharf and supplied the Royal Navy with baked goods. She attempted to get him to arrange for her to meet Capt. Sir James Wallace, the commander of the HMS *Rose*, patrolling at Newport. If Wallace was not available, she said she could meet with other individuals who happened to be prominent local Tories. For various reasons, one of which was a pending marriage to a local young lady, Wenwood found the presence of his former lover unwelcome. He convinced her to leave the letter with him for subsequent delivery.[15]

Apparently a man of slow and careful deliberation, he held the sealed letter for several weeks, no doubt weighing the benefits and disadvantages of getting himself involved in an obviously controversial situation. Finally, he sought the advice of a friend, one apparently with a more rash nature, who opened the letter and discovered the encrypted contents. However, no doubt recognizing that they had become involved in some potentially dangerous matter, rather than take any additional action they both thought about the matter for several more days. The matter was brought to a head for both these thoughtful individuals when Church learned the mistress had left the letter with Wenwood. He insisted she write a letter to Wenwood noting that she knew the letter had not been delivered. At this point the letter was taken to a Rhode Island rebel official, who immediately recognized what the letter represented and instructed Wenwood to take it to Gen. Nathanael Greene, the commander of Rhode Island forces surrounding Boston.

Upon seeing the letter, Greene took it, and the baker, to General Washington. Washington convinced Wenwood to visit the woman to try and obtain more details about the letter. But he was unsuccessful. Washington then ordered her arrest, interrogated her, and obtained the details of how she came to have the letter. Washington was most surprised to learn that Church had written it. He sent for Church, who admitted authoring the letter but stated it was innocent in nature.[16] On October 3, Washington received copies of the actual contents of the letter, which contained information on Continental Army strength. Church's cipher had been broken independently by an army chaplain and a militia commander. When questioned further, Church insisted he was only attempting to frighten the enemy and cause it to reconsider any offensive actions by providing the size of the Continental forces. This argument was not effective, and the generals Washington had gathered to investigate the matter decided to court-martial Church, who held the position of chief medical officer of the Continental Army at the time.

Here we run into another counterintelligence issue that exists to the present day: the lack of effective legislation to try and convict intelligence agents working for a foreign power. While the Continental Congress had legislated that an individual reporting to the enemy could be punished by a court-martial, it also limited the punishments granted to courts-martial. Thus the worst Church could get was thirty-three lashes or a fine of two months' pay. Were he an army officer, he could also be cashiered, but he was not considered to be one.[17] This was hardly a meaningful punishment, either for the individual involved or as a deterrent for others for such a serious crime as providing information to the enemy regarding military capabilities. Probably in frustration, because the decision was legally questionable, the Congress imprisoned Church. The case took various turns until 1780, when the Congress banished him to the West Indies. During the voyage his ship sank, and he was never heard of again.

It appears that the Continental Congress passed the legislation regarding reporting to the enemy in the belief that such an action would only be found at a very low level of significance. The patriotic colonial leadership could not, or rather would not, comprehend that within their ranks were individuals with various motivations allowing them to spy for the British. As the war progressed, they would be disabused of this view.

Just as Gage effectively employed intelligence collectors against the rebels, they in turn spied on him. By the fall of 1974, the Mechanics, led by Revere, were organized and active inside Boston. Much of their effort was related to early-warning reporting such as watching for indicators of British troop movements. Because the Mechanics comprised well-established tradespeople in Boston, their status and cover for action were natural.[18] In this manner they were easily able to monitor any indications of preparation for movements. In addition many British soldiers and their dependents took part-time jobs in the civilian community and naturally spoke with their employers and fellow workers about such matters as absences from work due to military activities.

An example of Mechanics reporting occurred in December of 1774. The organization learned that Gage was preparing to move two regiments to Fort William and Mary in Portsmouth to secure British munitions and cannon stored there. Portsmouth patriots were quickly warned, and local militia forces overpowered the small resident British garrison and removed most of the munitions and several cannon into the countryside.[19] However, they were also developing more in-depth information on Gage's plans and intentions through reporting, or cooperative, sources in his professional and social circles. Many Tory stalwarts had relatives sympathetic to the rebels. Also, many Boston tradesmen had long-standing business relationships supplying the British Army and Royal Navy. By monitoring British supply orders, the patriots were able to anticipate future plans and movements. Finally, social and family interactions offered significant opportunities for current gossip and nonpublic, but not secret, information on British plans and intentions.[20]

All of these collection capabilities played a role in the Mechanics' best-known intelligence success—the warning of the countryside about the British raid on Lexington and Concord. On April 15, 1775, patriots observed the Royal Navy's small boats being repaired, a clear indication that troops were to be moved from Castle William across the Charles River to the Massachusetts shore. By the next day other sources had confirmed that troops were to be sent to seize military supplies at Lexington and Concord. That day Revere rode to Lexington to warn Hancock and Samuel Adams. Local patriots in Concord also began moving military stores out of the village into the countryside to hide them. When the British finally embarked on April 19, most of their objectives had already been denied them. The story of Paul Revere's, and his fellow patriot William Dawes's, famous rides represents the final phase of this intelligence operation.

An interesting side note to this story is the possible role played by the New

Portrait of Margaret Kemble Gage, 1771, by John Singleton Copley.
She was the American-born wife of British general Thomas Gage and
was suspected of providing information on her husband's plans to the
Patriot "Mechanics" in 1775. Her husband subsequently sent her to
England. *The Putnam Foundation; Timken Museum of Art, San Diego;
and The Bridgeman Art Library*

Jersey–born wife of Gage, Margaret Kemble Gage. While no direct evidence exists that she passed information to the rebels regarding her husband's plans, there is ample information to demonstrate that she had both the capability and political leaning to do so. While it is possible that General Gage never discussed his plans with his wife, this probably was not the case with other family members. Gage's staff officer handling intelligence matters was Margaret's brother, Maj. Stephen Kemble, and her other brother, Samuel Kemble, was his confidential secretary. Rounding out the family's role in Gage's intelligence organization, his aide-de-camp for intelligence was Capt. Oliver DeLancey, Margaret's cousin.[21] Thus, while Gage may not have discussed such matters with his wife, he probably did with her brothers. Therefore it is possible—even probable—that Margaret learned of the plan for the raid. As to her political orientation, it was well known that she had sympathy for her countrymen and wished them no harm at the hands of her husband's troops.[22] Another fact that points to her possible involvement is the action of Gage after the Lexington and Concord expedition. He sent Margaret back to England alone, well before he departed Boston, and his further relationship with her is in dispute among historians.[23]

Dr. Joseph Warren also left hints of an informant within British ranks who would seem to have had access and a status similar to Margaret's. Warren was a very security-conscious individual, and the identification of his source went with him to his death at Bunker Hill. Also, the fact that he and Church were not on friendly terms, even though peers in rebel leadership roles, helps explain how his source remained secret. His source was close to the British commander and thus could only be met in emergency situations. In this case, the informant provided the information that the British objective of the troop movement was "to seize Samuel Adams and John Hancock, who were known to be at Lexington, and burn the stores at Concord."[24] Once it became clear that the British plan had been known to the patriots, several British officers felt that Gage had been betrayed by someone close to him and suspected his wife.[25]

While many aspects of the Mechanics' operational methodology were sound, as mentioned previously, their concept of operational security and vetting of members was a bit more idealistic than realistic. At each of their meetings at the Green Dragon Tavern in Boston, they would all swear an oath to protect the secrecy of their activities. Just as congressional leaders found it incomprehensible that any patriot could be seriously involved in reporting to the enemy, these Boston patriots were equally sure of the moral righteousness of their cause and their people. However, even if this secret oath was respected within the group, the British would still have learned of its activities thanks to Church. Revere explained the procedure: "We were so careful that our meetings should be kept secret, that every time we met, every person swore upon the Bible that he would not discover any of our transactions but to Messrs Hancock, Adams, Doctors Warren, Church and one or two more."[26] This statement demonstrating that Church had complete access to all the activities of the Mechanics is the most probable explanation as to why Gage did not simply arrest Revere and the other members of the group to stop their activities in Boston.

Gage's decision represented the intelligence approach to counterintelligence rather than that of law enforcement. With an agent inside the group, Gage was well informed of their activities and could monitor their actions and take appropriate measures to minimize their successes. However, if he were to eliminate the group through arrests, he could be sure that a new group would soon be established for the same purpose, and he would have no assurance that he could again place an agent in it with similar access to all its activities. This is a constant dilemma in counterintelligence, counterinsurgency, and counterterrorism operations—and a constant source of friction between law enforcement authorities focused on stopping the threat through arrests and imprisonment and intelligence officers who would prefer to monitor the group's activities and stop specific events through advance warning.

During this period Gage had many other spies and local Tories happy to share current intelligence on the rebels' activities. One of the most important was Joseph Galloway, who reported on activities of the Continental Congress. He was openly Tory in his political views and had been a long-time speaker of the Pennsylvania Assembly. He was an elected Pennsylvania delegate to the Continental Congress, a resident of Philadelphia, and a close friend of Benjamin Franklin. Whether you view him as a spy within the Congress or as a loyal Englishman reporting to his government's senior official in the colonies is moot considering the politics of the time. However, that he did provide Gage with detailed reports on the political actions and personalities in the Continental Congress until he left in 1775 is a matter of record.[27]

In 1775, many of the towns surrounding Boston were split in terms of political loyalty. Cambridge in particular was full of wealthy Tories, including many Crown-appointed colonial officials. One of them, Maj. Gen. William Brattle, the senior officer of the colony's Royal Militia, secretly reported rebel military activities in the area to Gage.[28] Well-established Tory families, and thus informants, were also present in significant numbers in such towns as Plymouth, Worcester, and Taunton. However, a particularly valuable service not always associated with intelligence work was also performed by a Tory loyalist, Henry Pelham, who, under the guise of sketching the landscape, actually sketched rebel positions surrounding Boston for Gage.[29] He was the half-brother of the better-known artist John Singleton Copley. Details of enemy positions, especially in a siege situation, are invaluable intelligence to a commander. While today this could be done by satellites, reconnaissance aircraft, or drones, in 1775 it required firsthand observation and the talent to reproduce the observation accurately on paper. Sketching of fortifications and military facilities has always been an important part of military intelligence collection.

However, Gage's intelligence efforts were not always successful. In the case of James Wright, the royal governor of the colony of Georgia, the patriots were able to confuse Gage through a classic disinformation operation. Wright had written to Gage stating that the colony was in danger from local rebels, and he feared they would seize his gunpowder. However, the patriots were able to intercept his letters and substitute forgeries. Wright's alarming letters became glowing reports of British stability in the colony. They stated that there was no serious rebel threat to British control of Georgia, and that its neighbor South Carolina was also firmly in British hands. A letter even recommended against sending any additional military forces to the area as it would be counterproductive. In addition to accurately forging the governor's signature, the patriots were also able to forge his official seal, a fraud not discovered until January 1776. Wright's forged letter claimed that just a few hundred British troops could have held Georgia for the Crown.[30] Instead the colony was a battleground throughout the war.

Once American forces isolated the British troops in Boston, intelligence on their plans and intentions became more difficult to obtain. British forces occupied the city of Boston, and the Boston Neck, connecting it to the rest of the colony, was heavily fortified. After the Battle of Bunker Hill, the British occupied the Charlestown area, which was also separated by a narrow strip of land from the mainland and heavily fortified. And the Royal Navy controlled the local waterways. Consequently, passing intelligence from inside British lines became more difficult. While some reporting capabilities continued to exist inside the city from the Mechanics' network, most patriot sympathizers were well known to the British and thus under suspicion, with their access to information restricted. Collection activities focused on tactical military subjects such as troop deployments, fortifications, supplies, and any military activities that could indicate offensive actions by the British. This type of information was gathered by observation and by conversations with British military and civilian officials and their sympathizers inside Boston. The Continental Army used

observation points on the hills surrounding the city to monitor troop movements and the status of various British fortifications. Local fishermen who sold
their catch to British naval officers also picked up useful information, as did individuals permitted by American authorities to enter Boston to settle business
and legal affairs there. Many had long-standing personal and business relations
with British officials, and their conversations produced a low-level, but relatively constant, flow of information on British supply issues, troop morale, and
general gossip regarding British intentions.

On July 15, within two weeks of taking command, Washington began
to establish his own reporting capabilities. His account book stated, "333^1/$_3$
Dollars given to ——* to enduce him to go into the Town of Boston, to establish a secret corrispondence for the purpose of movements and designs." At the
bottom of the page, he noted, "*The names of Persons who are employed within
the Enemys lines, or who may fall within their power cannot be inserted."[31] A
little over a week later, Washington obtained some valuable intelligence from a
British soldier who had deserted from the Twenty-Third Regiment on July 26.
This enlisted man, Thomas Machin, had specific knowledge of British fortifications in Boston based upon his personal experience there.[32]

One actionable piece of information available from individuals who had
been able to visit the city was the state of supplies within the British forces.
Even though the Royal Navy controlled the harbor, provisions for the troops
were poor and numerous reports made this an issue worthy of American exploitation. Through both leaflets and oral communications, the Americans conducted an orchestrated propaganda effort to convince the British troops that
food, health care, and personal freedoms were readily available on the American side. With the exception of the personal freedoms, this was hardly the case,
but then the point of propaganda is not necessarily to tell the truth. While this
campaign may have led to a few desertions from the British Army (perhaps in
the case of Machin), its real impact was to contribute to low British troop morale, which in turn led to inactivity on the part of the British command. While
Washington hoped to draw the British into a set-piece battle similar to Bunker
Hill and thus inflict significant casualties, the British refused to engage.[33]

Washington may also have been able to use a particularly valuable open-
source publication in his analysis of British strength and positions in the city—
a detailed map of Boston Harbor published in London on August 5, 1775.[34]
Containing significant British military information, including identification of
British military positions, it was believed to have been purchased by a French
company and then obtained by Washington. Its use to vet reporting-source

information and to develop collection requirements for reporting, as well as being a tactical map of British defenses, would have been of significant value to the Continental Army. Unfortunately, attempts to document when Washington actually obtained this map, and therefore determine if it was of any use during the siege of Boston, have been unsuccessful.[35]

In late 1775, Gen. William Howe made up his mind that Boston was not sustainable as a British base, and the British government agreed. The surrounding population was hostile, and therefore local supplies were difficult to obtain, and logistical support from Canada was poorly organized. As the military siege wore on into winter, the British began planning for a strategic campaign to end the Revolution. The plan was to split the colonies along the Hudson River, separating the radical political northern colonies from what was believed to be the more moderate colonies of the South. This strategic concept, which would reappear often during the course of the war and was the cornerstone of Benedict Arnold's value if he could deliver the American defenses at West Point, was militarily sound. The British could count on its navy controlling the external lines of communication at sea for troop movements, logistics, and command-and-control purposes. Thus forces could be moved to New York City and supplied there, as the southern anchor in the British line. Canada, still loyal to the Crown and a secure base for both troops and supplies, was the northern anchor. With British forces moving up the Hudson Valley, supported and supplied by the Royal Navy, and other British forces moving from Canada along the traditional lake route in northern New York toward the Hudson River, the northern colonies would be isolated. With the colonies split, the Congress might then have been forced into favorable negotiations—or even capitulation.

This plan was obvious to both sides, and its success would depend upon the British being able to bring adequate forces to bear on the weak Continental Army and local militia units in New York State. The first step for General Howe was to move British forces to New York City and secure that base of operations. By early March 1776, Continental Army observation posts identified British loading of artillery and military stores onto transports in Boston Harbor. Troop movements soon followed, and in the early hours of March 17, the last British soldiers departed the city. When American scouts entered the former British outpost at Bunker Hill, they found straw dummies in British uniforms left behind as a rear guard.[36] After the last British transport left its anchorage on March 27, the city of Boston would remain free of British occupation throughout the war, although the Royal Navy was a constant threat outside its harbor.

By the spring of 1776, the Boston area, and for that matter most of New England, had seen the last of the British troops on the ground—except for an occasional raid and the British presence at Newport. The focus of the war shifted to the middle colonies, with New York City and Philadelphia as key centers. Washington, readily recognizing that New York City was the British's next military objective, started moving southward with his army in early April. In addition to the military significance of the city and its port, New York also represented a vital commercial and economic center for the colonies, and its loss would be a serious blow to the struggling government and army. Also, while around Boston, Washington could count on intelligence support from the patriots' well-established political organizations.

This was not true in the New York City area, where Tory feelings were as common as patriot loyalties. Indeed, during this time period a serious Tory plot, thwarted through the counterintelligence efforts of John Jay and others, was planned to kidnap or possibly even kill Washington, as well as stimulate an armed uprising by Tory militias throughout the area.[37] Wealthy merchants and landowners in the city and along the Hudson Valley had long-established family and commercial ties with the motherland and had serious doubts that the independence desired by the patriots would benefit them better than the colonial system, taxes notwithstanding. Developing equally capable intelligence-collection agents would take time—and the British, while slow to get organized for their assault on the New York area, did not give Washington ample time.

However, at this time other intelligence activities were being organized in France. They would play the key role in creating the French alliance and assist in maintaining American military capabilities until French troops could arrive.

CHAPTER 4

COVERT ACTION IN EUROPE LEADING TO THE FRENCH ALLIANCE

M ost Americans think of the Revolutionary War only in terms of the conflict on the American continent. Yet European rivalries worldwide also played a strategically significant role, especially Britain's long-standing conflicts with France and to a lesser degree Spain. European support for the Revolution, once again particularly French, was of significant importance to an American victory. This aid was motivated not by any great commitment to American independence or the concept of political freedom as much as a desire to see Britain lose its American colonies and for France to gain prestige and power in international affairs.[1] American political leaders well understood this reality and skillfully manipulated French actions through America's first diplomatic mission abroad, the American Commission in Paris. The Continental Congress established this three-man commission with the objective of establishing a treaty of alliance against Britain. But while the treaty was being negotiated, the commission's efforts were employed in covert activities to support American military and political efforts against Britain. Its efforts were to be discreet, if not entirely clandestine, and its success or failure would play a significant role in determining the outcome of the War of Independence.

In terms of secret activities, Europe at that time was a difficult environment in which to operate. The intelligence capabilities of the major European powers were well organized and funded.[2] Almost from the day the first American representative arrived in Paris, the commission was penetrated by a well-managed and professionally conducted British spying effort. Nevertheless, its members succeeded in first obtaining covert French, and to a lesser degree Spanish, financial and military aid and in eventually negotiating a treaty that created a military and political alliance against Great Britain. They also aggressively conducted a range of covert actions against the British. These actions included political action, propaganda, and paramilitary activities such as privateering actions, sabotage of British naval facilities, and raids on Great Britain itself. These actions were covert in the sense that they were conducted in a manner that gave the French government plausible denial of responsibility for them, although the British were well aware they were organized by the Americans and sanctioned by the French.

It all started on a cold and windswept night in Philadelphia in late December 1775. Julien-Alexandre Archard de Bonvouloir, an agent of the French Foreign Ministry operating under the cover of a Flemish merchant, approached Ben Franklin through a trusted friend to inquire about the seriousness and resolution of the colonies' dispute with Britain. Franklin introduced him to other members of the Continental Congress's Committee of Secret Correspondence, which had been established on November 29 of that year for the purpose of communicating with foreign friends.[3]

During three secret nighttime meetings at Carpenters' Hall in Philadelphia between December 18 and 28, Bonvouloir was told that the Continental Congress would soon declare the colonies independent from Britain.[4] He was asked if France would support American military efforts against the British, open its ports to American ships, and assist the colonies in obtaining military supplies required for the conflict. He broadly hinted France would do so.[5] Based upon these conversations—and supported by contacts between a French agent in London and Arthur Lee, a colonial lawyer residing in London and supporting the patriots' cause—the committee dispatched Silas Deane, a Continental Congress delegate from Connecticut, to Paris in the spring of 1776 under the guise of a merchant.[6] Once Deane had verified the willingness of the French government to cooperate, the Continental Congress made plans to open the first American diplomatic post abroad, the Paris Commission.[7] However, because the French government could not formally recognize America as a country, the commission had to operate discreetly. Its dealings with the French government often had to be handled through individuals with no official connection to that government.

The French commitment to assist the colonies bore its first fruit even before

Silas Deane. *Library of Congress*

Deane arrived in France. Lee was corresponding with the Committee of Secret Correspondence and had been in touch with Pierre-Augustin Caron de
Beaumarchais, also a resident of London, since 1775. Beaumarchais was a most
remarkable man, well known then as a popular dramatist and accomplished
musician and best known today as the author of the plays *The Barber of Seville*
and *The Marriage of Figaro*, upon which the famous operas were based. He
was also a secret agent for King Louis XVI of France.[8] Lee worked closely with
Beaumarchais to lobby the French government to provide material assistance

for the colonies' military activities against Britain. In the spring and early summer of 1776, Beaumarchais advised Lee that the French government would be willing to send military supplies worth £200,000 for American use but was unwilling to openly side with the colonies against Britain.[9]

Deane began his efforts to obtain military supplies at a July 10 meeting with the French secretary of state for foreign affairs, Charles Gravier, comte de Vergennes. Vergennes arranged for Deane to meet Beaumarchais, who had returned to Paris. Beaumarchais was under instructions to work with Deane to obtain and ship weapons and other military supplies to the colonies in return for agricultural products. To accomplish this in a manner permitting the French government to exercise plausible denial, he established a proprietary company named Hortalez & Company, directed by its imaginary founder Roderigue Hortalez. This dummy corporation, with no apparent relationship to the French government, purchased and shipped military supplies to the colonies as a private business enterprise. Through this company, Beaumarchais laundered French and Spanish government financing for the military purchases.[10]

Up until this time, Continental Congress efforts to import military supplies had been largely unsuccessful. As early as the fall of 1775, Robert Morris, later the leading figure in financing the war for the Congress as a member of the Philadelphia Committee of Safety, had a contract from the Congress to purchase gunpowder and military supplies abroad for the army.[11] While he dispatched several ships to purchase and transport these supplies, his efforts proved mostly unsuccessful.[12] As the covert arrangements with the French developed, Morris worked with Franklin to arrange Deane's mission in Paris. As the flow of military supplies developed, he sent agents, under cover of commercial shipping companies, to the Caribbean and New Orleans to assist in shipping the goods to colonial ports.[13] He was also the key figure attempting to organize—not always successfully—shipments of colonial products for sale in Europe to pay for the imported military supplies. Thus Morris represented the American-based link to the Hortalez & Company enterprise.[14]

Beaumarchais financed Hortalez with a one-million-livre loan from the French government in June 1776. On August 11, he received another million from the Spanish government. Shortly thereafter, he obtained a third million from a group of French merchant investors anxious to purchase American agricultural products at cheap prices. The French government secretly guaranteed this commercial loan. Beaumarchais, utilizing the alias "M. Durand," rented a Paris hotel as the company's headquarters. The firm's ostensible business was trade with the West Indies. His business plan was to purchase military supplies

P. A. CARON DE BEAUMARCHAIS.

Pierre-Augustin Caron de Beaumarchais is best known for his theatrical works, but as a French secret agent, he established and managed a commercial cover company covertly providing military supplies to the Continental Army. *Library of Congress* from French arsenals on credit and ship them to the colonies directly or trans-ship them through the West Indies to the colonies if necessary. He planned to make the company self-supporting by charging a small commission on each shipment and accepting payment for the supplies in tobacco, rice, indigo, cotton, and other agricultural products from the colonies. He could resell these products in Europe at a significant profit.[15]

This large-scale transfer of gunpowder, weapons, and other military equipment from French arsenals simply could not go unnoticed by the public—or the British. So the French government created a cover story to explain its sale of these items to private merchants. King Louis XVI made a public decision in the summer of 1776 to modernize and reequip his army and navy. Thus he declared that all current older weapons, munitions, and supplies were to be sold to help finance the purchase of new military equipment.[16] While this story did not fool the British, it did publicly explain the purchase of these military supplies by individuals connected with Hortalez.

While Beaumarchais's business plan was sound in theory, on the American end there were serious problems obtaining the agricultural products from the individual states that were to pay for these military supplies. Through September 1777, Hortalez sent military supplies worth over five million livres to the colonies but received virtually nothing in payment.[17] Beaumarchais had to request additional funds from the government three times in 1777 in order to keep the company solvent. By the time France officially entered the war, Hortalez was heavily in debt because of nonpayment by the Continental Congress for supplies delivered.

However, while not succeeding financially, Beaumarchais did an excellent job providing the Continental Army with badly needed supplies. By the end of 1776, he had collected two hundred field pieces, three hundred thousand muskets, a hundred tons of gun powder, three thousand tents, large amounts of ammunition, and uniforms for thirty thousand soldiers.[18] In April 1777, the first Hortalez-chartered vessels arrived in Portsmouth carrying a large quantity of gunpowder, sixty cannon, twelve thousand muskets, and uniforms. This shipment was vital for supplying the Continental Army's Northern Army, operating in upper New York State, and it proved invaluable during that fall's combat with British forces under General Burgoyne.[19]

While all the military supplies transported to America by Hortalez were important to the ill-equipped Continental Army, the need for gunpowder probably was the most critical. The colonies simply did not have the manufacturing capability to supply an army with adequate amounts required for combat operations. As early as the aftermath of the Battle of Bunker Hill, the army surrounding Boston was reduced to but a few shots per soldier.[20] Even to support the militias around Boston prior to the combat at Lexington and Concord, the patriots had to raid Crown arsenals throughout New England to obtain adequate supplies of gunpowder.

In what could well be described as America's first paramilitary action overseas, in August 1775 Americans raided the Crown arsenal in Bermuda for its gunpowder. As an operation it was an initial success, but it also quickly demonstrated one of the major issues inherent in such activities: compartmentation of operations versus adequate coordination. The raid was the result of discussions among members of the Continental Congress, led by Franklin, and Col. Henry Tucker of Port Royal, Bermuda. He was the head of a powerful family on the island, as well as a strong supporter of American independence. Bermuda depended upon the colonies and Great Britain for its food supply, and Tucker was willing to trade the Crown's gunpowder, even if it was not his own, for a steady food supply for the island. On August 14, two American ships, one from South Carolina and one from Virginia, landed men on the island and with the help of Tucker's associates liberated the gunpowder.[21] The royal governor sent a dispatch to London noting that local assistance must have been rendered to the Americans, and while a reward for information on these individuals was offered, none was ever identified. However, Bermuda did have a regular supply of American foodstuffs shipped to them for purchase throughout the war.

Because of the secret activities involved in the planning and execution of this operation, knowledge of the raid was hidden from not only the American public, but also other American officials, including Washington. He, of course, had grave concerns about his munitions supply and was aware of the Crown arsenal in Bermuda. He also had plans to send a small force there to seize it. As he was rather busy around Boston at the time, he was not able to implement his plan until October 1775. When his group arrived on island, to their surprise they found that the gunpowder was gone.[22]

Lack of adequate manufacturing capabilities within the colonies also limited the production of most military supplies in large numbers. While small quantities of muskets and rifles could be produced locally, only Europe could provide the numbers and variety of weapons and munitions needed for warfare. In the desperate years of 1777 and 1778, until France officially entered the war, the supplies delivered by Hortalez constituted the vast majority of the military items used by the American army. One historian estimated that

80 percent of the gunpowder used by the Americans during that period was obtained through covert French supply channels.[23]

The American victory at Saratoga on October 17, 1777, was a major factor in France's decision to officially declare a military alliance with America and recognize the colonies as an independent nation. On February 6, 1778, representatives of both countries signed two treaties effectively making France an ally of the colonies against Britain. With this alliance, French government and merchant vessels began a constant flow of supplies to the colonies. The covert supply effort could be replaced by the overt support of an American ally.

While gunpowder and weapons were the most crucial military supplies required in the 1776–78 period, the French also provided covert assistance in several other important areas. This included provision of military officers with special skills and expertise, provision of European-built ships for military and paramilitary use, and the establishment of facilities at French ports to support American maritime activities. To ensure American covert activities were properly financed, the French king provided a clandestine loan of two million livres in January 1777. The terms of the loan contained no defined terms for repayment, and its stated purpose was appropriately vague: to permit the Paris Commission to conduct its business.[24]

By the fall of 1776, the Americans had developed a rudimentary command structure and a basic, if not very disciplined, fighting capability. However, it lacked experience in large-scale operations and areas of special military expertise such as artillery and engineering. The Continental Congress looked to France for assistance, and its representatives in Paris responded. In late 1776, Deane worked through Beaumarchais to identify French artillery and engineering officers willing to serve in the American army for compensation rather than belief in the cause. With the quiet assistance of the French military, seventeen officers, including Maj. Pierre Charles L'Enfant, later the designer of the city of Washington, were released from French military duty. Deane signed employment contracts with the men, providing them with senior ranks in the American army. This represented the start of a long tradition in the American military of hiring individuals with specific areas of expertise as contractors. This group departed the port of Le Havre in December 1776 on a Hortalez ship for the colonies, arriving at Portsmouth in April 1777.[25]

Up until France's formal recognition of the colonies' independence, commission members continued to sign employment contracts with individuals with needed skills. The talents and experience of these officers played a vital role in Washington's strategy, because his defensive positions and artillery capabilities were essential in facing a larger and more mobile enemy. Marie-Joseph Paul Ives Roch Gilbert du Motier, marquis de Lafayette, the best-known French officer to serve in the American army, left France to join Washington in 1777.[26] The young man had little military expertise to offer, and his primary motive was to obtain revenge against the British for the death of his father. But his noble heritage enhanced support for the American cause within the French court and among the French population in general.[27] He soon became a favorite of Washington's and evolved into a highly competent military officer.[28]

One French officer who accompanied Lafayette, perhaps in a mentor role, was Baron Johann de Kalb. He was born in Bavaria but joined the French Army and rose to the rank of general. He also handled other duties for the French government as an intelligence officer. He was first sent to America in 1768 to report on the growing political dispute between the colonies and the British government.[29] He was not entitled to the title of baron but had simply adopted it to enhance his position within the French power structure. With Lafayette's influence in the Continental Congress, based upon his strong ties to the French court, De Kalb was given the rank of major general. He spent much of his time in the Continental Army commanding the Delaware and Maryland Continental Lines forces and served with bravery under Gen. Horatio Gates in the South. He died of wounds on August 19, 1780, after quite gallantly leading a Continental regiment in battle at Camden, South Carolina.

These skilled foreign military officers provided much-needed expertise to the young Continental Army. And a few were even involved in intelligence operations.[30] However, more than a few American officers, and their political sponsors in Congress, were upset at the loss of promotion opportunities caused by the senior ranks and pay grades given to these individuals.

Not all of the foreign officers acquitted themselves well in the American service, but the majority did contribute to changing the American farmer-soldier into the disciplined Continental Line soldier. Particularly influential in this training was Gen. Baron Friedrich Wilhelm von Steuben, who became the inspector general of the American army. He is best remembered for the discipline he instilled in the American forces during the horrible winter at Valley Forge. Steuben was recruited into American service by Beaumarchais under somewhat dubious circumstances. Though of noble birth and with some limited military experience, Steuben had never risen above the rank of captain in his military service. But he impressed Beaumarchais with his enthusiasm, and he decided to dress Steuben in a general's uniform for his introduction to the American commissioners. The ruse worked. Upon his arrival at Washington's headquarters, Steuben's military bearing and martial appearance also greatly impressed the commander in chief. He was placed in charge of training the army, and he rose to the occasion.[31]

French covert assistance in the building and purchase of vessels for use by the colonies both for the carrying of supplies and for paramilitary activities against the British was another significant benefit for the American cause. While the colonies could readily produce ships capable of operating as a coastal force, larger ships had to be purchased from abroad, through middlemen in France. In 1777, three American warships were fitted out under supervision of members of the American Paris Commission.[32] In addition, dozens of other ships were purchased from French and other European owners and turned into supply vessels, privateer ships to attack British shipping, and even Continental Navy ships.

With the exception of two minor American-supported covert actions—one a paramilitary raid and the other a series of attempted sabotages—the British homeland was spared the violence of the Revolutionary War. These incidents resulted in only minor damage to British property, yet they were propaganda victories for the fledgling American cause, causing some public panic and providing solid talking points for those British politicians favoring an end to the conflict. These activities involved two colorful characters, one of whom would move on to become a true American hero. The other was hanged by the British, and his decaying body was left swinging at the entrance to Portsmouth Harbor in England for several years as a warning to others.

James Aitken, better known to the British as "Jack the Painter" because of his guise of a painter to scout out his sabotage targets, was responsible for the only American sabotage of a British military target in Britain during the war.[33] He was born in Edinburgh, Scotland, in 1752, and after some schooling and an apprenticeship in painting moved to London. There he fell in with bad company and had to sail for America before the law arrested him for being a highwayman. In America he developed a taste for the revolutionary writings of Samuel Adams and the Sons of Liberty. He returned to Britain in 1775 and once again fell into criminal activities. However, a conversation about the armed conflict in America rekindled his political passion, and by the next year he was ready to strike a blow for American independence. He decided to burn down as many British dockyards as possible. He started his plan by obtaining employment as a painter at Portsmouth, England, and then continued his casing of potential targets by visiting Plymouth, Chatham, Woolwich, and Deptford.[34]

According to Aitken's confession to British authorities, he traveled to Paris

in early November 1776 to seek assistance for his plans by contacting the supposedly low-profile if not clandestine American representatives there. He did
meet with Silas Deane, explaining his plans to destroy various dockyards and
the ships berthed in them.[35] Deane was cautious in his encouragement, at first
dismissing the operation as unrealistic. However, Aitken's enthusiasm eventually won him American support: three pounds cash, a French passport in a
modified version of his name issued by the French Foreign Ministry at the
commission's request, and the name of a contact in London.[36] Aitken returned
to Britain and in late November began purchasing materials and building his
incendiary devices. On December 6, he attempted to start a fire in the rope
house at the Portsmouth dockyard, but his device failed to ignite. The next day
he returned to the rope house, which contained the riggings for two ships, and
succeeded in burning it down.

He then returned to London and contacted the individual identified to him
by Deane, Dr. Edward Bancroft. Bancroft was a confidant of Deane's and would
soon become the Paris Commission's private secretary. However, in his spare
time Bancroft acted quite effectively as a British secret agent reporting on commission activities. On December 8, Aitken met with Bancroft and confided his
plans to set fire to other dockyards. Bancroft admitted an association with Deane
but would provide no assistance. He told Aitken to leave and not return. As Bancroft was a British agent, it would be expected that he reported the meeting, but
apparently no action was taken to stop Aitken.[37] This may have been to protect
Bancroft's cover.

Aitken next attempted to again penetrate the Plymouth dockyard but
found it too heavily guarded. He proceeded to Bristol and on January 15, 1777,
was able to set fire to the *Savannah*, a Jamaican vessel docked at the port.
The next night he burned a bookseller's warehouse. By mid-January, as Aitken
sought new opportunities, the British had developed a description of him and
circulated a misnamed wanted poster for "John the Painter," offering a £50
reward. He was arrested on February 3 for suspicion of burglary and quickly
recognized as "Jack the Painter."

To get adequate details for their legal case to convict Aitken of his crimes,
the authorities contrived a chance encounter between Aitken and an American
informer visiting Clerkenwell Prison. The informer subsequently befriended
him and visited him daily. Their relationship soon allowed Aitken to unburden
himself of all the details of his activities, which were provided each evening
to British authorities.[38] Aitken went to trial in early March. The case against
him was so overwhelming, with the informer as the principal witness, that the

jury rendered its verdict with little consultation. After his condemnation to death, Aitken asked to make his confession and that it be published. In it he provided details of his interactions with the Americans in Paris and mentioned his meeting with Bancroft in London. On March 10, 1777, he was executed at Portsmouth.

There has always been suspicion that part of Aitken's confession, when published, was written to accomplish British political and diplomatic objectives against the French and American governments.[39] But closer consideration should also be given to the public description of his interaction with Bancroft, the double agent working for the British. To support British secret activities, any publicized interaction would have to accomplish at least two British operational objectives: to demonstrate Bancroft's actions supported his role as an American agent by protecting American interests and also to make clear that he took no part in illegal activities and therefore did not have to be arrested. Interestingly, the published confession managed to accomplish these objectives, and Bancroft was subsequently hired as the commission's private secretary. Also interestingly, he partially explained his reason for moving to Paris to take the commission position as being the result of concern for his safety because of his involvement with Aitken.[40]

The only American paramilitary raid on the British homeland was planned and led by John Paul Jones, later of US Navy fame.[41] Jones arrived in France from the colonies in late 1777, and with the assistance of Franklin, began to seize British ships in the English Channel and the broader Atlantic Ocean. His ship, the *Ranger*, carried eighteen guns, a small detachment of marines, and a rather undisciplined naval crew comprising several nationalities. It was also reported to be the first ship to fly the American flag. As a young child, Jones had lived in the Cumberland seaport of Whitehaven and knew its harbor and fortifications well. He and Franklin believed this would be a perfect spot for an American attack on the British homeland. The harbor usually was crowded with hundreds of ships in close anchorage, and the element of surprise would be with the Americans.[42]

At midnight on April 22, 1778, Jones's raiding party left the *Ranger* by small boats and headed for Whitehaven. The plan was to arrive in the predawn hours, but the forty-man raiding party had only reached the harbor entrance when dawn broke. The objective was to burn the two-hundred-plus ships estimated to be in the harbor. Marine lieutenant Samuel Wallingford was to lead the party burning the ships while Jones's party attacked the fort and its gun battery.

However, the plan quickly went awry. One of the men, an Irishman named

David Freeman, apparently decided to change sides and split off from the group and began knocking on doors yelling, "Pirates!" Meanwhile, Wallingford's men had managed to set a fully loaded collier, the *Thompson*, on fire, and the flames added credibility to Freeman's cries. But a public house happened to be located opposite the *Thompson*'s berth, and once the men realized what they could loot there, their focus changed. (Apparently the famed discipline of the US Marine Corps was still in its developmental phase. Or more likely the problem was the sailors in the crowd.) While Wallingford managed to start fires in a few other ships nearby, most of his men were more interested in the liquor than their initial objective.

Jones, however, was successful in the attack on the fort and guns, easily surprising the garrison and spiking the guns to ensure a safe departure for the raiding party. In the town, with the raiding party absorbed in another kind of party, the citizens had formed a fire-bucket line and saved the *Thompson*, as well as the other ships set aflame. Realizing that the element of surprise had been lost, the raiding party prepared to depart even before Jones and his men arrived at the dock. Luckily, the officer in charge of guarding the boats, a former Swedish army officer, Lt. Jean Meijer, was a solid officer. He and Wallingford kept the boats at the pier until Jones arrived. The raiding party was then able to retreat to the *Ranger*, which had sailed to the mouth of the harbor.[43]

Jones was quite upset by his lack of success. He had hoped to turn Whitehaven harbor into a sea of burning ships. Instead, only one ship had been partly burned, and a few cannon had been spiked. The British later estimated the cost of the damage done at between £250 and £1,250. No casualties had occurred among the townfolk or the fort's garrison, and from a financial perspective the cost was minimal. However, the raid was a significant propaganda success for the Americans. A British town had been temporarily seized by a foreign military force—something that had not happened since the late 1600s. The raid caused concern in seaports all along the British coast and a general anxiety in the shipping industry.[44]

After leaving Whitehaven, Jones stopped at St. Mary's Isle, in Kirkcudbright Bay, and raided the home of the Earl of Selkirk in an attempt to hold him hostage for the release of American prisoners held in Britain. But the earl was in London, and Jones settled for taking the family silver hostage. Still frustrated by his lack of success, on April 24 he approached Carrickfergus Harbor at Belfast, Ireland. There, he encountered a British warship, the HMS *Drake*, and a battle ensued. After a heavy and lengthy engagement, the *Drake* surrendered. At that point, with British warships in pursuit, Jones sailed back to haven in France. He entered the harbor of Brest on May 8 and received a hero's welcome from the French.

Unfortunately, Franklin was not as pleased. The British had formally charged Jones with piracy for stealing the Selkirk family silver. Jones was forced to write a letter of apology and after the war did return the silver.[45] However, within a short time he was given command of the *Bonhomme Richard*, and the rest is US naval history.

Early in the conflict, the Continental Congress recognized the weakness of the mighty Royal Navy: It was not large enough to control the entire seacoast of the colonies, nor could it protect the vast British merchant trading fleets worldwide. Plans were soon implemented to use selected ports, outside of British naval reach, for importation of vital military supplies and as home bases for small American naval vessels that could harass British shipping. Other privately owned ships, commissioned by the Congress to act as privateers, plied the waters of the West Indies, attacking British merchants and the occasional smaller British warship, in Atlantic and Caribbean waters. Washington even personally invested in a privateering vessel with the hopes of capturing and selling cargoes and vessels.[46]

With Deane's arrival in France and the start of covert French assistance, efforts began to obtain use of French ports for disrupting British shipping in the waters around the British Isles. Franklin spent a significant amount of his time and effort during his first year in Paris negotiating French government cooperation to overlook its neutrality obligations regarding American use of French ports. Under a treaty with Britain since 1713, France was bound not to accept prize cargoes or vessels of British ownership or provide facilities to those attacking British vessels. Nevertheless, American-directed ships conducted such activities from French ports, with local officials' and merchants' collusion. And in the face of British diplomatic protests, the French government insisted it was doing all it could to halt such activities—a classic example of plausible denial afforded a government by covert actions.[47]

Franklin expanded Deane's efforts to harass British shipping. He established a system of American port agents at French harbors to handle resupply, refitting, and crew recruitment and to facilitate the disposition of captured cargo and ships. The French ports of Brest, Saint-Malo, L'Orient, Nantes, and Le Havre were used extensively by the Americans. The British, well aware of these activities through their numerous penetrations of the Paris Commission, issued strong protests to the French, with specific examples of the actions of certain ships and their masters.[48] But Franklin was able to maintain French support through his brand of personal diplomacy and kept his small fleet active and effective throughout the war.

From these activities America received military, economic, political, and psychological benefits. A portion of the funds obtained from the sale of the prize ships and cargo went to the American cause. These funds were used to purchase military supplies and European ships. Some captured ships were re-fitted and then used against the British. These actions also drove up British shipping insurance rates, making trade less profitable, and more worrisome, to a politically influential segment of the British commercial class.

The first American capture of British vessels in European waters took place in January 1777 and was achieved by Capt. Lambert Wickes, who had sailed to France carrying Franklin to his post in Paris. Wickes captured four small British merchant ships and sold them to French merchants. He also captured a Royal Mail packet operating between Falmouth and Lisbon, which greatly upset the British government and signaled the opening of a new phase in the war.[49]

Wickes's success encouraged Franklin. He instructed Deane to increase his efforts to attract more American sea captains to accept commissions to attack British ships. Deane then began recruiting French and Spanish seamen to serve as crews on these ships. By the end of 1777, numerous ships were plying their trade in the English Channel and the waters surrounding Britain. For example, Capt. Gustavus Conyngham was active all along the eastern coast of Britain and Scotland, capturing numerous British ships and a Royal Mail packet ser-vicing Holland.[50] In the same period, another American raider in the Irish Sea captured eighteen vessels, and John Paul Jones, operating as a Continental Navy commander, captured several more. As the war progressed and the profitability of attacking British merchantmen became more apparent, the number of let-ters of commission multiplied. While no accurate record exists regarding the number of British ships captured or destroyed by a combination of paramilitary and American-French naval vessels during the conflict, London insurance rates clearly indicate the risk became significant. This did not please the commercial shipping industry or its investors, who represented the ruling class in Britain. As ship losses mounted and increasing insurance rates reduced profitability, senti-ments within Parliament for a solution to the conflict grew stronger.[51]

While at the Paris Commission, Franklin used his knowledge of European, and particularly British, society to conduct propaganda and political-action operations in support of the American cause. Acting as an agent of influence within the French court and with the French public, he was able to negoti-ate great latitude for American activities, as well as increase French funding and military support. Within Britain, Franklin had the support of influential Whigs, many of whom had known him for twenty years or more. In his early days in London as a colonial agent, he had developed a wide circle of acquaintances through membership in social and scientific circles. He had been inducted into the Royal Society, a fellowship of eminent scientists and perhaps the most prestigious scientific academy in the Western world at that time, while serving as an agent for the Pennsylvania colony in London during the period 1757–62. These groups shared a common enlightened political liberalism then spreading through European intelligentsia. After returning to the colonies, he remained in contact with these individuals, keeping them informed of the colonials' view of the growing dispute with the British and encouraging their support for America's position.[52]

After arriving in Paris, Franklin and the other commissioners continued to communicate with these contacts through the use of mail drops at the addresses of other American sympathizers in Britain. Aliases were used to further disguise the identities of the British contacts. The correspondence provided a colonial spin to the latest news of the war and suggested political themes that the Whigs could use in parliamentary and private debates. The effectiveness of Franklin's efforts to use these contacts and their political and intellectual influence to sway public opinion was only marginally harmed by the fact that British intelligence was monitoring most of the communications thanks to its penetration of the commission. One of its spies within the commission had stolen a list of the cover names and addresses of the commission's contacts in Britain.[53]

Franklin's influential contacts included Lord William Petty Fitzmaurice Shelburne, a politician with close ties to the king who had served previously as the secretary of state. Another was Lord Charles Pratt Camden, a former lord chancellor. Franklin also had contacts in the financial sector. One such individual was Thomas Walpole, a powerful London banker and nephew of the famous Sir Robert Walpole.[54] After the alliance with France was formalized, Franklin sent a trusted agent, Jonathan Austin, to stay with Lord Shelburne and use his access to members of Parliament to lobby for the American cause.[55]

Franklin also obtained bits of information from these contacts, which he used in his efforts to influence the French toward an alliance. For example, in early January 1778, he received information that Gen. Lord Charles Cornwallis had reported to the British government that conquest of the colonies was impossible. Coming as it did about the same time as the news of the British defeat at Saratoga, Franklin immediately used this information as part of his effort to convince the French to formalize a military alliance with America.[56]

Franklin was also active in creating black propaganda, which hid the true authorship of the material. To facilitate these efforts, Franklin set up a printing press in the basement of the building housing the commission. He imported type and paper from Holland and even Great Britain in order to create documents as authentic as possible for his propaganda efforts. He produced pamphlets, false documents, and articles for publication in various newspapers and magazines throughout Europe. Some provided an American spin on political and military developments in the conflict, while others offered false information on British actions in the war. In most cases the information was purported to be from sources other than the colonies. Franklin also wrote a monthly column for a French magazine in Belgium, *Affaires de l'Angleterre et de l'Amérique*, which was actually a French government–funded and controlled propaganda sheet.[57]

Examples of his efforts include a letter written in 1777, supposedly by a German prince to the commander of his mercenary troops in America serving with the British forces. The letter questions casualty figures provided by the British government. The prince writes that he believes the actual figures to be much higher and that he was being cheated of money due him for his dead and wounded soldiers. He also advised the commander to let his wounded soldiers die, as he would receive a larger British payment for a dead soldier than a wounded one. He concluded that wounded soldiers were of no use to him, as they were only cripples unable to serve their prince. This letter was widely circulated in Europe and among German troops in the colonies. It was credited with causing some desertions in the colonies, recruiting problems in Germany, and also creating significant public debate in Europe over the British government's payment of "blood money" to foreign mercenaries serving with the British in America.[58]

Another example of Franklin's handiwork was a 1782 forged copy of a Boston newspaper, complete with current advertisements and local news, which contained an article reporting that the British royal governor of Canada was paying his Indian allies for each American scalp provided to him. The article also noted that many of the scalps sold to the governor were from women and children.[59]

Franklin also strove to influence European banking centers in order to enhance the credit standings, and therefore the purchasing power, of the Continental Congress and the individual colonies. He accomplished this by using influential contacts to embellish news of American successes and downplay British victories. His efforts were not always successful, as in the case of

D. BENJAMIN FRANKLIN
et vitæ inter Americanos acta
et magnis electricitatis periculis claris

Benjamin Franklin dressed in his "native" fur hat. While in Paris he often dressed plainly in public to enhance the image of his, and America's, character as simple and honest. *Library of Congress* the Dutch bankers and government. Franklin used Swiss journalist Charles Dumas to plant favorable stories in the Dutch press. However, his actions did little to arouse Dutch interest in taking sides in the conflict.[60] Dumas had been working for the American cause since early 1776 with the mission of influencing foreign leaders to support the Revolution. Franklin, while a member of the Continental Congress's Committee of Secret Correspondence, authorized him to do so in a letter dated December 19, 1775.[61]

Franklin's efforts to forge French court and public opinion were highly successful and the result of hard work in both the public relations and political influence areas. From the day he arrived in France, he cultivated the image of the enlightened American struggling for independence from the despotic British monarch. The clothes he wore and the manner in which he conducted himself in public were all carefully crafted to advance this image. As a political agent, he worked French officials and members of the influential aristocracy skillfully, carefully, and endlessly.

Franklin's most important influence operation against the French government took place in the period of late 1777 to early 1778. When news of the American victory at Saratoga reached Europe in late November 1777, pressure on the British to seek a peaceful solution to the conflict increased significantly. British agents were sent to France to sound out the commissioners regarding negotiable terms. Franklin skillfully flirted with the British representatives, meeting personally with one of their agents and speaking encouragingly of the British proposals with commission and French colleagues. At the same time, he officially advised the French of his meetings but provided them only selected portions of the conversations. He recognized that French spies would report the full details of his meetings and his subsequent comments to colleagues. Upon comparing Franklin's reports and information from their monitoring of his activities, the French became concerned that reconciliation might be possible. That would jeopardize France's military and commercial strategy meant to weaken the British through the loss of its American colonies. By early 1778, the French royal council had decided to negotiate a military alliance with the colonies, as well as a treaty of commerce and amity. If this decision was driven by concern that the Continental Congress would accept British terms, it was totally unfounded. The terms offered by the British would never have been accepted by the Continental Congress, but Franklin's orchestration of the meetings with the British agents painted a different picture.[62]

While the commission was successful in its mission, it is worth noting that from another intelligence perspective—that of counterintelligence—it was pretty much a disaster from the start. Its physical security was poor, its personnel security nonexistent, and its three commissioners had no real counterintelligence awareness. Because France was a friendly country providing covert assistance to the Revolution, the three Americans apparently felt comfortable and secure under the French government's protection. They underestimated the ability of the British intelligence service to operate against them in a third country, and this underestimation of the enemy had its usual result.

Diplomatic historian Samuel Flagg Bemis describes the diplomatic environment in Europe as America sought foreign assistance in its fight with Britain: "The capitals of Europe were full of international spies. The technique of deciphering intercepted dispatches attained a high degree of perfection. Corruption was the conventional instrument of diplomatic success. The art of dissimulation and deception was a necessary part of the equipment of any minister of foreign affairs. . . . It was this cynical and brutal international world of the eighteenth century into which the United States of America was to be delivered."[63]

The British coverage of the commission was highly professional, comprehensive, and aggressive. It included the theft of documents, penetration agents in the commission, development of access agents with close ties to commission members, and manipulation of the principle targets based on personality assessment information. The British were able to obtain a nearly complete picture of American-French activities supporting the war in America and of American intentions regarding an alliance with France. Tactically, the British used this intelligence somewhat effectively against the American cause. From their coverage of shipping activities, the British were able to seize badly needed supplies destined for Washington's army. The British minister in Paris also used timely and accurate intelligence on American supply efforts and paramilitary activities in the English Channel to force the French government to become less blatant in its support for these activities.

Perhaps the greatest irony in the intelligence history of the war is that while British intelligence activities were highly successful in collecting information regarding American-French plans and intentions in both a timely and comprehensive manner, British failure to use this information effectively in its policy formation and implementation negated most of its value.

In the written instruction to Deane by the committee, Franklin provided the names of several trusted individuals in Europe worthy of contact, including Dr. Edward Bancroft.[64] The American-born Bancroft was an old friend of Franklin's, as well as a respected scientist and businessman in Britain. The two had met in London in the early 1770s when Franklin was a colonial business agent. He had acted as a mentor to Bancroft, sponsoring him for the British Royal Society in May 1773 and involving him in a land speculation deal in the colonies. Franklin believed him to be well connected in Britain and sympathetic to the American cause. Deane had also known Bancroft, having tutored him for a brief period.

Within two days of Deane's arrival in Paris, Lord Stormont, the British minister in Paris and the local head of British intelligence, advised London that "Nathan Rumsey," the British code name for Deane, was there.[65] Stormont was instructed to keep Deane under surveillance. Shortly after his arrival, Deane wrote to Bancroft and arranged to meet with him in Paris on July 8, 1776. Deane was impressed with Bancroft and discussed with him the status of negotiations with the French regarding an alliance. Bancroft and Deane continued their discussions until late July, when Bancroft returned to London.[66] They then maintained an active correspondence while he was in London.

Shortly after Bancroft's return to London, American-born businessman Paul Wentworth called on him to discuss his visit with Deane. Wentworth had been a businessman in London for many years and had befriended Bancroft in the late 1760s. In 1769, he hired Bancroft to work on his Surinam plantation for a few years. Around late 1774, as political problems grew in the American colonies, Wentworth was working for British intelligence, reporting on colonial activities and on other Americans in London.[67]

It is not clear whether Bancroft was under British control before his trip to Paris to meet Deane. Some historians speculate he had been recruited as early as 1772. However, his specific reporting efforts against the American Commission in Paris can be traced to August 1776.[68] Whether a previous relationship had existed or surveillance on Deane had identified Bancroft as a potential agent, Wentworth's visit resulted in Bancroft providing an account of Deane's mission to France. This report, dated August 14, provided detailed intelligence on American plans, as well as operational information that could be used to monitor American-French activities through other intelligence resources. It was well received by the British, and two days later Stormont was advised of the full extent of Deane's mission in France.[69]

In October, Bancroft returned to Paris to visit Deane. This trip resulted in additional reporting to Wentworth regarding American-French planning for secret French military aid and the status of discussions on a treaty of alliance. Bancroft now enjoyed Deane's complete confidence, and this reporting demonstrated to Wentworth that Bancroft's access to American and French secret planning was valuable. Shortly thereafter, Wentworth formalized British intel-ligence's arrangements with Bancroft to act as a spy on the American activities in France, using his access to the American Commission in Paris. The terms of agreement are noted in a December 1776 letter from Wentworth to William Eden, the undersecretary of state in the Northern Department of the British Foreign Ministry and the official responsible for coordinating intelligence col-lection in the ministry against the commission:

> Dr. Edwards [Bancroft's cover name] engages to correspond with Mr. Wentworth and to communicate to him, whatever may come to his knowledge on the following subjects. The progress of the Treaty with France and of the assistance expected, or commerce carried on in any of the ports of that kingdom. The same with Spain, and of every other court in Europe. The agents in the foreign islands in America, and the means of carrying on the commerce with the northern colonies. The means of obtaining credit effics and money; and the channels and agents used to supply them; the secret moves about the courts of France and Spain, and the Congress agents, and tracing the lives from one to the other. Franklin and Deane's correspondence with Congress, and their agents; and the secret, as well as the ostensible letters from the Congress to them. Copies of any transactions, committed to papers, and an exact account of all intercourse and the subject matter treated of between the courts of Versailles and Madrid, and the agents from Congress. Subjects to be communicated to Lord Stormont. Names of the two Carolina ships, mas-ters both English and French, descriptions of the ships and cargoes; the time of sailing, and the port bound to. The same circumstances repre-senting all equipment in any port in Europe together with the names of the agents employed. The intelligence that may arrive from America, the captures made by their privateers, and the instruction they received from the deputies. How the captures are disposed.[70]

As compensation, Bancroft would receive a salary of £500 a year, a recruit-ment bonus of £400, and a pension of £200 a year. By 1780, his annual salary had increased to £1,000.[71]

As noted previously, by the time of the American Revolution the concept and practice of collecting intelligence was well established in the British gov-ernment. While no centralized organization issued requirements and ana-lyzed reports, these responsibilities were handled by King George III through his prime minister, Lord North. The two major elements of intelligence collection on American activities in France and the rest of Europe were Eden's network operating out of the Foreign Office and the Admiralty intelligence reporting to the secretary of the Royal Navy. Eden concentrated on political intelligence and the navy on shipping intelligence. In the case of American activities in France and throughout Europe, these reporting areas often overlapped. Eden specifically targeted American-born British subjects in England for recruitment.[72]

In Paris, Lord Stormont ran several reporting sources on American activities at French ports. These sources included John Barton & Company, a British firm at Bordeaux; David Allen, A. Keith, and John Williams, a distant relative of Franklin's, at Nantes; and John Hunter at Rennes, who also covered activities at Brest, Saint-Malo, and L'Orient. These agents' reporting was passed through the British Foreign Office intelligence network. Stormont also controlled agents targeted against the French government and the American Commission, with the able assistance of Horace Saint Paul, another senior British official at the mission, and Thomas Jeans, a personal assistant to the minister, who did much of the actual operational work with the British agents. Stormont's agents included one in the archives section of the French Foreign Ministry, who was able to provide official minutes of the first meeting between Franklin and Foreign Minister Vergennes on December 28, 1776.[73]

While other British agents were establishing access to the commission and its members, it was Bancroft, as the commission's private secretary, who had the broadest access to American activities and thus was the centerpiece of the British spy network. In his 1784 detailed statement to the British secretary of state for foreign affairs, Lord Carmarthen, Bancroft pressed his claim for a generous pension based upon his services. His own words clearly described the wide access he had within the commission:

> I went to Paris, and during the first year, resided in the same house with Dr. Franklin, Mr. Deane etc., and regularly informed his Government of every transaction of the American Commissioners; of every Step and Vessel taken to supply the revolted Colonies, with Artillery, Arms etc.; of every part of their intercourse with the French and other European Courts; of the Powers and instructions given by Congress to the Commissioners, and of their correspondence with the Secret Committees etc. and when the Government of France at length determined openly to support the Revolted Colonies, I gave notice of this determination,

and of the progress made in forming the two Treaties of Alliance and Commerce, and when these were signed, on the Evening of the 6th of Feb'y, I at my own expense, by a special Messenger, and with unexampled dispatch, conveyed this intelligence to this City, and to the King's Ministers, within 42 hours, from the instant of their Signature."[74]

The commission officially opened in late December 1776, with Franklin as the de facto head of the mission. It was located in the Hôtel de Valentinois, in the Paris suburb of Passy. Unfortunately, there were serious personality clashes within the commission. The split was clear from the start: Franklin and Deane against Lee. Personal and business rivalries existed, and the sometimes brittle emotional personalities of the individuals made for an unpleasant environment.[75]

This situation provided British intelligence with opportunities to manipulate the three commissioners and the working environment within the commission. Had mutual trust and respect existed, the commission might have been more aware of the behavior of its employees and looked more objectively at why the British were so well informed of its plans and activities. According to an American historian, "from 1776 to 1781, it is not too much to say that the British Foreign Office was far better informed of American activities than was Congress itself. Franklin's embassy at Passy, it now appears, was almost a branch office of the British Secret Service."[76]

Unfortunately for the Americans, the commissioner with the most active counterintelligence suspicions was also the least liked in the commission's fellowship. Lee had a reputation for being suspicious, and Franklin's personal and professional dislike and distrust of Lee stood in the way of his giving objective consideration to Lee's suspicions of British agents in the commission. In a letter to a friend, Franklin said of Lee that "in sowing suspicions and jealousies, in creating misunderstandings, and quarrels, in malice, subtility, and indefatigable industry, he has I think no equal."[77] However, Lee's suspicions, while correct about Bancroft, were not as focused on his own staff and associates, which also included British agents.

The lack of personal and professional trust within the commission was readily apparent to the French, and Bancroft made sure that British intelligence was well aware of the situation. An experienced intelligence service such as Britain's would have collected personality assessment data on all the commissioners and have had excellent profiles on Franklin and Lee from their time in England. With this information, an intelligence service would be in an excellent position to identify and insert additional agents into the commission's staff, using the commissioners' personality traits to make these individuals attractive to them.

During the period prior to French official involvement in the war, one of the most time-consuming tasks of Franklin, as the senior commission member, involved constant negotiation regarding the mechanisms of the nonattributable military supply shipments and privateering activities involving French ports. The British spies within the commission, as well as other agents located at various French ports, kept British intelligence well supplied with accurate information and details on these activities. In turn, the British ambassador in Paris, Lord Stormont, made strong and frequent official protests citing specifics to the French government.[78] These protests forced the French government to take additional measures to disguise its involvement but had little real effect on the activities.

With the commission and its three distinct personalities representing such a rich and concentrated target, British intelligence moved quickly and effectively to move Bancroft into a commission staff position. Bancroft, at Wentworth's direction, traveled to Paris in January 1777 and further ingratiated himself with Deane and Franklin. On returning to Britain, he expressed confidence that he could obtain a position within the commission. This suited British intelligence, and a cover story was created to justify Bancroft's move to Paris. British intelligence used a public incident, which could have proved a threat to Bancroft, as the justification for his decision to move to Paris and take the position of private secretary. His ostensible reason to leave Britain related to the publication in the *London Chronicle* on March 15, 1777, of Jack the Painter's confession. The confession included the facts that Deane had given Jack a letter for Bancroft and that Jack had told Bancroft of his activities.[79] Deane and Franklin accepted Bancroft's statement that he no longer felt safe in Britain after this public exposure of his association with Jack. He departed London on March 26 and joined the commission as private secretary, with access to all its papers. Surprisingly, the French, who had agents keeping an eye on the Americans, also believed the cover story.[80]

As Bancroft was now able to report from inside the commission, British intelligence searched for other Americans who could also gain the trust and confidence of one or more of the commissioners. Having more than one reporting source against the same target offers obvious advantages in terms of vetting the accuracy of reporting, as well as increasing its overall comprehensiveness. One England-based British intelligence agent, the Rev. John Vardill, an American

Anglican clergyman and a former assistant rector of Trinity Church in New York City, recruited two such agents: a businessman named Jacobus Van Zandt (also known as George Lupton) and Capt. Joseph Hynson, a Maryland sea captain.[81] Van Zandt was directed to travel to Paris and develop a relationship with Deane. Van Zandt came from a merchant family and used his knowledge of business to discuss possible business opportunities with Deane, who was always on the alert for a profitable deal.

Deane often invited Van Zandt into his living quarters, which gave him the opportunity to steal various documents that Deane kept there. Overall, much of what Van Zandt reported from Deane was also being reported by Bancroft, and his information served as a useful cross check on the latter's reporting. At least one piece of Van Zandt's reporting proved to be of significant value to the British: He was able to provide a list of the cover names and addresses used by the commission to correspond with its contacts in Britain.[82] However, Van Zandt's questions soon became too obvious, and the business deals Deane had hoped for were not forthcoming. Deane dropped contact with him in early 1778. Having lost his access, Van Zandt was terminated by Vardill.

Vardill had better luck with Captain Hynson, who managed to befriend Franklin and Deane for over six months. Hynson was originally spotted by his British girlfriend and her landlady in London, part of Vardill's network identifying potential agents, after he boasted of being tasked to obtain an English ship to sail to America for transfer to the American navy. He also bragged of involvement in the movement of secret correspondence from the American commissioners in Paris to the Continental Congress. Vardill recruited him, using a combination of threats and financial rewards, specifically to obtain the official correspondence between the commission and the Congress. Hynson's contributions to British intelligence included military shipping information and American plans to purchase European ships for American use. His sources of information were Deane and Franklin, American sea captains involved in moving supplies and vessels to the colonies, and William Carmichael, an assistant to both Franklin and Deane.[83]

Hynson's most important intelligence success was his theft of the commission's official correspondence to the Continental Congress from January through June 1777. This correspondence, which he had been scheduled to carry, was subsequently entrusted to another American seaman, Captain Folger, who was prepared to sail earlier than Hynson. During a social drinking session in mid-October, Hynson replaced the correspondence in Folger's dispatch pouch with blank papers, and the correspondence was not discovered

as missing until Folger reached the American shore. Hynson passed the correspondence to Lord Stormont's assistant.[84] Hynson was rewarded with a one-
time payment of £200 pounds and a lifetime pension of £200 pounds per
year. British Foreign Ministry intelligence chief Eden personally delivered the
correspondence to King George III.[85]

Carmichael, a source of Hynson's and a probable recruitment target of the
British, was an American businessman from Maryland residing in Europe who
volunteered to help the commission in a clerical position. He served as an assistant to both Deane and Franklin from late 1776 through 1777. His duties,
in addition to preparing papers for the commission, involved handling commercial and military shipping procedures and activities related to American
privateers operating from French ports. He also had a mistress in London who
lived in the same house as Hynson's mistress.[86] There is no firm evidence that
Carmichael was under British control, but he told Hynson of activities at the
commission and details of American shipping and privateering plans knowing
that Hynson was passing this information to the British. He was well aware
that Hynson was in touch with a British intelligence officer, Lt. Col. Edward
Smith. Thus he was close to the edge of actively assisting the British, if he did
not actually cooperate with them.[87]

French monitoring of Carmichael's activities finally caused the French government to apply pressure upon Franklin to remove him from his position at
the commission. Under the guise of carrying dispatches back to the Congress,
he was sent home.[88] However, his potential cooperation with the British was
never investigated. He became a representative to the Continental Congress
from Maryland for a year and then in 1779 became a secretary in the American
legation in Madrid, serving under John Jay. Interestingly, Jay, perhaps because
of his previous counterintelligence work, came to distrust Carmichael as they
worked together.[89]

While these other espionage activities were taking place, Bancroft was reporting both quantity and quality intelligence using a classic tradecraft communication method to pass his intelligence to the British ambassador in Paris.
Lord Stormont, employing his secretary Jeans, had established a dead-drop
site in the Tuileries gardens for Bancroft's use. Effective use of this tradecraft
requires careful planning of not only the concealment capabilities of the site,
but also the normal daily routine of both individuals involved.

To use the site, Bancroft was to prepare cover letters of a social nature
addressed to a Mr. Richards and signed by Edward Edwards, his operational
alias. He would then write his actual report in secret ink between the lines of

the cover correspondence and place his letter in a bottle with a string attached to it neck. His drop was scheduled for after 9:30 in the evening, ensuring darkness, each Tuesday when he took his regular stroll through the gardens. When he reached the south terrace, there was a box tree that had a hole by its roots. As he passed this tree, he would quickly slip the bottle down the hole, ensuring the end of the string was at the base of the tree. After an appropriate period of time to allow Bancroft to exit the area, Jeans would stroll by the tree and retrieve the bottle using the string. He would remove the letters and replace them with coded instructions and taskings for Bancroft's next report. Once again after an appropriate amount of time to allow Jeans to exit the area, Bancroft would again pass by the tree and retrieve his message from Stormont. He used this method to pass hundreds of pages of intelligence to the British.[90]

Just as there was no security vetting of commission personnel, there was also no real physical security at the commission itself. The public had access to the mansion, with documents and papers spread all over the office areas, and private discussions were held in public areas. Commissioner Arthur Lee was appalled by the situation and wrote: "Count Vergennes had complained that everything we did was known to the English ambassador, who was always plaguing him with the details. No one will be surprised at this who knows that we have no time or place appropriate to our consultation, but that servants, strangers, and everyone was at liberty to enter and did constantly enter the room while we were talking about public business and that the papers relating to it lay open in rooms of common and continual resort."[91]

However, as previously noted, Lee's counterintelligence concern was so broad that it was ignored. And while he did carry it to extremes, an incident early in his career as a commissioner probably contributed to his already suspicious nature. He was the victim of a document-theft operation by British agents.

In June 1777, Lee went to the court of King Frederick the Great in Berlin to seek assistance for the Revolution. Learning of his arrival, the British ambassador in Berlin, Hugh Elliot, used a German servant from his mission to bribe several employees of the hotel where Lee was staying. Elliot was a young and rather inexperienced diplomat, but he had a flair for intelligence work.

Elliot had the hotel employees observe Lee's habits and daily schedule for several days. They reported that he spent many hours each day writing in his journal. The minister quickly decided that he wanted the information in that journal. He tasked his German servant to obtain a key to Lee's room from the hotel employees and to duplicate it. On June 26, Elliot was advised that Lee was to travel that day to the country for a social occasion. His servant stole Lee's journal from his room and took it to Elliot's residence, where several people were waiting to copy it.

The copying went slower than anticipated, and much remained to be copied about the time Lee was to return to the hotel. Elliot decided to stop Lee from returning to his room until the copying had been completed. At this point, his sense of operational security became somewhat flawed. He went to the hotel and waited in the lobby until Lee arrived. He then approached Lee casually and engaged him in conversation. He told Lee that when he had heard him speaking English, he was so happy to hear a familiar language that he had to talk to him.

Two hours later, Lee finally broke away and got to his room. He immediately noticed the loss of his journal and reported the burglary to the local police. Meanwhile, Elliot hurried back to his residence and retrieved the journal. He then donned a disguise, returned to the hotel, and gave the journal to one of the employees in his pay. She returned it to Lee, claiming that it had been left at the door to his room. The ensuing investigation identified Elliot as having been involved, and King Frederick publicly blamed the British minister for the theft. In the diplomatic démarche that followed, King George III resorted to plausible denial, and publicly rebuked his minister. Privately he rewarded Elliot with £1,000 for obtaining such valuable intelligence.[92]

Lee's lack of security in protecting his secret journal, regardless of his public counterintelligence pronouncements, also extended to his personal staff. Like the other members of the commission, Lee used his personal judgment of an individual's character and loyalty as the only vetting tool. In the case of Maj. John Thornton, a British army officer on inactive duty, Lee accepted a recommendation from Franklin that Thornton become Lee's private secretary. Thornton had successfully completed a mission to Britain for Franklin regarding the condition of American prisoners of war held there, and he was able to convince Lee that through his contacts in Britain he could provide Lee with useful intelligence on British military activities and planning. Lee subsequently passed his information on to the Congress. Because Thornton was a British agent, the information had been provided by British intelligence.[93] However, Thornton's tenure was short-lived because within a few months of his hiring, Franklin received word from contacts in London that the major was a spy.[94] Under pressure from Franklin, Lee dismissed Thornton.

While all three commissioners share in the counterintelligence disaster, Franklin, as the mission head, has to bear primary responsibility for it. By the time he arrived in Paris in late 1776, he was elderly and had little interest in the commission's administrative aspects. Franklin was widely recognized as a statesman, scientist, and intellectual. While highly respected, he was also vain, obstinate, and jealous of his prerogatives and reputation. He had decided that his role would be that of an agent of influence among both the politically powerful and the French public.[95] He found it convenient to allow Deane to handle the commission's housekeeping affairs while he moved among the wealthy and powerful social elite.[96] Also, the commission was under the protection of the French government, and Franklin underestimated British capabilities to operate in a friendly third country. In any event, he did nothing to create a security or counterintelligence consciousness at the commission.

In addition, Franklin's personal association with Deane and Bancroft and his dislike of Lee caused him to brush aside Lee's accusations against both men. Intellectually, however, he realized that spies posed a serious threat. In January 1777, in response to a letter from a lady friend, Juliana Ritchie, warning him of spies, he wrote back to her:

> It is impossible to discover in every case the falsity of pretended friends, who would know our affairs; and more so to prevent being watch'd by spies, when interested people may think proper to place them for that purpose; I have long observ'd one rule which prevents any inconvenience from such practices. It is simply this, to be concern'd in no affairs that I should blush to have made publick, and to do nothing but what spies may see and welcome. When a man's actions are just and honourable, the more they are known, the more his reputation is increas'd and establish'd. If I was sure, therefore that my valet de Place was a spy, as probably he is, I think I should not discharge him for that, if in other respects I lik'd him.[97]

Because Franklin was involved in numerous activities that he would not want to have been made public, such comments seem somewhat ingenuous. His attitude, however, is all too familiar among some policymakers and statesmen. His ego may have overwhelmed his common sense. Like many government officials before and after him, he may have believed that he knew exactly what he was doing and that his judgment required no additional verification. If this is correct, then he had forgotten a basic rule that he stated years earlier as Poor Richard: "If you would keep your secret from an enemy tell it not to a friend."

The second, most important commissioner, Silas Deane, was an aggressive

Yankee merchant with a well-honed taste for personal profit. His aggressive activities in establishing transport of military supplies via Hortalez & Company and the somewhat vague manner in which he made agreements with the French over payments and profits for these supplies allowed his enemies to criticize his behavior. Lee, and his family and political allies, led the attacks that caused Deane to be recalled in early 1778.[98] The subsequent congressional investigation made Deane extremely bitter, and in 1781 Bancroft, whom Deane still considered a friend, convinced him to write a series of letters expressing concern for the American cause and urging an accommodation with the British short of independence. British intelligence then arranged for these letters to be published in a New York City newspaper.[99] Historians still debate the degree to which Deane was subsequently controlled or manipulated by British intelligence through Bancroft after he was recalled from the commission.

The third commissioner, Arthur Lee, had difficulty getting along with people because of his huge ego.[100] He was neither liked nor trusted by either his fellow commissioners or by Vergennes. While he did have a suspicious nature, his attitude toward counterintelligence was erratic. He suspected everyone until he developed a personal relationship with them, and then they became loyal based upon that relationship.

As is usually the case with a counterintelligence disaster, there is sufficient blame to share among all the participants.

And a final note about Dr. Edward Bancroft. He remained with the commission as private secretary until early 1783. He returned to Britain and resumed work in the field of chemistry and died in 1821. His activities as a British agent against the American commission remained secret until the 1880s, when B. F. Stephens, an American researcher, found information in British official files that exposed his role.[101]

CHAPTER 5

NATHAN HALE AND THE BRITISH OCCUPATION OF NEW YORK CITY

In early February 1776, Washington instructed Gen. Charles Lee to take command in the New York City area and with local militia to start constructing fortifications and developing a plan for its defense. In addition to only the poorly armed and trained militia, Lee also had little in the way of artillery and nothing capable of stopping British naval ships from controlling the sea lanes around the city. The geographical location of the city dictated that whichever side controlled the sea would control the land. This meant the Americans could not successfully defend the area.

Lee developed his defensive plan with the objective of making the British Army pay as high a price in men and materials as possible to take New York.[1] He built numerous fortifications, on high ground where possible, but because of the lack of manpower and armament, these positions were inadequately constructed and did not have proper artillery support. When Washington arrived in the city on April 13 with about ten thousand Continental troops, he immediately made efforts to improve the fortifications. But he made no serious changes to Lee's defensive plan.[2] His still poorly disciplined and poorly supplied forces continued to be at a disadvantage in terms of time and armament.

When Howe's army departed Boston, they sailed northward to the British base at Halifax, where they were resupplied and awaited additional troops from Britain. Other than make requests to local commanders for coast watchers to look for any approach of a British fleet, Washington was too busy with purely military matters to concern himself with creating an intelligence network in the greater New York City area.

It was mid-June when Howe sailed toward New York City with some nine thousand men. On July 2, his advance guard landed on Staten Island and easily drove off the local militia force. There Howe established his base of operations while awaiting additional troops. By mid-July, Washington was able to obtain from British deserters accurate intelligence on Howe's forces on Staten Island and on his anticipated reinforcements.[3] Ten days later, a British fleet easily entered the mouth of the Hudson River because of the ineffectiveness of the American batteries. Throughout the next six weeks, the British built up their troop strength on Staten Island and established control of the sea lanes around the city.

The Americans did have at least one intelligence agent residing on Staten Island who was in a position to observe British activities and troop presence. But he could not travel through British lines to pass along his information, and the Americans were unable to find a courier who could travel there and back. Finally, on August 20, a courier was able to meet the agent and return on the 22nd with fairly accurate information on the size and capabilities of the British forces.[4] Based upon a notation in Washington's expense reports, the courier was Lawrence Mascoll, of whom little else is known.[5] Based upon other comments in Washington's papers and the later intelligence role played by the Mersereau family in New Jersey, it is believed that the collection agent was John Mersereau, the youngest son of Joshua Mersereau, a patriotic merchant already supplying intelligence to Washington.[6] John was known to reside on Staten Island during that time.

For intelligence to be useful it must also be timely, and in this case, because of the lack of a functioning clandestine communication system, it arrived too late to assist Washington in his defensive preparations. On August 23, the British moved fifteen thousand troops onto Long Island, with more to follow, and began to attack the weak American positions. Washington's only intelligence on the attacking force came from his scouts, and because of the fact that these localized reports could only describe the British presence each scouting party saw, American commanders had the impression that the attacking forces were only about half the actual British strength.[7] Through the use of flanking movements, the British rapidly advanced until reaching American positions at Brooklyn Heights. Here Howe ordered a halt for reasons that seemed to have to do with his concern over excessive casualties, perhaps a legacy of his experience at the Battle of Bunker Hill where his victory was at the cost of over a third of his force.[8] This gave American forces the opportunity to vacate the fortifications and with the help of a fog, retreat across the water into Manhattan. But the American army, outnumbered and lacking supplies, remained in danger. Washington recognized that with British control of the waterways surrounding the city, he would soon be trapped on the island. However, before he could order an evacuation he needed the consent of Congress and wanted the agreement of his general officers. By the time he got his consent and agreement, the British had crossed from Long Island to Kip's Bay on Manhattan. This September 15th attack quickly scattered the militia units defending the bay, and the rout soon spread to the Continental Army units as well. Once again, Washington had no useful intelligence regarding the British move. His army scouts reported that the landing would take place farther north.[9]

Since late August, Washington had been operating with little tactical intelligence and no information on British plans and intentions. As soon as he arrived on Manhattan, he took steps to remedy this intelligence vacuum. He called in Col. Thomas Knowlton, an officer who had distinguished himself at Bunker Hill as well as in other military actions, and instructed him to select a group of men to conduct tactical reconnaissance for the army. This unit came to be known as Knowlton's Rangers. A member of that unit was to become not only better known than the rangers, but one of the most famous figures of the war. Nathan Hale was the commander of one of the unit's four companies.

The Office of Strategic Services, the Central Intelligence Agency's World War II predecessor, placed a great deal of value in recruiting its officers from the Ivy League colleges. In the early days of the CIA this was also the case. These organizations felt that men—and in those days it was primarily men—from such an academic, and usually moneyed, background had the right mix of intellect, ethics, willingness to take risks, and discipline to conduct intelligence operations effectively. Or, in other words, according to the story I was told as a young case officer, they could lie, cheat, and steal on a par with anybody in the world. That may have been true in the mid-twentieth century, but this was not the stuff of which Yale graduate Nathan Hale was made.

As is often the case with individuals singled out by history for symbolic reasons, Hale's legend is more drama than fact. Nevertheless, it should be clear that he was a true patriot and in this sense deserved to be honored for his willingness to die for his country. He is a hero in this regard. However, from an intelligence perspective, he was a lousy spy. His selection, training (or lack thereof), and how he conducted his mission were horrible by both intelligence and commonsense standards.

A metaphor for Hale's popular legend can be found in the numerous statues of him that inhabit such locations as the CIA headquarters compound and numerous other sites around the country. His noble features look resolved, and his bearing is reserved but firm. However, while the face and body represent an artistic inspiration of a patriotic legend, it has questionable resemblance to his actual likeness. As no drawings or paintings of him prior to his death have been found, his image is based upon descriptions and drawings from friends after his death.[10] If he had been a successful spy, history might never have heard of him, and it is doubtful that he would have statues about the country honoring him. Most intelligence officers and agents are happy just to get a decent pension and not be subsequently indicted for their professional activities as political perspectives shift within the government.

Hale was born on June 6, 1755, in Coventry, Connecticut, to a family with very early ties to America. He was the great-great-grandson of John Hale, a prominent figure in the Salem Witch Trials of 1692. His father was a well-to-do farmer and community leader. Both parents were staunch Puritans who considered religious values an essential part of one's life. Nathan and his brother Enoch were sent to Yale College in 1769. At that time, Yale focused on an education based upon religion and the classics. Its living conditions were basic, and its primary purpose was to train young men for the clergy. In fact, in 1757 it included a church on its campus—a first for a college in the colonies. Hale's reputation was that of an intelligent, religious, athletic individual with a gentle and kind nature.

Traditional CIA psychological personality profiles used to identify operations officers would find many of these traits useful, but a recruiter would want to dig a little deeper regarding the kind and gentle characteristics prior to employment. Empathy is important in intelligence work but so is objectivity in viewing those individuals around you. Being too trusting of individuals without proper vetting is an occupational hazard that has ruined a good many operations. Hale's life up to the point when he started his spy mission is quite well documented by correspondence, papers, and numerous biographies, most scholarly but some more patriotic than facts would support.

Within the culture of the time, his religious beliefs, with their emphasis on honesty in one's personal life, posed a serious question regarding Hale's suitability as a spy. Both his family and his educational experience ingrained in him a strong sense of personal integrity that made it difficult for him to lie

This statue, familiar to the public from numerous placements about the country, represents an idealized likeness of Nathan Hale. No illustrations of Hale from his lifetime exist. This photograph is of Hale's statue at the US Department of Justice. *Library of Congress, Carol M. Highsmith Archive*

effectively—not a good trait for an individual sent behind enemy lines to collect intelligence. However, it seems that this aspect of his personality was given the same amount of serious consideration as other important elements involved in planning a successful collection mission—that is, very little.

After college Hale became a teacher, and by late 1774, was the master of the Union School in New London. Being a patriot, he also joined the local militia and was elected to the post of first sergeant. However, when armed conflict broke out in April 1775, he did not join his militia unit in marching to Boston. Whether his reason was commitment to a teaching contract or uncertainty regarding the nature of the conflict is not clear. However, this changed in July when he received a letter from a close friend and college classmate, Benjamin Tallmadge. Tallmadge had gone to Cambridge for a firsthand look at the standoff around Boston between the British and the colonial forces. The letter, dated

July 4, 1775, was an emotional argument for joining the colonial forces: "Was I in your condition . . . I think the more extensive Service would be my choice. Our holy Religion, the honour of our God, a glorious country, & a happy constitution is what we have to defend."[11] Soon after receiving the letter, Hale joined the Seventh Connecticut Regiment as a first lieutenant and within weeks marched off to Boston. That Tallmadge was a most convincing communicator is not surprising. His natural talents were recognized by Commander in Chief Washington early on, and he eventually became the senior case officer for arguably the most sophisticated American spy network of the period, the Culper Ring in New York City. While both Hale and Tallmadge shared a deep commitment to their personal ethics and their Christian religion, Tallmadge would demonstrate a more pragmatic approach in his subsequent intelligence activities.

When the army was reorganized in January 1776, Hale was commissioned a captain in the new Nineteenth Connecticut Regiment and that spring moved with the army to the New York City area. In September, when Washington decided to form a ranger-like unit to conduct tactical reconnaissance of British activities, he was invited to join that unit. Up to that time, there was only one recorded incident of Hale's involvement in intelligence activities. While he was with the army in the New York City area, his army account book noted that he paid a man for secret information, with no additional detailed stated.[12]

Knowlton's Rangers is considered by the US Army to be its first military intelligence unit, and the "1776" on the army intelligence emblem represents this unit.[13] However, the existence of Knowlton's Rangers was short-lived. While Hale was on his secret mission, Knowlton's unit was sent by Washington to scout British lines about two miles south of Continental lines at Harlem Heights on September 16. It met a unit from the famed British regiment the Black Watch, and during the bloody engagement Knowlton and many of his men were killed and wounded.[14] This action effectively destroyed the unit. Two months later, the remaining rangers were captured by the British at Fort Washington, the last remaining Continental fort in Manhattan, while covering Washington's main army's retreat into New Jersey.

The British campaign to capture Long Island and Manhattan probably represented the low point of Washington's military skill and leadership during the Revolutionary War.[15] He was not well informed regarding British tactical movements and constantly sought better intelligence on British plans and intentions. Various records indicate Gen. Hugh Mercer tried to collect intelligence on Staten Island in mid-July, and Gen. William Livingston sent Lawrence Mascole (possibly the same individual as Lawrence Mascoll) on a similar mission several weeks later.[16] And as previously noted, General Livingston finally was able to send a courier to Staten Island to get reporting, probably from a member of the Mersereau family, whose intelligence collection efforts two years later were quite successful.[17] However, such information was of little value to Washington as he rapidly withdrew his forces from Brooklyn to Manhattan.

By early September 1776, Washington was desperate for intelligence. His troops were trapped in Manhattan, facing advancing British forces while surrounded by the Royal Navy. His letter to Gen. William Heath of September 5 clearly conveys his state of mind: "I do most earnestly entreat you and General Clinton to exert yourselves to accomplish this most desirable end. Leave no stone unturned, nor do not stick at expense, to bring this to pass, as I was never more uneasy than on account of my want of knowledge on this score."[18] On September 8, Washington received some intelligence from Col. Isaac Nicoll, the militia commander of Fort Constitution, on the western side of the Hudson River. And New York governor George Clinton sent two agents, George Treadwell and Benjamin Ludlum, to Long Island on a collection mission that ended on September 12.[19]

In addition to the above activities, Washington instructed Knowlton to send a spy behind British lines to collect intelligence on troop movements and fortifications. Knowlton's first choice for this mission was James Sprague, an officer whom he believed had the skills to accomplish the mission. However, Sprague refused the mission.[20] Knowlton's next move was poorly documented, but it is clear that he publicly assembled several of his officers and requested a volunteer. No one did. While not volunteering for anything is a military tradition, in this case the requested duties clearly fit the definition of being a spy. For gentlemen of that period, being a spy was considered both dishonorable and disreputable. This was the reason that Sprague turned down his commander's request.[21] Hale either arrived late to this meeting because of an illness or attended a second officers' assembly and volunteered then. The facts that an intelligence-collection mission behind enemy lines was discussed publicly and the individual undertaking it accepted in public did not represent good operational security. And this serious error could have doomed the operation before it even started. Handling the selection of a candidate in this manner calls into question Knowlton's understanding of even commonsense security requirements for human collection operations behind enemy lines.

In a further breach of operational security, Hale discussed the mission with his fellow officer and old Yale classmate Capt. William Hull. Hull subsequently noted that he tried to convince Hale not to accept the mission but recognized it was Hale's personal decision to make. However, Hull also noted that Hale was a poor choice based upon his personality. He wrote it was "not in his character: his nature was too frank and open to deceit and disguise, and he was incapable of acting a part equally foreign to his feelings and habits."[22]

With his decision made, Hale left camp on September 15 and with his old friend and current sergeant Steven Hempstead traveled to Norwalk, Connecticut, to arrange boat passage to Long Island. It is undocumented as to what degree he received instructions on how to implement his collection mission. There are reports, undocumented but plausible, that he met with Washington just prior to his departure.[23] In a professionally planned mission, all aspects of Hale's cover plan, collection requirements, methods of recording his information, and detailed escape plans would have been thoroughly reviewed with him. While he had about a week between volunteering and departing, no record exists of any such operational preparation.

The population of Norwalk was considered to be friendly to the patriotic cause, with most of the town of Dutch ancestry, but there were also Tories in the area. On September 16, Hale was discreetly ferried to Long Island by Capt. Charles Pond of the sloop *Schuyler*. Pond was a trusted patriot and a mariner experienced in navigating the sound around British naval patrols.

Hale's mission would be short, ending in his death with no successes. In fact, his original collection requirements were rendered useless by the British rapid advances against Washington's army. It was only well after the Revolution that efforts began to publicize Hale and his mission.[24] It was a botched mission from its start, with little chance of meaningful success because of poor planning, poor execution, and, only recently learned, an effective counter-intelligence effort by a brutish British Tory officer well known during the French and Indian War.

For an intelligence activity to be successful, its planning must be well thought out, with careful attention to all details of the activity. The agent must have a cover for status and a cover for access to justify his or her actions. Collection requirements must be specific and focused on identified targets, with methods provided to conceal and pass the collected information in a secure manner. Both the entry into enemy territory and the return to friendly territory should be carefully planned and timed, with backup arrangements also in place. These elements of planning are not new and were known and used routinely in intelligence activities long before the Revolutionary War. In Hale's mission the mistakes made were beyond amateurish.

The first obvious mistake was in the area of what is known as operational security: protection of the operation, its purpose, and its implementers from hostile knowledge. To announce the intended secret mission at a large forum and then identify the individual to be used in that same forum threatens the security of both the mission and the individual involved. While there is no evidence that any of Knowlton's officers knowingly reported the mission to the British, with so many people holding this information it is probable that some or all of it became part of idle conversation or gossip. Spying is a dramatic topic, and it is human nature to want to tell others something exciting. Anyone who has lived within an embassy social environment can attest to the fact that the cocktail game of "spotting the spook" is active and well. While harm is seldom meant by such gossip, it can often cause great damage to the intelligence mission. The relationship between gossiping and resultant damage is much easier to understand in military operations than in intelligence activities. The poster of a sinking ship in flames with the caption "Loose lips sink ships" carried a much clearer message than can be publicly presented for an intelligence mission.

Thus, even prior to Hale's departure his mission was potentially threatened. A second issue was the decision that Hale would operate in his true name. This decision was apparently based on the fact that he wanted to carry his Yale degree as proof of his schoolteacher cover. His extended family, like many in the colonies, was split in its loyalties in this conflict. Of particular note, one of his cousins, Samuel Hale, was a senior British official active in the New York City area.[25] He was well aware of Nathan's membership in the Continental Army, and if he were to receive word of his cousin's presence in British lines, it can be assumed that he would have taken appropriate action. In fact, as the Hale legend began to grow after the war, much speculation focused on Samuel having played a key role in identifying Nathan as a spy.[26] While there are no records that Samuel did learn of Nathan's mission until after he was captured, sound operational planning does not leave such matters to chance. Murphy's Law that anything that can go wrong will go wrong is particularly applicable to intelligence operations, as any reader of the popular press knows well.

The next issue that should have been addressed was the covers to be used: cover for status, cover for action, and cover for access. These covers represent the seemingly overt rationale for the individual's identity, activities, and reason to be in a position to fulfill whatever requirements are the mission's objectives. In Hale's case these covers had little credibility. He was to act like a schoolteacher looking for work inside the British lines. Considering the interest most British soldiers of the time had in any intellectual pursuit, his stated purpose for wandering around the camps and fortifications was not very convincing. Another problem was his physical appearance. While his actual appearance was not known, it was known that he readily stood out in a crowd, as his height was above average, and he had a powder burn from a musket-flash accident on his right cheek.[27] Because his cover for status was that of a schoolteacher, this powder burn would cause any British soldier to wonder why a schoolteacher had such a mark characteristic of someone in the military. A third issue was that he had been stationed in the city for several months as a Continental Army officer and therefore might easily be recognized by almost anyone who might have seen him in uniform during that period. His lingering about in a specific location or repeatedly moving about an area, both of which are necessary to obtain accurate details of camps, troops, and fortifications, was unlikely to go unnoticed. It is the little gray man in history, one whose presence and activities fit so well into the background of the scene that he is ignored, who is successful specifically because he is just part of the crowd. Hale was not in this mold. Basically, his cover was weak to say the least.

Matters regarding note taking, to record the details of British troop strength and fortifications, also seemed poorly considered. Considering the broad scope of information Washington wanted from Hale's mission, notes to retain specifics would be a necessary requirement. Yet apparently the only idea presented to Hale was hiding his openly written notes and sketches under the soles of his shoes.[28] This was a common method of hiding important papers and other valuables during the period, so any semiprofessional search of his person would uncover this hiding place. And after his capture it did. Other more discreet and less detectable methods were both available and would have fit well with his cover. Schoolteachers would be expected to carry some books and papers with them, and notes written in them, either in primitive but readily available invisible ink or as margin notes in code, would have been a preferable option. That such simple solutions were not used further demonstrates the mission's lack of planning.

Finally, we must address the most basic issue of this operation: the suitability of Nathan Hale for the mission. Previous evidence of his lack of understanding, or at least practice, of the concepts of secrecy and compartmentation has been provided. But it was his personality that probably sealed his fate. Hale was a miserable liar and, possibly based upon his religious beliefs, had great trust in the honesty of his fellow man. Unfortunately for him, Robert Rogers, the commander of Rogers's Rangers during the French and Indian War, was very good at not telling the truth and was not an honest man by anyone's definition.

While all the mistakes involved in the planning and implementation of the operation contributed to its failure, it was a counterintelligence officer who put the pieces together and neutralized the operation. In the counterintelligence business, not unlike criminal investigations, human errors are the keys to success. However, it still takes a disciplined and skilled individual to recognize the errors and, more important, make sense of them.

A major challenge in writing any history or commentary regarding intelligence is that successful activities seldom see the light of day, while failures readily become public knowledge. This makes it easy to assume most intelligence activities fail and that other events took place without intelligence insights. Governments tend to release information on intelligence matters only decades, or more, after their conclusion, and then individuals involved are often still protected for logical reasons. Also, the individuals involved have their own reasons for often keeping their activities secret. This was true during the Revolutionary War period. This was a war where your neighbor might well be secretly on the other side and where personal vendettas might be pursued under the guise of patriotic or loyalist actions. Thus, once the conflict ended, many felt it best to forget the past. This sentiment may have been one of the reasons that it took two-hundred-plus years for Rogers's role in Hale's capture to come to light.

In 2003, the Library of Congress published an article by J. Hutson based upon a manuscript donated three years earlier that had been in the Tiffany family for generations.[29] This family had been Tories during the war, and the manuscript described why and how Robert Rogers became involved in Hale's mission.

Rogers grew up in the New Hampshire frontier area and as a youth in the mid-1740s experienced the brutal Indian attacks on local settlements by tribes supportive of the French. When the French and Indian War began, he had accumulated a great deal of experience in exploring the wilderness and learning the Indians' way of warfare. He was a captain in a New Hampshire regiment known for its aggressiveness and ability to scout enemy activities deep within French territory. In 1756, the British commander in North America selected Rogers to lead a new unit to harass the French and their Indian allies within their own territory. He did this well and applied the brutality he had seen as a youth to his actions against both the French and the Indians.

After the war ended, Rogers did not settle down well. He married but failed in a series of business ventures, and in the mid-1760s moved to London. His business ventures there also failed, and he ended up in a debtor's prison. After

Robert Rogers, famed leader of Rogers's Rangers during
the French and Indian War, joined the British side
during the Revolution and functioned as a ranger and
counterintelligence officer. *Library of Congress*

his release, he recognized the increasing political tension in the American colonies between the Whigs and the Tories and thought his talents might be both valuable and profitable back home. However, once back in September 1775, Rogers did not find a welcome from either side. General Gage, the British commander, personally disliked him based upon interactions during the French and Indian War, and the patriots were, understandably, suspicious of an individual who had shown no interest in their cause to date.

Nevertheless, Rogers, still deeply in debt, tried to play both sides to see who would give him the better deal. When Gage was replaced by General Howe in late 1775, Rogers approached him and offered his services, claiming the patriots had sought his service. Howe was agreeable. Rogers next sought out Washington and let it be known he was interested in the Continental Army. Washington had already been warned about Rogers's interactions with the British authorities and was suspicious. He next appeared in February 1776 in New York and convinced the recently arrived General Clinton, Howe's deputy, of his worth to the Crown. Attempting to leverage this for a better deal with the Continental Congress, Rogers found himself arrested and questioned by Washington. On July 6, he was moved to New Hampshire for further investigation. En route he escaped his guards and several days later managed to seek safety aboard a British ship in New York Harbor. On August 6, General Howe reported that Rogers had been commissioned to raise a battalion of rangers for the British forces.[30] The official name of this unit was the Queen's American Rangers, although based on his fame in the French and Indian War they were often simply called Rogers's Rangers. Rogers insisted on appointing his own officers, and his views of what he needed in the way of talent contrasted sharply with the British view that officers were to be gentlemen. His men were hard, tough, and definitely not gentlemen. For that matter, neither was he.

A lasting public image of Rogers resulted from a movie starring Spencer Tracy as Major Rogers in the feature film *Northwest Passage*, released in 1940. It was a heroic role featuring Tracy fighting the Indians and their French allies on the American frontier. And it did portray the barbaric fighting style of the frontier. However, while depicting a tough and disciplined leader, Tracy's portrayal was much more gentle and honorable than the real Rogers. Considering the period when this was made, as the shadow of Germany in Europe and Japan in Asia was spreading fear regarding the future, Tracy's character is understandable, and movies are not meant to be accurate—just entertaining.

By September 16, Hale had moved across the sound to Huntington, Long Island, to start his mission. Rogers's unit's mission was to monitor American activities on the Connecticut and Long Island coasts. He was to seek additional volunteers for the British and undertake raids against colonial supply points and troop movements. In addition to his Rangers, he had a ship for patrolling the sound and had established a well-paid network of informants on both shores.[31] On that night Rogers was aboard the HMS *Halifax*, a brig carrying sixteen guns, commanded by Capt. William Quarme, and positioned off Huntington. Quarme received word that two rebel vessels had been observed the previous day and that their actions seemed suspicious. About the same time, a Tory informant in Norwalk reported the presence of a rebel sloop, the four-gun *Schuyler*, and two Continental Army men. It was noted that only one of the men departed with the sloop while the other headed back toward Continental lines. Rogers became suspicious, but the information reached him too late to allow him to try to intercept the sloop.[32]

Upon arriving on Long Island, Hale would have noticed British movements indicating the invasion of Manhattan and realized that the objectives of his original mission were being overtaken by events. He then apparently decided to head toward Brooklyn and American lines. But his observation and collecting methods and his behavior were suspicious enough to draw attention. Rogers, having conducted numerous reconnaissance missions himself, deduced that any rebel spy would have to move along the coast to return to friendly lines. In mid-morning on September 18, Rogers landed at Sands Point, Long Island, and started on the trail of the spy. He soon learned that a stranger was asking questions about the loyalty of the local population.[33]

By September 20, Rogers had identified Hale as the suspicious individual and observed him from afar. He continued to surveil Hale until Hale took a room at a tavern. That evening, as Hale sat down for dinner, Rogers casually joined him at the table. After some initial polite conversation, Rogers confided in Hale that he was a Continental soldier being detained on the island and that the local population was Tory in their political sentiments. While nervous at first, Hale warmed to his new friend, and Rogers confided that he was also collecting information on British movements for use by the American forces. Hale then explained his secret mission, apparently believing he was with a fellow American patriot.[34] Rogers, desiring to get Hale to confess in front of witnesses, suggested they meet for breakfast the next morning at Rogers's place of lodging. Hale readily agreed.

The next morning, Hale joined Rogers and several of his rangers, identified as fellow rebels, for a meal. Other rangers surrounded the tavern as Rogers engaged Hale in talk about his mission and collection activities. During the conversation, Hale stated that he had been sent by Washington to collect intelligence on British troops and fortifications on the island. He also admitted that he was an officer of the Continental Army. Rogers then ordered his arrest, obviously to Hale's surprise.[35] From the tavern he was taken, by Rogers's ship, to General Howe's Manhattan headquarters. Upon being searched, Hale was found to be carrying notes and possibly drawings in the soles of his shoes detailing his collection activities. He was also in civilian clothing. With this degree of proof of his activities, and his comments to Rogers as attested to by several of the rangers present at the tavern, Hale's guilt as a spy was obvious. Howe signed Hale's death warrant.

The next morning after breakfast, Hale was marched to an artillery park next to the Dove Tavern and placed atop a ladder with a rope around his neck connected to a tree branch. He was given the opportunity to make a final declaration. While popular myth has him speaking a patriotic "I only regret that I have but one life to lose for my country," there is no documented record of what he actually said. The oft-quoted sentence is from a popular play of the time, *Cato*, by Joseph Addison. These words became part of the public image of Nathan Hale years later as his friends worked to build his legend.

The best-documented evidence available regarding Hale's final words come from a September 22 entry in the personal diary of British captain Frederick MacKenzie: "He behaved with great composure and resolution, saying he thought it the duty of every good officer, to obey any orders given by his commander in chief; and desired the spectators to be at all times prepared to meet death in whatever shape it might appear."[36] These words reflect Hale's sense of both patriotism and religion. However, it slightly glosses over that he did volunteer for the job rather than take it under orders. He justified his decision to accept the mission during a conversation with his close friend Captain Hull with words that far better reflect his personality than the "I only regret" quote: "I am not influenced by the expectation of promotion or pecuniary reward, I wish to be useful, and every kind of service, necessary to the public good, becomes honorable by being necessary."[37] Most intelligence officers could agree with that statement and that motivation.

That he died with dignity and conviction seems apparent. Throughout history the spy or intelligence officer who has undertaken a mission out of love of country or ideology and is subsequently captured and put to death usually is reported to have died with both of these characteristics. However, individuals motivated by money or other personal interests or gain who are involved in intelligence work and are caught and put to death are more often described as dying with far less grace and dignity. All other conditions of the death sentence being equal, this makes good sense. Personal commitment over personal gain tends to be respected even among enemies.

From the official British perspective, one of Howe's officers noted the execution in the orderly books: "A spy from the enemy (by his own full confession) apprehended last night, was this day executed at 11 o'Clock in front of the Artillery Park."[38]

The Continental Army first learned of Hale's capture and death the evening of September 22, when an officer sent by Howe to give Washington a note proposing a prisoner exchange mentioned it to Washington's adjutant general, Joseph Reed, and Gen. Israel Putnam and Capt. Alexander Hamilton. Because of the nature of the mission, Hale's death was only officially noted as "killed on 22nd September."[39] There was no formal announcement made of Hale's death by the army. Hale's family did not know of his death until September 30, and then it was only a rumor.

At the time, while a few army officers aware of Hale's fate were angry and ready to seek revenge on British prisoners, the public was unaware of his mission or fate. His story was first provided in some detail, but not necessarily factually, in the *History of New England* by Hannah Adams in 1799. However, it was not until 1824, in *Annals of the American Revolution* by Jedediah Morse, that Hale's story caught traction with the public. At this point, the patriotic theme took over and overshadowed the fact that his mission and activities were that of a failed spy.

As in any business, there are lessons learned from a failure, and in the intelligence profession a damage assessment is usually conducted of a failed operation to identify mistakes and avoid them in the future. In this regard, from an intelligence perspective there are two fundamental questions regarding Hale's mission: Who was responsible for the operational plan, and why did it fail?

Historical documents identify only three individuals who might have been involved in the operational planning of the mission: Hale, Knowlton, and Washington. Hale's involvement in planning the mission is probably the easiest to identify and understand. He would have been asked how he wanted to present himself in terms of his identity and cover story because he had, at least, to be at ease regarding these aspects of his cover. Otherwise, based upon his education and background, it seems doubtful that he would have knowledge of other tradecraft elements such as cover for action, disguise, concealment of information collected, observation methods, and so forth. However, his basic knowledge as a military officer would have given him the skills necessary to recognize and describe British fortifications and units. There is, however, no evidence of specific reporting requirements—only that he was to report on

British activities that he observed. So it seems a safe assumption that Hale played only a minor role in the operational planning that preceded his mission.

As to Knowlton, all the evidence would seem to give him even a smaller role in the matter. He was instructed by Washington to find a volunteer and managed to do so in a manner devoid of any operational security. His skills seemed better fitted to military reconnaissance than behind-the-lines intelligence-collection missions.

Thus we are left with Washington and his role in planning Hale's operational mission. Hale's sergeant and close friend Hempstead, who accompanied him as far as Norwalk, many years later stated he remembered that two meetings with Washington were held.[40] Yet as previously noted, no record of them seems to exist. He also stated that Washington provided Hale with a document instructing all American owners of vessels plying Long Island Sound to provide whatever assistance Hale required of them.[41] This would explain why Captain Pond assisted Hale in such a timely manner. Other than this, nothing is known of Washington's involvement.

The only conclusion one can draw from the available information is that no one took any real responsibility for planning the mission. Thus, as the commander in chief who ordered the mission, Washington must take ultimate responsibility. Why was it so lacking in even commonsense planning? A logical explanation might well be that Washington was too focused on the military situation to devote adequate time to this intelligence operation. That would be understandable, as Washington's first priority was to avoid destruction of his army in the face of the British offensive. One biographer, Edward G. Lengel, notes that he was quite emotional during this period and at his lowest point during the Revolution in terms of his management and leadership abilities.[42] Other analysts of Hale's mission believe that Washington did not know how to plan properly a behind-enemy-lines mission. And they consider Hale's failed mission a learning experience for Washington that manifested itself later in his creation of much better organized and productive intelligence-collection networks.[43]

My study of Washington as an intelligence officer causes me to rate him overall as a capable manager, implementer, and consumer of intelligence during the Revolutionary War. But in this case, for whatever reason or reasons, his inattention caused a failed mission and wasted a life. While a military commander expects to trade lives for objectives, the intelligence game is a bit different. The idea there is to get information that saves lives. An intelligence agent is a special tool, and if lost there is no certainty that it can be replaced. When Washington's headquarters was advised of Hale's death, there is no record of any comment or statement by Washington. Perhaps this is another indication of his lack of professional attention to Hale's mission.

As to the second question—what caused the mission to fail?—again there is no single absolute answer. This is usually the case in damage assessments because the actual capabilities of the enemy service are seldom fully known. As noted earlier, so little realistic planning went into this operation that its potential for success was extremely low from its inception. The relatively recent reporting on Rogers's role is insightful and demonstrates how various operational mistakes create the atmosphere for failure. Records indicate that, probably because of the small-town nature of Norwalk, as well as its frequent use as a berthing location for American ships, Hale's activities were observed and reported to the British. This information stimulated Rogers's instinct and motivated his investigative efforts to identify the rebel spy. Hale's suspicious behavior among the local population only assisted Rogers's efforts to identify him. Rogers then orchestrated the chance meeting in the tavern. After that, Hale's naive and honest personality sealed his fate. It is also possible that Hale, after several days of stressful isolation and now believing that he was in the company of a friend, may have allowed alcohol to affect his judgment a bit. While there is no information to document this, Hale did have a reasonable regard for drinking both while at Yale and during his time as a teacher in New London.[44]

However, professional credit must also be given to Rogers for his role-playing and ability to develop the trust and rapport with Hale necessary to get him to accept him as a confidant. Such skills are not common in all personalities and are highly sought after in the profile for case officers. A significant portion of case officer training in most intelligence organizations is devoted to developing and refining these skills. Rogers appears to have developed them naturally. Thus, while both were engaged in intelligence activities—Hale as a collector and Rogers as a counterintelligence officer—it was hardly a fair fight.

About the same time that Hale was captured and hanged, another American was sent behind British lines to collect on activities. His name was Joshua Davis, and he returned safely and was paid for his efforts, which apparently were successful, on September 29, 1776. Not surprisingly, little else is known about him or his specific mission.[45]

Did Hale's failure motivate Washington to focus more of his personal time on intelligence operations? Probably not. For the next several months his primary effort was to prevent his retreating army from disintegration in the face of the continuing British offensive. However, his intelligence efforts would continue and with slightly better results.

CHAPTER 6

John Jay's Efforts at Counterintelligence

There is little question that the rights of the individual as opposed to the authority of the government was one of the key issues that eventually led to American independence from Britain. This view of individual rights continues to this day to be one of the strongest characteristics of American national culture. And in societies where such views are held, the intelligence discipline of counterintelligence is always the most controversial and difficult for intelligence officers and law enforcement personnel.

In popular Revolutionary War history, Nathan Hale's capture and the unraveling of Benedict Arnold's plot to give up West Point are the most recognizable counterintelligence cases (British counterintelligence in the former and American counterintelligence in the latter). But both examples focus on the defensive side of the counterintelligence discipline: exposing or catching the spy. There is also an offensive side to counterintelligence. In my training this was exemplified by double agents, individuals offering to work for one side but in actuality working for the other, and recruitment of members of enemy intelligence and security services. Double agents can be used both for false reporting to manipulate enemy actions and for positive collection of enemy plans and intentions. This book contains many examples of Washington's use of double agents for both purposes. However, I was able to find only a few examples of American recruitment of British intelligence officers. This is not surprising, as such counterintelligence recruitments can be the most difficult to conduct because they are focused on targets with very high internal-security sensibilities and therefore require significant professional expertise in their planning, development, and execution.

However, the American side in the Revolutionary War did not even have a basic counterintelligence capability above local levels. Throughout the war British intelligence efforts were highly successful in learning American military and diplomatic plans and intentions.[1] This fact was well recognized and of constant concern to the Americans, as reflected in comments Washington wrote to Col. Josiah Quincy on March 24, 1776: "There is one evil I dread, and that is, their spies. I could wish, therefore, the most attentive watch be kept. . . . I wish a dozen or more of honest, sensible and diligent men, were employed . . . in order to question, cross question etc., all such persons as are unknown, and cannot give an account of themselves in a straight and satisfactory line. . . . I think it a matter of importance to prevent them from obtaining intelligence of our situation."[2]

Why neither the American civilian or military authorities created a centralized counterintelligence service is probably related to a wide variety of practical, cultural, and philosophical issues. Practically, the Continental Congress and Continental Army were usually struggling just to maintain their existence for much of the conflict because of internal political issues, as well as British military pressure. Creating a centralized counterintelligence structure would be a low priority compared to this. Culturally, this was a time when a gentlemen's honor was considered paramount in society, and religious and formal oaths were usually considered adequate testaments of loyalty. And considering that governmental interference in the life of the individual was a tenet of the patriots' reasons for independence, an intrusive government effort of a counterintelligence nature would have been difficult to justify.

However, for a brief period New York State did have such a centralized organization, although it functioned only in a limited region along the Hudson River above New York City. It was officially known as the Committee and First Commission for Detecting Conspiracies and was headed by John Jay.

While the Revolutionary War is usually portrayed as a war of independence from a foreign power, in reality it was an insurgency against an established government by a force that, at best, had the active support of only about a third of the population. This type of a situation poses especially difficult problems for counterintelligence, from both an ethical and practical perspective. The question of who is a traitor, and to whom, becomes a political issue rather than a legal one, depending upon which side controls the territory. Also, this type of conflict fosters individuals' capabilities to settle personal, business, and political disputes under the guise of counterintelligence accusations. Unless a

While best remembered as the first US Supreme Court chief justice, John Jay was also head of an effective counterintelligence organization in New York early in the Revolution. *Library of Congress. Reproduction of a painting by Joseph Wright that appeared in* Century Magazine, *vol. 15, 1889, 825.*

structure is created to provide an objective adjudication of such accusations, with an established set of fair procedures and standardized punishments, counterintelligence becomes nothing more than an excuse to use emotion and rhetoric to condemn one's enemies. For a brief period, Jay managed to create and implement such a counterintelligence effort, but for most of the war, actions taken in the name of counterintelligence were conducted along the lines of mob rule, with little burden of proof for accusations and verdicts rendered outside the rule of law.

While the majority of this chapter deals with Jay's activities, during the war there were numerous examples of Washington and other generals attempting to identify British spies and local loyalists in their areas of operation. As early as June 5, 1776, the Continental Congress created a Committee on Spies to establish procedures for dealing with persons providing intelligence information to the enemy. The committee's report, dated August 21, reflected the belief that honorable gentlemen would not be involved in such activities and focused its recommendations on lower-class individuals who might report basic information on American fortifications and encampments. Such spies were to suffer death or some other such punishment, as military courts-martial should decide.[3]

As is true in government and military organizations today, American military commanders would periodically issue warnings of enemy spying to keep the troops alert. Often this was based on a local incident wherein a spy had been identified, but it also became a standard part of the commander's instructions to his troops. This type of defensive counterintelligence is necessary but often loses its effectiveness when the warnings become commonplace rather than focused on a specific incident or threat to which individuals can relate. From the intelligence-vice-security perspective, the key to effective counterintelligence is offensive operations to identify and neutralize the enemy's activities.

Jay's efforts, for a short period of time, demonstrated that a fair system of adjudication of counterintelligence allegations coupled with an aggressive offensive approach to penetrating enemy organizations could prove highly successful. And as with most organizations, his personality and behavior set the tone. He is one of the least recognized Founding Fathers, and some would even place him on the second tier of political leadership of that period. However, when his career is reviewed, his importance in the establishment of the government and the country becomes clear: member and president of the Continental Congress, key negotiator of the treaty ending the Revolutionary War, secretary of foreign affairs under the Articles of Confederation, first Supreme Court chief justice, twice New York governor, a key contributor to the *Federalist Papers*, and the first counterintelligence manager for the patriots' cause.

Jay was not of British descent; his family came from French and Dutch backgrounds. He was born into a well-to-do colonial family and educated in the law at King's College, now Columbia University. His family background and his education made him more moderate in his approach to the political relationship with Britain than many of his peers. After having established a legal practice, he first came into public office in May 1774 as a member of the New York City Committee of Fifty. This committee was created to correspond with the leadership in the other colonies regarding how to respond to the closing of Boston Harbor by the Boston Port Bill. He was nominated to the committee because he was considered to be politically conservative, and the city leadership did not want mob violence to hinder trade.[4] He subsequently represented New York at the First Continental Congress in Philadelphia and was a voice for negotiation with the British government. John Adams described Jay's approach as first negotiation, then suspension of commerce, and only after that, war.[5] As late as the fall of 1775, Jay still believed that independence was not the correct path for the colonies, yet he had also become a member of the New York Committee of Observation with responsibilities for keeping public order while organizing the arming of the citizenry to oppose British taxation.[6]

Jay's moderate political approach continued to stand in contrast to such radicals as Samuel Adams and Patrick Henry. However, when Jay learned on November 9, 1775, of the king's refusal to even receive the Congress's Olive Branch Petition, which he had drafted in a final attempt at a political solution, he began to accept that independence might be the only solution.[7] Nevertheless, the following month he was in discussions with Lord Drummond, who was in Philadelphia as a private citizen, regarding a possible plan of accommodation that could avoid war.[8] While he was unwilling to completely give up hope for a political solution, the realities of the situation also had him meeting in the same time frame with Julien-Alexandre Achard de Bonvouloir, the French secret agent who was seeking to determine American intent and vaguely offering French assistance against Britain.[9]

By spring 1776, Jay had departed Philadelphia believing he might better serve his state by attending the New York Provincial Congress. He quickly became involved in how to deal with loyalist groups in the state assisting the British. In May the Provincial Congress published lists of suspected Tory operatives, and subsequently, mobs began publicly assaulting these individuals. Continental troops had to be called in to establish order. Shortly thereafter, Jay was assigned to investigate the danger of loyalist activities.[10]

His first investigation involved a Tory plot to assist a British occupation of New York City. The plot was directed by two officials in the British government structure for the New York colony: the royal governor of New York, William Tryon, and the New York mayor, David Matthews. The plot was both well organized and had ample financial support from the Crown. It included sabotaging military defenses and city infrastructure, as well as recruiting agents within the city to assist the British forces upon entry. Part of the plot involved members of Washington's own Life Guard, troops who acted as his personal bodyguards. Because of their involvement, this plot became known as the Hickey Plot, after Thomas Hickey, a noncommissioned officer in the unit. The British plan was to either capture or kill the general, thus crippling the American army's command structure and perhaps even forcing its surrender. Jay's committee investigated the plot and was able to expose it and arrest many of its members before it could be implemented. Hickey was executed, and Matthews was placed in jail, but Tryon was safely on a British warship in New York harbor.[11]

Based upon success in that investigation, fellow New York State legislators selected Jay to head a committee with counterintelligence responsibilities for a large portion of the Hudson River Valley, where the contest for the population's loyalty was fierce. The committee was appointed on September 26, 1776, and began its activities in early October at Fishkill, on the eastern side of the Hudson sixty miles or so north of Manhattan. Jay first served as its secretary and then became chairman. The committee was charged with "inquiring into, detecting, and defeating conspiracies . . . against the liberties of America, . . . to send for persons and papers, to call out detachments of the militia in different counties for suppressing insurrections, to apprehend, secure or remove persons whom they might judge dangerous to the safety of the State" and "to enjoin secrecy upon their members and the persons they employed."[12]

With his disciplined legal mind and his personal commitment to an objective and fair investigative process, Jay proved an excellent choice. He did so in the face of a personal determination that after the Declaration of Independence, those who were not committed to the struggle for independence were traitors. Nevertheless, he committed himself to a legal and orderly process based upon "rigid impartiality."[13] And when local groups acted against alleged Tories without proper authority and process, their actions were denounced, and such individuals were admonished publicly.[14]

Most of the committee's time was taken reviewing allegations of loyalist activities, and most cases were handled by asking the individual to take an oath of loyalty to the patriots' cause. Those who did were released, and those who refused were usually placed under some type of supervision or forced to move into areas controlled by the British.[15] Some of Jay's decisions affected friends of his, and in a letter to one who had refused to take a loyalty oath and was forced to move to British lines, Jay explained his approach to his responsibilities: "Your judgment, and consequently, your Conscience differed from mine on a very important Question. But though as an independent American, I consider all who were not for us, and You among the Rest, as against us, yet be assured that John Jay did not cease to be a friend of Peter Van Schaack."[16]

While the committee's process took place outside the established colonial legal system, it included many of the protections in that system. The committee tried hundreds of cases, and accurate records of the proceedings were kept. Under Jay's leadership the committee's procedures went a long way toward legitimizing the counterintelligence process, at least in the Hudson Valley. When the committee ended its term on February 27, 1777, local commissioners were appointed for various jurisdictions, and the counterintelligence process became decentralized.[17] In geographical areas where military operations were conducted, military courts took over counterintelligence investigations and prosecution responsibilities during the war.

The committee's authority to investigate, capture, and try suspects anywhere in the mid–Hudson Valley region gave Jay the opportunity to track groups and individuals regardless of their status or influence with local authorities. As his experience in counterintelligence investigations grew, he expanded the committee's role from primarily adjudication into offensive counterintelligence operations. He took the responsibility for organizing and directing a clandestine network of operators who did more than report on suspicious groups—they penetrated those groups and learned their composition, plans, and leadership.[18]

At the height of its activities, the committee had some dozen agents investigating various groups and individuals.[19] Their procedure in penetrating Tory groups usually involved false names and always feigned sympathy for the British cause. Their responsibilities were to gather evidence regarding the group's plans against the American government, to coordinate the actual arrests of the individuals—often by developing some ploy to assure assembly at a given location—and then to testify in the trial regarding what they had learned. To counterintelligence officials, this procedure of "identify, penetrate, and neutralize" represents the basic elements of the profession to the current day.

The exploits of one of the committee's counterintelligence agents, Enoch Crosby, are well documented and were well known by the early nineteenth century.[20] Records of his operations provided an accurate—if perhaps overly dramatic—insight into how the committee's agents operated. Crosby was in constant danger of being killed by the Tories if unmasked as an American agent or being harmed by unwitting patriots while associating with Tories. He operated in an area where much of the countryside was ungoverned by either side. Its residents were usually clustered in small villages, where all locals were well known. The physical and social proximity among the population meant that Crosby became widely known rather quickly. As a result, the danger increased with each operation, and his ability to function clandestinely diminished with each mission.

Crosby was born in Harwich, Massachusetts, but moved about quite a bit, which probably helped him develop the interpersonal skills so important in his role playing as a penetration agent. Crosby grew up in Southeast, a small town then in Dutchess County and now in Putnam County, New York. He was, by profession, a shoemaker and had learned the trade in a Connecticut town now known as Kent. He was living in Danbury, Connecticut, when the war began.

Enoch Crosby was the best known of Jay's counterintelligence agents.
He operated in the contested Hudson River Valley and undertook
daring missions using a variety of covers. This portrait of Crosby was
painted many years after the Revolution, in 1830, by Samuel Lovett
Waldo. *National Portrait Gallery, Smithsonian Institution*

He volunteered for a Connecticut force that became part of the Benedict Arnold–led invasion of Canada. After the invasion failed, Crosby returned to civilian life in poor health from the rigors of the campaign. By August 1776, his health had recovered, and he enlisted again. This demonstration of commitment and loyalty to the American cause was another indicator of his suitability for counterintelligence work. To face the dangers of working alone within a hostile group while living a false role requires not only courage but also a strong commitment to one's mission and a belief in its rightness. Nevertheless, Crosby became a counterintelligence agent for Jay quite by accident.

While on his way to the American camp at Kingsbridge after his reenlistment, Crosby was mistaken for a fellow Tory sympathizer. He immediately recognized the position he was in and used his interpersonal skills to further gain the man's confidence. He was soon introduced to other Tories, and he learned that a Tory militia company was being formed to join the British in New York. He even was able to learn the names of the officers of the unit. With this information, he advised his new friends that he must continue his journey to the British lines. Once out of sight, he headed for the residence of Squire Young, whom Crosby knew to be a member of the New York Committee of Safety, which was focused on public law and order in the state. Upon hearing his story, Young took him to White Plains and introduced him to members of John Jay's committee.

The committee recognized the opportunity offered by Crosby and convinced him not to return to the army, but rather to work with the committee as a counterintelligence agent.[21] Crosby was assured that his regimental commander would be quietly informed why he had not reported for duty. Then a cover story was developed to get Crosby back with the Tory company. He was to be arrested by the Americans as a loyalist and would then escape back to his Tory friends.

The cover story explaining his escape involved Crosby feigning the need to use the outhouse at the jail and then leaping over a fence into a cornfield, which hid his further escape into the countryside. Appropriately dramatic musket volleys were fired by his guards to announce his escape. He then returned to his Tory friends and explained the difficulties he had encountered trying to get to British lines. Within a few days, the Tory militia was ready to move, and Crosby was able to again visit Young's residence, where he met representatives of Jay's committee and briefed them on the Tories' plans. He then returned to the Tory camp and was subsequently "arrested" when an American ranger unit raided the camp. To maintain his cover story of Tory sympathies,

Crosby remained in jail for about a week. Once the others were captured, he was moved to a separate location, where he was set free.[22]

Pleased with Crosby's success, the committee dispatched him on another mission, on which he posed as a traveling shoemaker. Based upon information provided by the committee, he sought work with a family suspected of Tory activities and once again quickly learned of the formation of a Tory militia company. He was invited to enlist once he expressed his loyalties to the Crown but expressed a hesitance, claiming he did not want to join unless he knew who his companions would be. This ruse caused the militia organizer to show Crosby the names on the enlistment rolls. When Crosby stated that he still did not see the name of anyone he trusted, the organizer took him to a field and lifted a stone, revealing a hiding place for a logbook containing the names of other members of the group whose names were too sensitive to place on the regular rolls. He also showed Crosby a hollow haystack in the field where militia members would hide when patriots were in the area.[23]

That evening Crosby reported this information to his contacts in White Plains and by morning returned to the Tory household. That day he joined the Tory militia but asked not to sign the official muster roll until the unit had reached British lines. That evening, as the militia members assembled at the house, an American ranger unit raided the gathering and arrested all of them, including those who sought to hide in the haystack. Crosby, along with others, was found hiding in a closet in the house. The captives were taken to Fort Montgomery, where Crosby was discreetly instructed to continue to play the role of a Tory until plans for his "escape" could be made.

While under arrest at the fort, Crosby was seen by a former teacher who was a friend of his father's as well. The teacher was shocked to see Crosby involved with the Tories and immediately informed Crosby's family of the son's shameful loyalties. As there was no safe way to tell his family of his true activities and commitment to the American cause, he had no choice but to continue to play his role under arrest.[24] During a secret meeting with members of the committee, his future activities were discussed, and he was given the name "John Smith" to use in signing his covert correspondence with the committee.[25] He was also instructed to arrange his own escape and did so by forcing open a window in his room. However, he had only gone a short distance when he encountered a sentry unaware of his true loyalties and had to make his escape under fire. Failure by the committee to develop and implement an escape plan almost cost the committee the loss of a valuable agent. It also almost cost Crosby his life.

His next operation caused him to travel in late October to Marlboro, on the banks of the Hudson River, where he arranged to be introduced to a British officer raising a loyalist force. He was accepted as a recruit and was told the company was to meet at a hill near Cornwall, New York. On November 4, he sent a report to Col. William Duer, one of the committee's senior members, providing a plan to arrest the gathering. He suggested that an American ranger force hide in ambush in a barn near the hill until the group of some thirty Tories arrived near midnight on the 5th. The raid took place as planned, and Crosby once again found himself under arrest by the same rangers as before and from whom he kept escaping. This time the rangers decided to jail him in a secure room located in the house of John Jay at Cornwall. He was placed in irons, and sentries were placed at the only door exit.[26]

As Jay was away and no one else there knew of his activities, Crosby's chances of escape were poor and serious punishment likely. But he was able to gain the sympathy of a housemaid who provided the sentries with drugged brandy and then opened the door to allow him to escape. He fled the area, with which he was well acquainted, seeking to establish contact with one of his committee contacts. However, he was captured by two patriots and threatened to the point that he had to produce, from a sealed compartment in his vest, a document identifying him as an American agent. This convinced the duo to release him. But as he started toward Duer's home, he met a Tory who suspected Crosby was a patriot and was ready to detain him. Having played the loyalist role so well in the past, Crosby was able to talk his way out of that problem. He did reach Duer, after first checking that none of the rangers were in the area, and Duer sent him to a safe location in Dutchess County to live with a German family.[27]

A few days later a doctor, who, it turned out, had supplied the housemaid with the drugs used on Crosby's sentries at Jay's quarters, arranged a meeting for him with members of the committee. Upon arriving at the doctor's house, he was met by that maid, who reminded him how powerful the drugs had been.[28] While Crosby only reacted with surprise at seeing her again, this incident could place his escape from Jay's house in another perspective. It is possible that Jay, having recognized the danger from not having a plan in place for Crosby's escape, arranged with the maid to implement a plan that would permit his safe escape without making more people—that is, his captors—aware of his true activities.

Jay arrived later that night and instructed Crosby to return to the German family and await further orders. Jay was well aware that Crosby's numerous recent operations had raised his profile among the Tories in the mid–Hudson

Valley and that his usefulness in that area was diminishing.[29] In addition to concern about the Tories and the British, his frequent escapes from American units raised questions about how he would be treated by them if captured again.

In December, Crosby was sent to northwestern Connecticut to report on Tory activities but was soon sent back to New York to investigate reports on a Tory militia company gathering in the Fishkill area. His controlling officer was Nathaniel Sackett, a counterintelligence officer working for Jay's committee.[30] By early January, Sackett had adequate information to alert a local American militia company to prepare for action. However, while he prepared the operational plan to seize the Tories, he almost forgot an important detail, which could have had serious consequences for the committee's best agent. In his January 10, 1777, instructions to the American militia commander Capt. Peter van Gaasbeek, Sackett noted: "I had almost forgot to give you directions to Give our friend an opportunity of making his Escape Upon our plan you will Take him prisoner with this party you are now wateing His name is Enoch Crosbey Alias John Brown I could wish that he may escape before you bring him Two miles on your way to Committee. . . . By no means neglect this friend of ours."[31]

Meanwhile, as he was so good at doing, Crosby had convinced the Tories of his loyalty to the Crown and joined their ranks. Also as usual, his interpersonal skills enabled him to elicit details of the local Tory organization, its members, its safe sites, and the identities of British agents operating in the area. As Crosby was ready to send his message to conduct the raid, he was unable to get word to Sackett. However, he was able to contact a local American militia commander and was able to have the Tories arrested. Again, out of sight of the other captives, he was released.

But this would be Crosby's last operation. Regardless of the alias he used to identify himself as a loyalist, his face was too well known among Hudson Valley Tories and the British to permit him to continue his activities. He was sent to Albany to lower his profile, handling administrative duties involving the transfer of seized Tory property. Shortly thereafter, he was allow to resign from the committee, which was about to disband itself. He had served as a covert agent for the committee for some nine months.[32]

Finally, he was able to tell his family of his true activities, and he attempted to settle back into civilian life with his brother in the Hudson Valley highlands. However, when he found the area did contain loyalist sympathizers, fear for his personal safety caused Crosby to return to the Continental Army.[33] He served in the New York Line until the war ended.

For many years it was believed Crosby was the model for the hero Harvey Birch in America's first espionage novel, *The Spy*, published in 1821 by James Fenimore Cooper. Cooper publicly denied this. But Crosby readily accepted this role and enjoyed the attention the novel and a subsequent play based upon it brought to him. The truth was that Cooper and John Jay were neighbors in the Hudson Valley after the war and often discussed activities of the committee. The plot for *The Spy* was a compilation of various counterintelligence operations described by Jay to Cooper.[34]

However, a book about Crosby's adventures was published in 1828, seven years before his death. It was titled *The Spy Unmasked; or Memoirs of Enoch Crosby, Alias Harvey Birch*. Although its author, H. L. Barnum, was guilty of some poetic license, it is possible that Crosby assisted him with the book's content, but this has not been documented.

Regardless of the drama provided in the literary works supposedly describing Crosby's operations, his activities as reflected in records of the committee and his Revolutionary War pension deposition speak highly of his commitment and courage as a counterintelligence agent.

Jay's subsequent contribution to the structure of American government in the debate over its future form after the Revolution and his role at the Supreme Court are well known and well documented. However, Jay's writing in one section of *The Federalist Papers* demonstrates that his experience in the counterintelligence field gave him a solid appreciation for a government's requirement for protection of sources and methods. Here he argued strongly for the right of the executive branch to conduct intelligence activities in secret:

> There are cases where the most useful intelligence may be obtained, if the persons possessing it can be relieved from apprehensions of discovery. Those apprehensions will operate on those persons whether they are actuated by mercenary or friendly motives, and there doubtless are many of both descriptions, who would rely on the secrecy of the President, but who would not confide in that of the Senate, and still less in that of a large popular assembly. The convention has done well therefore in so disposing of the power of making treaties, that although the President must in forming them act by the advice and consent of the Senate, yet he will be able to manage the business of intelligence in such a manner as prudence may suggest.[35]

While Jay's committee did represent the most organized counterintelligence effort of the war on the American side, similar investigations were a common practice at the local level in both military and civilian circles. And the primary operational cover for action, that of an individual claiming Tory sympathies, was often used. Most of these activities used an individual as a penetration agent for only one operation because they were conducted against a specific group or person and the agent's true name, and family background and location, were well known. Because records on these activities, when maintained, were decentralized at the local level, it is difficult to find a strategic vice tactical achievement in most of them. In many cases, records at local historical societies and libraries are often vague in detail to protect those involved, who probably after the war had to live in the same areas with relatives of their targets.

Military counterintelligence activities were also numerous and constant but again decentralized to the local command level and thus difficult to collate for military or intelligence mission accomplishments. In the Hudson Valley the American military authorities caught fewer British agents than Jay's committee. However, there was one British agent, Daniel Taylor, a young British officer who agreed to act as a clandestine courier through American lines in hopes of promotion, who merits mention.

Taylor's capture took place just before Gen. John Burgoyne's surrender to Gen. Horatio Gates at Saratoga and involved the British general Sir Henry Clinton's attempt to advise Burgoyne of his slow progress moving up the Hudson from New York City as he attempted to draw American forces away from Burgoyne. From a military perspective, the communication carried by Taylor when captured, written October 8, 1777, was of no importance and was overtaken by events. Yet the tradecraft used in the concealment of the message was one of the British's better methods. The message, written on silk, was placed inside a small silver ball and concealed in Taylor's hair, which was braided in the style of the time. Silver was used in case the courier was forced to swallow the ball when threatened with capture.[36] This was a concealment device not readily available to combat commanders in the field, and its use usually indicated a message from a senior British officer and therefore of strategic value.

Taylor departed with the message the evening of the 8th, unaware that an American double agent had already provided his name and description as a British courier. He was captured just below Newburgh, New York, because of his confusion over the uniforms of troops he met. He happened to run into a unit of Col. Samuel B. Webb's Connecticut Regiment that was wearing captured scarlet uniforms. Thinking he was among loyalists, he made various comments to try to ascertain which side they were on. These comments made the Americans suspicious, and when they questioned him he demanded to be taken to General Clinton. They did so, but General Clinton turned out to be George Clinton of the Continental Army, not Sir Henry Clinton. Upon being questioned by the wrong Clinton, the young officer panicked but was able to swallow the ball just as he was being restrained. Having seen him swallow something, the American reaction was simple: A doctor was called to administer a draught that caused him to vomit up the ball. However, he was able to grab the ball and swallow it once more. At this point Clinton said another draught would be given and that if Taylor interfered again, he would be immediately hanged and his stomach cut open to obtain the ball. Taylor saw the logic of cooperating; the ball was recovered and the message obtained. He was, after a brief court-martial, hanged anyway.[37]

British correspondence during the war indicated that the silver ball device was used by various senior commanders throughout the war. Yet there are few other mentions of it having been discovered by American forces. One such mention involved a very successful American double agent, Capt. David Gray, who, for over two years acted as a clandestine courier for Tory intelligence officers in New York City and for Sir Henry Clinton. He was issued a silver ball concealment device for some of his trips.[38] If the army had had a more centralized approach to counterintelligence, the use of this silver ball as a concealment device could have been made known throughout the military by the fall of 1777. And it would seem probable that searching for this method of concealment would have yielded more information of value than was found without this specific knowledge.

While individual counterintelligence efforts by the Americans did yield valuable results, the overall effort was uncoordinated and therefore ineffective in many aspects. There is little doubt that the excesses of some local efforts did much to discredit counterintelligence as an activity regardless of Jay's short-lived committee. After the war America made no attempt to create a military or civilian counterintelligence organization, and such an enterprise did not reappear until the time of the Civil War—and once again this became a wartime organization only, quickly to be terminated after the conflict. One indication of the need for such a centralized enterprise after the Revolutionary War was represented by the fact that in the early nineteenth century, the most senior US Army officer, Gen. James Wilkinson, was a paid agent of the Spanish government.[39]

CHAPTER 7

WASHINGTON ESTABLISHES HIS INTELLIGENCE CAPABILITIES

While Jay was establishing his counterintelligence operations against Tory groups, Washington was quickly being pushed out of the New York City area by a series of British attacks. By mid-summer, the Continental Army had been forced off Long Island and was pushed into lower Manhattan. In mid-September, Washington was able to momentarily stop the British advance at the Battle of Harlem Heights. But not for long.

By late September 1776, Washington's only option was to react to British movements in the manner best suited to saving his remaining forces. While the army had fought with some discipline and even managed a small victory, it was defeated at the Battle of White Plains in late October and forced most of the army across the river into New Jersey. Only Fort Washington, a poorly constructed defensive position located on high ground on the Manhattan side of the Hudson River, remained in American hands. Luckily for Washington, Howe once again halted his advance to reorganize and resupply his troops.

However, in mid-November, British forces again outflanked American positions and attacked the fort, forcing surrender of almost three thousand American soldiers. A few days later, the British captured Fort Lee, on the New Jersey side of the Hudson. While the garrison escaped, they left behind badly needed military supplies. The British assault continued aggressively, and Gen. Lord Cornwallis reached Newark, New Jersey, on November 28. On December 7, Washington made a strategic retreat, crossed the Delaware River, and established a defensive position for his demoralized and suffering army, which had dwindled to fewer than three thousand men. The next day, Cornwallis took the city of Trenton, but there Howe stopped and began arranging his army into winter quarters. Had he continued to chase Washington, it could well have meant total disaster for the American army. With the end of the British campaign of 1776, Washington and the army were in great despair and fearful of the future.[1] But Washington was about to take the offensive, and solid intelligence was there to help him succeed.

By mid-December 1776, Washington had instructed his commanders to develop local reporting sources to gather intelligence on the enemy in New Jersey.[2] Solid intelligence on the enemy can be a great equalizer for a smaller force in combat. Its most obvious benefit is accurately identifying enemy locations and positions. This tactical intelligence is of great importance to the infantryman who must face the enemy. However, it is strategic intelligence that wins wars or, better yet, avoids them. Its impact extends well beyond a specific battle. The intelligence that gave Washington the confidence to attack Trenton and Princeton in late December 1776 and early January 1777 was to have a strategic effect in the war. It enabled him to save his army from dissolution and keep it in the field, at least for that winter.

In mid-December, for the first time since departing the Boston area, Washington had accurate, well-corroborated intelligence on the enemy forces at Trenton and Princeton, including their strengths, their defensive postures, their recent combat histories, and their fatigue levels. He also knew the personalities and attitudes of the enemy commanders. This gave him the confidence to undertake a series of attacks in which his weak and still poorly organized force had a solid chance for victory. That is the key to strategic military intelligence: The leadership has to feel confident of victory and then take decisive action. Luckily, and probably because of the leadership at the regiment level and below, Washington's small force was composed of men still willing to fight.

Once the British forces settled into winter quarters spread around New Jersey, they found themselves in much more hostile territory than they had experienced in the New York City area. The military situation was similar in environment to any occupying force in an insurgent's territory. While the British did have some supporters and there were others willing to cooperate for personal gain, the Americans controlled most of the countryside. That said, Trenton was a town with a strong Tory presence. However, the New Jersey Militia, which was well armed (including cannon), well led for the most part, and willing to fight on its own terms, made life difficult for the British garrisons. The militia used its area knowledge and skirmish-and-harassment tactics to make it costly for British forces to obtain supplies and patrol outside their lines. This meant that the militia also was well aware of British positions and fortifications, their supply situation, their strength, and their combat effectiveness.[3]

When Washington convened his senior officers to decide on the Trenton attack, he had comprehensive intelligence from his own scouts and New Jersey Militia scouts, as well as their contacts within Trenton, regarding the enemy and the mind-set of the commanding officer, Hessian colonel Johann Rall. I also believe he had an agent with personal knowledge of the situation in the town and of Rall's thinking, a man named John Honeyman. Washington had specifically sent Honeyman on a mission both to collect intelligence on the forces at Trenton and to plant false information on his army's activities just as the attack was moving forward. Washington knew the Hessian forces had been in almost constant combat since the Battle of White Plains and that the New Jersey Militia had been harassing them constantly, further weakening their combat effectiveness. He also knew that Rall held the American army in low regard. Rall had ignored orders from senior British commanders to construct fortifications around the town, believing that if the Americans dared to come, he would simply drive them off. In fact, someone who attended the first of Washington's two planning meetings did report to Rall that an attack was forthcoming. He responded, "Let them come."[4]

Even with excellent intelligence, Washington did not have an easy time moving his forces back across the Delaware River and coordinating the various elements engaged in the attack. Popular history tends to depict the Hessians as undisciplined and even drunk from Christmas celebrations the night before. This was not true, although it seems likely that Rall, who did enjoy his alcohol, may have responded to the attack a bit slowly because of his drinking on Christmas. Rather, the Hessian sentries were surprised and pushed back into town by a much larger American force than they had experienced previously. Also, the Continental Army regulars did attack with both discipline and bravery. The actual battle was of short duration, with the majority of the Hessians fleeing the town. Rall died of wounds in American captivity as the battle ended, having tried gallantly if ineffectively to rally his confused forces. Almost nine hundred Hessians were captured, along with their weapons, supplies, and cannon. American casualties were few but did include a wounded relative of Washington's, William Washington, who was a company-grade officer.[5]

Whenever intelligence regarding the attack on Trenton is discussed, the role of the American spy John Honeyman must also be considered. The oral story of Honeyman's actions is quite detailed, fits in well with the information known about the tactical situation at Trenton, was characteristic of what Washington had the experience to do, and from an intelligence officer's perspective, makes sense. But researchers have been unable to find independent documentation to support the Honeyman family's story. Thus a debate has developed regarding his role and intelligence contribution.

As someone familiar with the compartmentation and secrecy of clandestine activities and records, and also well aware of Washington's strong sense of operational security to protect his sources and methods, I do not find the lack of government or army documentation surprising. Nineteenth-century American historians—who were closer to the conflict, could speak with individuals claiming firsthand knowledge, and were more culturally focused on how events were recorded in those days—believed the Honeyman story to be true, if perhaps somewhat less than completely factual in detail. For example, William S. Stryker, considered one of New Jersey's foremost military historians of the war, accepted Honeyman as a valuable intelligence agent of Washington's.[6] This held true through the mid-twentieth century, with respected researchers such as John Bakeless including Honeyman in his book.[7] However, David Hackett Fischer's carefully documented work does not include Honeyman and explains in detail his issues with the lack of documentation.[8] Another writer well versed in the period, Alexander Rose, author of *Washington's Spies*, declared that "John Honeyman was no spy" and explained his perspective on the issue.[9] I subsequently wrote in response, describing why an intelligence officer would put more faith in the story, even without full documentation, than someone outside the profession.[10] Whether or not Honeyman did any or all of what his family's oral and written history reflects, his story is representational of Washington's aggressive efforts to use intelligence to leverage a critically needed victory at a time of military crisis. In this sense at least, the story of John Honeyman deserves to be included in this narrative.

Washington first met Honeyman in Philadelphia at the start of the war when Washington was there to attend the Continental Congress as a representative from Virginia. Honeyman was a veteran of the French and Indian War and understood what type of intelligence was vital to military planning. They met again as the American army was retreating across New Jersey, and Honeyman was asked to assume the role of a cattle salesman in the area around Trenton, to observe British activities and develop a relationship with the British forces there. He did so and by mid-December was selling meat to the Hessians at Trenton and had some business and a social relationship with Rall. With free access within enemy lines, he was able to collect intelligence on Hessian strength, disposition, defensive positions, patrolling patterns, and general health and morale. His interaction with Rall enabled him to understand the colonel's arrogant disrespect for the Continental Army and thus his lack of concern and preparation for any offensive actions by the American army. In order to provide a pro-British cover story for Honeyman, Washington even issued a warrant for his capture as an individual cooperating with the enemy. An unintended consequence of creating the cover story was that local patriots began to harass Honeyman's family. To ensure their protection, Washington provided a letter to the family noting that even though Honeyman was a Tory, his family was not to be harmed.

In late December, Honeyman was "captured" and taken to Washington, where he provided his complete intelligence report on the enemy at Trenton. In addition to incorporating this intelligence into his plan of attack, Washington also instructed Honeyman to escape and report back to Rall about his capture and escape and that from his observation the American army was inactive in quarters for the Christmas period. He did so and then left the area before the fighting began. Soon thereafter, he rejoined his family in the Griggstown area of New Jersey but remained under suspicion of Tory sentiments till the end of the war.

Even as Washington was planning his attack on Trenton, he was also collecting intelligence on the enemy at Princeton. When he emphasized the importance of intelligence collection to his commanders in mid-December, Col. John Cadwalader of the Pennsylvania Militia took the order seriously and became a constant source of intelligence on British activities. He had his forces, mostly composed of local militiamen, patrol and scout aggressively to ascertain British movements. As Washington decided his next move after the success at Trenton, Cadwalader reported a fortuitous development: He had found a "young gentleman" willing to enter Princeton to collect intelligence and report back. This agent was quite successful, and by the first of the year he provided Washington with a detailed report on the British forces in the town. The report provided the key information Washington would need for his attack on the town. While describing British force positions, it noted that the western approaches to the town were well patrolled and guarded, as the enemy expected Washington to approach from that direction, but that the eastern side of the town was unguarded.[11]

With this intelligence, supported by other intelligence collected through the interrogation of captured enemy soldiers as they retreated from Trenton and close reconnaissance by local militiamen, Washington again had the confidence to take his still-understrength forces on the offensive. This was also a particularly critical time for Washington even after the Trenton victory because with the end of the enlistment period for many of his units, especially those from New England, his army was in the process of disintegrating. Only through a personal appeal from Washington, and the promise of a bonus of an extra month's pay, was he able to maintain a force of fewer than six thousand men, about half of them militiamen. As Washington was developing his plan, the British counterattacked at Trenton, and only thanks to a series of disciplined skirmish engagements were the American forces able to hold a defensive position outside the town on the evening of January 2, 1777.

However, Washington was about to take one of his boldest moves of the war. That night, leaving behind a few hundred men to create the appearance that his army was encamped, he flanked the British force and attacked Princeton, over ten miles to their rear. In addition to the "young gentleman's" intelligence on the unguarded eastern approach, a party of British dragoons had been captured on January 1, and their interrogation provided comprehensive intelligence on the size and disposition of forces at Princeton.[12] As a result, Washington knew both the strength of the British and the weakness of their position. Based upon his intelligence, Washington attacked the town from the east and forced the British garrison to withdraw. By early afternoon of January 3, the American army was moving out of Princeton, having burned whatever military supplies it could not carry along.

With his army moved to the relatively safe area of Morristown, New Jersey, Washington's campaign was over for the winter. He had accomplished a great deal in the face of near disaster. Intelligence had played significant roles at both Trenton and Princeton, and Washington clearly recognized this. He would now spend more of his personal time developing intelligence networks to support his war against a superior force. Following up on his earlier instructions, Washington moved to avoid an earlier intelligence error. In the face of the military demands of command during the battles around New York City, he had failed to create a stay-behind reporting capability in the area. He ordered Gen. Thomas Mifflin to organize such networks around and in Philadelphia, clearly aware that it would soon be a British target for occupation.[13] He also kept his militia commanders in New Jersey and their civilian Committee of Safety counterparts focused on monitoring British activities and reporting tactical military intelligence such as enemy supply issues, their defensive positions, British garrison patrolling routes, and early warning indications of enemy movements. Continental Army officers also maintained a high state of reconnaissance, with commanders such as Gen. Israel Putnam dressing his scouts in civilian clothing at times to give them access to forward areas near British lines.[14] This was particularly dangerous as these soldiers could be tried as spies rather than prisoners of war if captured. To reduce this risk, Putnam only used his men in civilian garb when they were intimately familiar with the locales in which they were working.

For the foreseeable future Washington would face an enemy who controlled better lines of communication and supply—the sea lanes—than the internal, poorly developed roads he had to use for both supply and maneuver. His plan would be to attempt to draw the enemy into battle where the ground was favorable and his forces well matched to British strength, otherwise he would avoid contact and use harassment by the local militias and his scouting units to keep the British uneasy. This type of defensive warfare, which characterized the period of 1777–78 before French intervention, could only succeed with accurate and timely intelligence that would allow Washington to anticipate British movements rather than respond to them. During this period his official correspondence began to reflect the growth in his intelligence-collection activities.

But as he settled into winter quarters, Washington's first problem was to create the perception in the enemy's mind that his forces were larger than was the case. To accomplish this he used both physical and written deception tactics quite effectively. This began early in 1777 when Washington's small force, numbering somewhere between three and four thousand men, was encamped in the Morristown area.

Washington's deception plan consisted of at least four separate operations. The first involved captured British officers who were being returned to their side from the Princeton area. General Putnam instructed his troops to place lights in the windows of all the empty residences and the college halls to give the impression that American troops were billeted there. He also had units from his force parade about the area, reforming into different configurations to give the impression of a much larger force. Upon returning to their lines, the British officers presented an inflated picture of the size of the occupying American force based upon what they thought they had observed. The second operation involved similar activities—changing troop formations, marches and countermarches providing the image of a larger force at the main American camp at

Morristown—but here meant to influence the reporting of local Tories back to the British. The third involved the use of patriotic locals posing as travelers through the area who reported large numbers of American troops when questioned by British patrols.

The last operation was the most carefully orchestrated of the deception pieces, and played a significant role in convincing General Howe that the American forces were too large to confront in a winter campaign. A New York merchant known by Washington to be of Tory sympathy arrived at Morristown with a tale of mistreatment by the British in New York and claimed that he was passing through as a refugee. Washington arranged for the merchant to be well treated at his headquarters. It was then arranged for each brigade commander to prepare a false roster that inflated their unit's strength. These reports were sent to the American headquarters and placed on the desk of the officer entertaining the merchant that evening. During the course of a social evening, Washington arranged to have the officer called away "unexpectedly," allowing the merchant the time to read the army's present-strength reports that just happened to be there. The next day the merchant took his leave and hurried back to report to Howe.[15] Even though Howe received more accurate reporting from other sources, the merchant's firsthand account of seeing American army strength reports made the greatest impression on Howe.

The original British plan for 1777 was to split the colonies by seizing the Hudson River Valley: An army under Gen. John Burgoyne was to move southward from Canada by way of Lake Champlain, Howe was to send troops northward from New York City up the valley, and a small force under Col. Barry St. Leger was to move eastward from western New York, with all to meet around Albany. However, new British government leadership decided to modify the plan. Howe was ordered to capture Philadelphia. This meant that his forces would have to both support the Canadian force moving into central New York State and garrison Philadelphia as a base for operations against Washington's army.

Ordering Howe to support both military actions without providing him with additional forces turned out to be a mistake—a very serious mistake. It eventually led to the strategic American victory at Saratoga on September 19, 1777, a victory that helped convince the French to enter the conflict on the American side. The reasons for the defeat of the two separate elements of the British campaign had mostly to do with British overconfidence, poor knowledge of the terrain they had to navigate, and the level of resistance they anticipated from local militias and the Northern Army. And intelligence also played a role. Ironically, an even more important role was played by the future traitor, Gen. Benedict Arnold.

The Americans were well aware of the British plan to move southward from Canada, but their knowledge of Burgoyne and Howe's plans to coordinate activities was significantly increased thanks to the capture of a British courier, William Amsbury, in mid-June. By the 15th, he had been questioned by the Northern Army commander Gen. Philip Schuyler, and details of Burgoyne's plans were sent to Washington the next day. The courier was also carrying a letter to Gen. John Sullivan of the Continental Army, whom the British mistakenly believed might be willing to join their side. In an effort to deceive the British, Schuyler answered the letter pretending to be Sullivan and included false information regarding American strength in Washington's army in New Jersey, as well as enlarging the forces available to General Putman in the New York highlands and his own forces. He was able to send the message back to the British by using an unwitting deserter, who believed a Tory-sympathizing officer was assisting his desertion in return for delivering the communication.[16] Schuyler's objective was to affect British planning regarding the sending of forces from the New York City–New Jersey area northward to meet up with Burgoyne's forces. The effect the false letter had on the British is unknown. However, the more detailed knowledge of Burgoyne's plans was a factor in Washington's decision to send reinforcements to the Northern Army in August. These troops, especially the sharpshooters led by Gen. Daniel Morgan, would be an important factor in the coming battle at Saratoga.

While focusing on Burgoyne, Schuyler was also concerned about the British force under Colonel St. Leger, which had landed at Oswego, New York, on Lake Ontario on July 25 and was moving eastward along the Mohawk Valley to connect with Burgoyne. This force comprised some eight hundred British and Canadian soldiers and about a thousand Indians. The first major obstacle in St. Leger's path was Fort Stanwix, now Rome, New York, also known as Fort Schuyler. He arrived at the fort on August 2 and laid siege to it. This siege was broken in late August thanks to Benedict Arnold, who had been placed in command of five hundred Continentals and instructed to relieve the fort.

However, Arnold did not use his force to raise the siege—he used a combination deception-and-disinformation operation. In August, the Americans had captured an emotionally disturbed Dutchman who had been involved in loyalist activities. From his previous experience, Arnold knew of Indian superstition regarding individuals who behaved like the Dutchman, and he also knew that the bulk of St. Leger's force was composed of Indians. He used a member of the

Dutchman's family as a hostage to ensure the deranged man acted as instructed and sent a trusted Indian loyal to the American cause along to support the story he wanted told, as well as to further control the Dutchman. Making it appear that he had escaped, the Dutchman and his companion reached the Indian camp. The Indians immediately recognized his strange behavior and believed a spirit was communicating through him. He told them the story that Arnold had provided: The Americans were approaching with two thousand troops, and they were coming only to punish the British forces. The Dutchman's Indian companion confirmed he was speaking the truth.

Because the Indians supporting St. Leger were already unhappy with the amount of plunder and scalps they had been able to accumulate, the news of having to fight a larger force caused them to reconsider their commitment to the campaign. While St. Leger was initially able to convince them to think about remaining, their discipline soon broke down, and they began taking British supplies and sneaking away. Without his Indian allies and believing he was facing an American force three times his number, he ended the siege on August 22 and returned to Canada. The threat to the Mohawk Valley and a joining of the two British forces had been avoided by an intelligence ploy.[17]

Meanwhile, Burgoyne's advance southward continued. On August 19, General Gates replaced Schuyler as commander of the Northern Army, which was now being reinforced by New York and New England militias. By the middle of September, his army was in well-fortified positions around Bemis Heights, near Saratoga, watching Burgoyne's British and Hessian troops cross the Hudson River in preparation for battle. There were actually two battles related to the British defeat at Saratoga: Freeman's Farm and Bemis Heights. The former took place on September 19, when Burgoyne moved to flank the American positions on the heights. Here again, Arnold played an important role in stopping British progress. But they did capture the farm at the cost of significant casualties.

The second and decisive engagement took place on October 7, with Burgoyne attacking Bemis Heights. While the Americans were in good position and quite well fortified, the aggressiveness of the British did create some panic, and for a time various American units gave way. Arnold, who had been relieved of command by Gates earlier, was in his tent when the battle began. Impetuous as usual, he took a horse and rode toward the gunfire in time to rally the Americans and drive the British force back to their pre–September 19 positions. By October 13, Burgoyne found himself facing superior numbers of Americans, with heavy casualties and the loss of much of his officer corps.

Morgan's sharpshooters had done an excellent job of targeting officers, knowing that this would throw their troops into disarray and confusion. Burgoyne surrendered, giving the Americans their most important strategic victory of the war until Yorktown.

There was a particular intelligence-mission connection to the victory at Bemis Heights, although its importance existed more in the sense that it confirmed information Gates already knew from more traditional military reconnaissance activities. But it also did provide an early warning of Burgoyne's intent and timing to attack the heights. It involved Gates convincing a local resident to go into British lines and obtain intelligence on troop strength, artillery capabilities, combat readiness, and planned actions. Alexander Bryan was well known as a patriot to the local committee of safety, which recommended him to Gates to serve as a scout based upon his local knowledge. Gates convinced Bryan to undertake the dangerous intelligence mission—going into enemy lines—by promising to provide medical assistance to Bryan's ill son and pregnant wife. Bryan was able to sneak into the British camp and did learn of Burgoyne's planned attack. At some point, perhaps because his interest in military details seemed more than a local farmer should exhibit, he fell under suspicion. He had to quickly sneak away and was able to report to Gates, allowing the Americans some advance warning of the attack. The sad part of this story is that Gates failed to fulfill his part of the agreement and did not send medical aid to Bryan's family. Bryan's son died of the illness, and his wife lost the child.[18]

The British campaign from Canada had, from a strategic perspective, been the focus of Washington's and Howe's armies as soon as the campaign season began in the spring of 1777. Both armies maneuvered to keep the other from sending reinforcements to the Hudson Valley. In late July, the British army departed from Sandy Hook, New Jersey, and Washington suspected that Philadelphia was their target, but he had no intelligence on British plans, and once the fleet sailed he would have little intelligence on its movements.[19] On August 25, only a few days after Washington learned the fleet had entered the Chesapeake Bay, Howe landed his forces at Head of the Elk, where the Elk River enters the bay, and marched northward toward Philadelphia. Here again, his scouts, local militiamen, and patriotic residents were not productive in identifying Howe's plans.

As Washington marched his army through Philadelphia toward the British force, he soon faced one of the most basic tactical intelligence problems of any commander: He and his officers were not familiar with the countryside where they would have to fight. The Battle of Brandywine on September

11 near Chadds Ford, Pennsylvania, reflected this basic intelligence failure on Washington's part. He had only an inaccurate map of the area, and despite his orders, the local militia failed to conduct aggressive scouting of the British movements.[20] Washington was badly defeated. In a report to the Congress, he admitted that his defeat was the result of poor intelligence.[21]

While Washington was determined to stop Howe from capturing Philadelphia, Howe was slowly and deliberately moving toward his objective. Again Washington's reconnaissance and scouting activities, particularly those that were to be conducted by the militia, failed to give him any advantage. On September 26, the British captured Philadelphia, the home of the Continental Congress, which fled into rural Pennsylvania. Thanks to prior planning by Washington, his intelligence picture on the enemy was about to improve significantly. While the city and its surrounding area held many prominent and wealthy Tory families, it also contained networks and individuals prepared to collect intelligence on the British.

In the case of Philadelphia, and New York after British occupation, Washington had given clear orders to establish intelligence capabilities within the cities—stay-behind resident collectors, as well as individuals with seemingly legitimate reasons to enter and exit the cities on a frequent basis both to observe and report and to courier out intelligence from the resident agents. As he managed the development of these capabilities, Washington also used three young men who would prove to be talented, aggressive, and capable intelligence officers: majors Benjamin Tallmadge, John Clark, and Allen McLane. They protected the identities and methods of collection of their agents, planned their operations carefully, and were personally discreet in noting details of their intelligence responsibilities. What we know of their activities comes from official correspondence and postwar private papers. Tallmadge focused his efforts on New York City, and Clark and McLane focused on Philadelphia. McLane also became a key player in the intelligence operation that lead to the capture of Stony Point in the summer of 1779.

Interestingly, Tallmadge and Clark, both new to intelligence operations, had worked together in early 1777 on a collection operation on Long Island. Tallmadge had the responsibility of inserting Clark onto Long Island from Connecticut, where he remained for several months reporting on British positions and activities.[22]

Major Clark's Philadelphia operations involved a large network of collectors, primarily individuals with personal or commercial connections to the city that permitted then frequent visits.[23] They included farmers selling their products to the British forces, merchants with business interests in the city, some resident agents with social connections to Tory and British leaders, and at least one double agent he developed to provide Howe with disinformation on Washington's army while collecting intelligence on British activities. Some of his agents pretended to be Quakers, as the British believed the Quakers were nonpolitical and therefore less of a threat to them. Clark also used women as part of his network. The quantity of his reporting and its frequent updating at critical times indicated a widespread collection base. But even in his official correspondence, he used vague descriptions of his agents, such as "old woman," rather than actual identification by name or position.[24]

His creation of a double agent to use against Howe was a particularly professionally crafted intelligence operation, which received warm praise from Washington. In a report of November 3, Clark explained that he had created a false intelligence source for Howe—a mythical individual of Tory sympathy who resided outside of Philadelphia—and had selected a trusted friend to courier his information to British authorities in the city. For the courier, Clark chose an individual whom he knew could handle the stress of British questioning and play his part well.[25]

His approach to crafting a double-agent operation was classic: He created a trust in the enemy that the source was on its side and then provided the source with information, appropriately crafted, that seemed accurate and would stand up in the face of other reporting the British might get. Accomplishing those objectives was a complex and disciplined operation. But Clark also added the objective of having the courier develop a capability to gain intelligence on British plans and intentions from his reporting relationship and free access within the city. Clark concluded his report by noting that Howe had accepted the offer. He also suggested that Washington prepare papers with disinformation regarding the strength and condition of the Continental Army that the courier could pass to Howe as the first report from the Tory source. Washington quickly responded the next day, endorsing the operation. He stated that he wished to use Clark's double agent to pass several items: information that General Gates, now firmly in control of upper New York after the Saratoga victory, was sending large reinforcements to Washington's army, that Washington planned to raise the New York militias and attack New York City, with Gen. John Dickinson and New Jersey militias attacking Staten Island at the same time, and that after taking New York City, Washington would call up the Pennsylvania militias and attack Philadelphia. All these themes were of both interest and concern to Howe at that time.

It is unclear when or if this disinformation was actually passed to the British, and the duration of the double-agent operation itself was not further discussed in existing official correspondence. The last mention of the double agent was in a report dated November 22, when he reported that there were only five thousand troops in the city, provided their dispositions, and commented that this was a weakened force.[26] Regardless of the actual impact this operation may or may not have had on Howe, its creation and planning denoted a high degree of aggressiveness and professionalism that seemed to characterize all of Clark's intelligence efforts.

Clark's reporting to Washington in November and December 1777 was quite well documented and demonstrated the apparent ease with which his agents were able to observe activities in the city and then pass through British lines to report their intelligence to him. He maintained an operating base just outside of the British area of control, and in addition to receiving and collating intelligence from his collection network, he also debriefed travelers and enemy deserters on intelligence requirements. While Clark seemed to have little problem with British security regarding his agents' travels, he had more problems with local militias attempting to stop trade with the British. Because he could not advise the various militia officers of the identities of his agents and the true purpose their travel into Philadelphia, he had to develop cover stories that plausibly explained their business or personal reasons for their travel. At one point, Clark even obtained a packet of blank British passes to use to facilitate his agents' travel between army lines.[27] However, at least from the British perspective, other accounts made it clear that because the occupying forces required food supplies from the countryside, as well as intelligence reporting from their own sympathizers in the surrounding area, British perimeter security was quite loose in allowing travel in and out of the city.[28]

As would be expected of a military intelligence operation, the focus of Clark's collection was directed at the order of battle and warnings of troop movements. Even his resident agents had little access to Howe's plans and intentions beyond a tactical level. Yet he was consistently able to report on British casualty figures after skirmishes with American forces, British supply problems, details of troop dispositions both in the city garrison and in the forward defensive positions, reinforcements arriving in the city, and the state of readiness of the enemy. He successfully advised Washington of British movements against Fort Mercer on the Delaware River, which permitted the Americans to withdraw from that untenable position without losses, and provided advance warning of Howe's movement toward Washington's camp at Whitemarsh, about thirteen miles northwest of Philadelphia, ensuring the American army was not caught by surprise.[29] As British supplies became low in December, Clark was able to report specific information to Washington regarding the strength and targets of British foraging parties seeking food from the surrounding countryside. This enabled local militia units to harass them and limit their efforts.

By early 1778, Clark's health failed him, and he asked to be relieved of his responsibilities and given a less demanding position.[30] While many of his agents continued to collect intelligence, the network never regained the productivity it had attained under his direction. Luckily, other American spies were working to ensure Washington was kept advised of British activities while he and his small army languished at Valley Forge in the winter of 1777–78.

The Darragh family of Philadelphia was the source of some of this information, and their reporting efforts were definitely a family enterprise. Lydia, the wife, did most of the collecting, while the husband, William, used a family code to write down the information. John, the younger son, acted as the courier, carrying the messages sewed into his clothing through British lines to visit his older brother, Charles, in the Second Pennsylvania Regiment of the Continental Army. Charles decoded his father's message and passed the intelligence on to army headquarters. In this case, as with Honeyman, official records of the activities and reporting of the Darraghs are circumspect. The few details known are from Lydia telling a daughter about the family's activities after the war and the daughter taking careful notes of the story. From an intelligence officer's perspective, the explanation of the courier method, the cover for action used, and the fact that unidentified individuals providing intelligence as reported in official documents fit into her story make that story believable. It seems doubtful that someone not engaged in intelligence activities could provide such details. One scholar recently conducted collative research on the story and, like other historians of the Revolutionary War, believes its validity.[31]

The reporting from the family seemed focused on basic military activities that could be observed in the normal course of movement about town. The Darraghs were Quakers and as previously noted, considered less a security threat because of their beliefs. Only one specific early-warning intelligence report is mentioned in the daughter's written account. The British would on occasion use the Darragh home as a site for meetings, and on the night of December 2, Lydia overheard discussion of the British plan to quietly move toward Washington's forces at Whitemarsh and attempt to engage him in a surprise battle. Because of the immediacy of the intelligence, the next morning Lydia traveled through British lines under the guise of going to purchase flour from a nearby mill, sought out an American military officer, and told him of the British action. This intelligence was forwarded to Washington and corroborated similar reporting from Clark's agents. The written account of Lydia's actions fit well with the American officer's report of how and where he obtained his intelligence on the British advance toward Whitemarsh.[32]

Maj. (then Capt.) Allen McLane's intelligence collection focused on early warning of enemy movements through reconnaissance activities.[33] But he also employed residents near to the British lines to report on their routine defensive, patrolling, and foraging activities. Mention of these potential agents is noted in a November 22, 1777, letter from Washington agreeing to fund such sources, while setting some terms for the arrangements.[34] Apparently he also did, on occasion, run agents into Philadelphia for brief visits to observe enemy activities.[35] Official records also indicate that in late January 1778, he was operating around Germantown and using individuals, under the guise of trading with the British, to collect intelligence. And in May, as Washington became aware of British planning to leave Philadelphia, McLane was ordered to stop all personnel entering or leaving the city and debrief them for all intelligence possible. He was to send his consolidated report of each day's intelligence obtained to Washington's headquarters the following morning.[36]

While Washington had numerous intelligence reports on British departure preparations, on May 18 he obtained firsthand intelligence on the matter. The previous evening, some fifty American prisoners of war had escaped from a Philadelphia prison and made their way to his headquarters the next morning.[37] Their eyewitness accounts of British activities added useful perspective to the timing of the enemy's departure. Washington also ordered General Lafayette to take a force of two thousand men and move to an observation position on Barren Hill, where he might discern where the British planned to go and when they would be departing, with the intention of attacking their rear guard.[38]

There are two specific instances where McLane's reporting can be cited as of particular value: enemy movement toward the American camp at Whitemarsh[39] and advance warning of a British attempt to capture a senior officer at an observation post overlooking Philadelphia. The latter reporting, on the attempt to capture General Lafayette at Barren Hill, which resulted in the Frenchman quickly departing the site, was especially valuable.[40] The capture of Lafayette, a favorite of both Washington and the French court, would have been a significant propaganda victory for the British. McLane's reporting enabled his escape.

Allen McLane, a Continental Army officer from Delaware, became a senior intelligence officer for Washington, particularly in the Philadelphia area. *Library of Congress. Wood engraving originally appeared in John Thomas Scharf,* A History of Delaware, 1609–1888, vol. 1 (*Philadelphia: L .J. Richards, 1888*).

McLane also happened to be the first American officer to enter Philadelphia as the British departed. On June 18, 1778, at Washington's instruction, he led a small force into the city to determine the status of the evacuation. In the process he was able to capture several British officers who were still engaged with their local female lovers—apparently having lost track of time.[41]

References exist to other individual agents working for various army and militia officers, but their identities and activities are not well documented. For example, a Pennsylvania officer, Capt. Stephen Chambers, was involved in running a network of local residents between Philadelphia and Valley Forge in early 1778. Based upon his military affiliation, it can also be assumed that he operated a reconnaissance element, protecting the army's encampment by monitoring enemy troop movements in the area between the city and the camp.[42] But records on his specific actions are scarce.

There is a bit more information on another family, the Leverings of the Wissahickon Creek area outside Philadelphia, who were involved in similar observation and early-warning intelligence reporting. They were also associated with a local partisan group, the Green Boys, who harassed and frustrated British patrols and foraging parties so aggressively that the British made several efforts, unsuccessfully, to kill them. One family member, Jacob Levering, would enter Philadelphia disguised as a Quaker farmer selling his agricultural products to the British Army and collect whatever information he could observe or elicit from his British contacts. He would then return home, prepare his report, and have a younger brother courier it to American forces.[43] Local legend in the area also connects another individual, Molly "Mom" Rinker, to intelligence collection. According to the story, she used to sit atop a rock in the Wissahickon Valley from which she could observe British troop movements on the outskirts of Philadelphia. She would than use the Green Boys' channels to the American military to pass along her observations.[44] However, no written records of the time support this story, and it lacks adequate details to provide further authentication.

By early 1778, the British government had decided that its army should withdraw from Philadelphia back to New York City. General Howe was replaced by Gen. Sir Henry Clinton, and the British began preparation in May for evacuation. By June 18, they were out of the city. As they marched northeastward in two bodies, militia units constantly harassed them, making their march difficult. Washington decided to send a strong force, some four thousand men, to follow Clinton's section closely. However, his lack of cavalry significantly hindered his ability to identify the location and size of the moving

British forces.[45] The British troops were suffering from both high summer temperatures and a lack of drinking water, as well as the constant skirmishing with militia. By June 26, Clinton's troops were exhausted and demoralized. Washington decided to attack, and on the 28th the Americans faced Clinton's troops at the Battle of Monmouth. The battle was confused from the start and included the only documented instance of Washington publicly berating one of his generals in the heat of battle.[46] The result was a draw, but the British did withdraw from the field, enabling Washington to claim the battle as an American victory in which his army had stood up to and defeated a large regular British force. Clinton then marched his troops to Sandy Hook, where they boarded ships to New York City.

British headquarters would remain in New York City for the remainder of the war. There, awaiting Clinton, was an even more comprehensive American intelligence presence than Howe had faced in Philadelphia.

CHAPTER 8

BENEDICT ARNOLD:
HERO TURNED TRAITOR

Even after over two hundred years, over which time hundreds of Americans have betrayed their country, Benedict Arnold remains America's best-known traitor. Treason is the only crime defined in the United States Constitution, and his actions might be the reason why. After George Washington, Arnold's name is one of the best remembered from the Revolutionary War. His name and story are much more familiar to most than that of Benjamin Church and even Nathan Hale.

Arnold has been described as the prototype of the American spy, reporting from inside an organization where he was trusted. He did it for ego and financial reasons rather than any commitment to ideology, which made his actions particularly abhorrent. Arnold's story has a similar lineage to the modern-day spy Robert Hanssen, the Federal Bureau of Investigation special agent who provided information to the Russians.[1] Both were seen as competent professionals by their peers, if perhaps somewhat arrogant in personal behavior, and both attained senior positions of authority and responsibility within their career fields. Both had egos that motivated them to betray their profession, their colleagues, their country, and their personal ethics. If they had obtained the professional recognition they felt they deserved, they might well have ended up as respected leaders in their organizations' histories.

However, in both cases the recognition was never sufficient. Had it been in Arnold's case, today he would probably be remembered and honored as one of the greatest heroes of the American Revolution. There is an old story, often told, in which a group of Continental Army soldiers are discussing what should be done to Arnold if he were captured, now that his treachery had been exposed. The group decides that his right leg that was wounded severely at the Battle of Saratoga should be cut off and buried with full military honors, while the rest of him should be hanged and thrown in an unmarked grave.[2] Indeed, in the battlefield at Saratoga, there is a monument to his leg.[3]

Arnold's family was well rooted in New England by the time of his birth. One of his ancestors assisted Roger Williams in the establishment of Rhode Island, and another relative was governor of that colony ten times.[4] Thus Arnold came from solid and proud New England stock. It is probable that his arrogance developed as a result of the pressure on him to justify his place in family history. In any event, to understand how he went from a patriot to traitor, it is necessary to understand some of the background of his life.

Because of his place in American history, Arnold's personal history has been well researched, and countless books and articles written describing—and in many instances trying to explain—his life and actions. His espionage activities with the British are also quite well documented in the Sir Henry Clinton papers at the William L. Clements Library at the University of Michigan.[5]

Arnold was born on January 14, 1741, at Norwich, Connecticut, and officially named Benedict Arnold V. His family was prosperous and well respected in the local community. However, as Arnold grew up, his father's business interests fell into disarray, and eventually he faced the humiliation of having a drunken father who had become a subject of ridicule in the community.[6] His first taste for military life was near the end of the French and Indian War, and while he saw no combat action, he did develop a liking for military life—if not military discipline. His personal leadership skills were evident from an early age, as was his physical prowess. He was apprenticed to a wealthy family, a Dr. and Mrs. Lathrop, and through their support embarked on a commercial career. His enterprise soon took him into a traditional New England trade, practiced by virtually all the prominent commercial families and many of the future leaders of the Revolution—smuggling products into the colonies to avoid paying British taxes.[7]

His entrance into the politics of the patriot, or Whig, element came through involvement with the Sons of Liberty in Connecticut.[8] He found that his business interests were adversely affected by British taxation policies, and he became a local leader in political activities in opposition to the Stamp Act in 1765. By the early 1770s, as the Sons of Liberty became more influential in colonial political and military organizations, so did Arnold. In March of

1775, when a charter was issued to form the Connecticut governor's Second Company of Foot from militia members, he was elected captain of the unit. A month later, when news of Lexington and Concord became known, he called for Connecticut support to the patriots surrounding Boston. When the town voted to remain neutral, he collected a group of men from the Sons of Liberty, members of the Second Company, and some Yale students and seized the local powder supply by intimidation. He then marched off to Boston with his group.[9]

Within a few days, Arnold met with members of the Massachusetts Committee of Safety, including Samuel Adams and Dr. Joseph Warren, leaders of the Sons of Liberty who would have known of his activities with that organization in Connecticut. He briefed them on his view that British cannon at Fort Ticonderoga, at the southern tip of Lake Champlain, would be easy to capture. Warren obtained the approval of the commander of the American forces surrounding Boston, Gen. Artemus Ward, and of the Massachusetts Provincial Congress to send Arnold to seize the cannon. Ironically, Arnold's instructions from the Massachusetts Committee of Safety to capture the fort were given by Dr. Benjamin Church, General Gage's spy within the Boston patriots' leadership.[10] On May 3, Arnold began his journey to the fort. In the early hours of May 10, the fort was taken by a joint force of Arnold's Massachusetts troops, Ethan Allen's Green Mountain Boys, and a small group of Connecticut men.

However, Allen's announcement of the capture of the fort gave himself most of the credit: "I Took the Fortress of Ticonderoga with About one Hundred and thirty Green Mountain Boys. . . . Col. Arnold Entered the fortress with me Side by Side."[11] It was not much of a battle, the small garrison was caught by surprise, and the feeble British resistance was quickly overwhelmed. In retrospect, Ethan Allen, the leader of the Green Mountain Boys from the area north of New York that would become Vermont, gave Arnold more trouble than the British.[12] Allen had decided on his own authority to seize the fort and as a strong personality did not look kindly on sharing command with Arnold.

With the capture of the fort came more confusion over the chain of command in a civilian government structure that was disjointed and confusing, to say the least. Also, the rivalry between Arnold and Allen over command responsibilities continued. However, Arnold soon moved quickly and aggressively to seize control of Lake Champlain from the British. He captured the British sloop HMS *George*, the largest warship on the lake, as well as its home port in the province of Quebec, St. John's. Once again, these were bloodless victories based upon solid planning and the element of surprise. He wanted to move on to an invasion of Canada, but decisions were made to place others in command above him, and he was questioned about his expenditures by Massachusetts provincial officials. Interestingly, it was Dr. Church as head of the Massachusetts Committee of Safety who ensured that Arnold's momentum against the British was halted.[13] Frustrated by these issues, he decided to return home.

The issue of Arnold's use of public funds became a recurring theme throughout his American military career. Eventually, between reimbursement by the provincial authorities and the Continental Congress (at the recommendation of George Washington), Arnold received pretty much the reimbursement he claimed. However, whether it was simple inattention to financial details or a liberal attitude toward his authorities and privileges, Arnold was not good at documenting his expenses. Regardless of the reason, the frequent questioning of his expenditures was a constant point of sensitivity to his ego and became a key motivation for his offer to spy for the British.

After returning home and settling family issues related to the death of his first wife, Arnold traveled to Boston and sought an interview with Washington. He had a plan for an invasion of Canada and spent several days briefing Washington on its details. He and Washington developed both a personal and professional rapport during these meetings and began what became a close relationship. When Washington had assumed command of the army, his "Virginia gentleman" perception of what constituted sound officers was shocked by the New England officers he met. Most had been elected by their troops, had only a vague knowledge of military tactics, and demonstrated a lax attitude toward military discipline. Arnold's detailed planning, knowledge of European military tactics and strategy, and disciplined military persona greatly appealed to Washington. He gave Arnold the rank of colonel in the Continental Army and approved the campaign with its objective of capturing the city of Quebec.[14]

That campaign was a failure. Problems with extremely difficult logistical and weather conditions, poor discipline among troops and some officers, inadequate forces and armament, and some strong military resistance from the British garrison, especially its artillery units, combined to defeat the American force. Arnold, leading from the front as he always did, was seriously wounded in his right leg during combat. His failure to capture the city, however, was overshadowed by his developing reputation as a military leader and his growing relationship with some well-placed friends. In addition to Washington, Arnold also had an ally in the Continental Congress, Silas Deane, who got him promoted to brigadier general.[15]

In addition to having been wounded, Arnold was also being ignored, he felt, by the new campaign commander, Gen. David Wooster. When Wooster was replaced, Arnold suffered another blow to his frail ego when Maj. Gen. John Thomas, who had been promoted over him, took command. Nevertheless, once recovered and now reporting to a third commanding officer, Gen. John Sullivan, he continued to perform his military duties quite well. When the American troops were finally ordered to retreat, he was given the responsibility for the rear guard of the army. He handled this role competently, and throughout the entire ill-fated Canada campaign documents clearly support the fact that Arnold was a talented and brave military officer.

In July of 1776, those left of the Quebec campaign forces were at Crown Point in poor shape. His new superiors, Gen. Philip Schuyler and Gen. Horatio Gates, accepted his typically aggressive plan to build a Continental naval force to halt any British movements from Canada into northern New York and the Hudson Valley. Once again under difficult resource restraints, he did an excellent job of creating the force, based no doubt on his knowledge gained from his commercial shipping ventures before the war. However, his constant demands for additional resources did try the patience of his superiors. He was also called before a court-martial proceeding to explain his actions during the campaign in Canada. While most of the charges were based on interpersonal disputes among the officers and on colonial politics, Arnold, who never suffered criticism passively, created additional drama in his testimony and finally challenged several of his critics to duels. Wisely, the court refused to allow the challenges. With General Gates's support, the charges against him were dropped.

By August, with command of the naval force given to him by Gates, Arnold was preparing to engage the British on Lake Champlain. The decisive battle for control of the lake took place on October 11 and 12 at Valcour Bay. Initially, Arnold employed some clever tactics against a more powerful British naval force and managed to inflict serious damage. But by the second day of battle his capabilities were spent, and he had to retreat by land to Crown Point and then destroy what he could there prior to falling back to Fort Ticonderoga. As 1776 ended, the British controlled the lake, but Arnold's tenacious actions delayed the British until winter weather made further campaigning unrealistic—buying precious time for the American cause.[16] Once again his military leadership, this time in a naval warfare scenario, was most impressive, even as his interaction with his peers and superiors continued to reflect his view—quite possibly accurate—of their inferior competence and lack of support.

Arnold accompanied Gates as veterans from the Northern Army were added to Washington's weak forces in Pennsylvania, where Washington gave him responsibility to organize military resistance to a British attack on Rhode Island. However, in mid-February 1777, Congress promoted five brigadier generals to major general, all of whom were less senior and arguably less competent and experienced than Arnold. These promotions had everything to do with colonial politics, as the Congress attempted to motivate each colony's willingness to supply resources and manpower to the army. Washington even told Arnold in a letter of April 3 that the promotions were the result of politics and not personal merit.[17] Nevertheless, Arnold was angry and hurt. When the Congress did promote him in May, his concern over the date of commission as a seniority issue caused him to submit his resignation to the Congress. However, a new British campaign to geographically split the colonies by controlling the Hudson Valley enabled Washington to offer him a command position that would, for the time being, soothe his wounded ego.

Arnold returned to the Northern Army as commander of one of the two wings of the undermanned force. As recounted in the previous chapter, the British plan was to have Gen. John Burgoyne lead a force down from Canada by way of Lake Champlain to Albany, with Col. Barry St. Leger's smaller force of British regulars, loyalist militiamen, and Indians moving eastward through the Mohawk Valley, and Gen. William Howe sending troops up the Hudson from New York City. The Northern Army commander, General Schuyler, assigned Arnold the task of stopping St. Leger's force at Fort Stanwix in the Mohawk River Valley. In his campaign Arnold used a mentally deranged Dutchman to cause the British's Indian allies to desert, forcing St. Leger to retreat and ending any possibility of British reinforcements for Burgoyne's troops.[18]

However, when General Gates took over the Northern Army from General Schuyler, he reduced Arnold's responsibilities to that of a division commander. Because of intercolonial and personal army politics, Gates did not trust Arnold. On the eve of the Battle of Freeman's Farm, the first of the two battles near Saratoga where Gates was determined to stop Burgoyne, they became involved in a bitter argument over Arnold's use of militia forces under his command. Gates countermanded some of Arnold's decisions, apparently without advising him of it, and Arnold was furious.[19]

On September 19, 1777, the battle began with Burgoyne attempting to outflank the Americans. Arnold again performed bravely and skillfully. However, Gates restricted his attempts to lead an attack, which might have routed the British, and the battle ended with the Americans back behind their defensive line and the British in control of the battlefield.[20]

Arnold again lost his temper a few days later when Gates reassigned some of Arnold's troops without informing him beforehand. This action, as well as Arnold's belief, quite possibly true, that Gates should have been more aggressive during the battle, caused him to burst into Gates's headquarters and demand an explanation. Obviously, Gates was not pleased at Arnold's behavior, especially in front of his staff. Arnold asked Gates for permission to leave the army and travel to Philadelphia to meet with Washington—sort of a letter of resignation but with none-too-subtle threats that the argument was not over. Other senior officers attempted to calm down the men, but neither Arnold nor Gates apparently saw the British as greater enemies than each other at that moment.[21]

Facing logistical issues, Burgoyne did not attack but remained on the battlefield, hoping for additional troops from New York City. On October 7, he ordered a reconnaissance in force, which became the Battle of Bemis Heights, the second battle near Saratoga. Slowly, the Americans engaged his force, and the British began to take serious casualties. Arnold, removed from any command responsibilities by Gates, heard the combat and fumed at his situation. In frustration, he mounted his horse and rode toward the gunfire. He managed to round up some stragglers and reserves and led them against a Hessian unit. He then went into a somewhat deranged mode, moving rapidly about the battlefield and eventually into the British defensive lines. His dramatic presence on the battlefield inspired the American troops. But he was then shot in the right leg, shattering his femur—the same leg in which he had been wounded during the battle for Quebec. Carried from the field, he refused to allow the field surgeons to amputate as they recommended. This wound left him disabled and in constant pain for the remainder of his life.[22] It effectively ended his combat career.

Gates was not pleased with Arnold's actions, as he had directly disobeyed orders, and he gave Arnold no official credit for his actions in the Battle of Saratoga. However, Arnold's actions did become public knowledge through the letters and comments of others in the army, further strengthening his reputation as a military hero. A historical appraisal of the battle indicated that Arnold's actions did contribute to the American victory, as popular history suggests.[23] However, an objective evaluation might well decide that his military leadership and skills demonstrated during the Lake Champlain naval campaign marked his most significant contribution to the American cause.

Although after the battle the Congress voted to restore his original place on the seniority list, there are no indications that this in any way soothed his anger over the original slight. The recovery period from his wound ended in early May 1778, when he returned to active duty at Washington's headquarters at Valley Forge. Washington was well aware that the British were about to leave Philadelphia and offered Arnold the post of military governor of the city. As one recent counterintelligence review of the Arnold case noted, that decision by Washington placed Arnold in a post that "played to none of Arnold's talents and all his flaws."[24] Arnold accepted and began planning how to administer the city under martial law. In mid-June, he led American forces back into Philadelphia.[25]

The former home of the Continental Congress had been occupied by the British since September 26, 1777, when General Cornwallis led his troops into the city. The British commander in chief, General Howe, had established his headquarters there, and the Tory Joseph Galloway became the city's civilian manager and superintendent of police.[26] Galloway had always been a loyalist but had also been a member of an early session of the Continental Congress from Pennsylvania and had used his access to other patriot leaders to report on their actions and personalities to General Gage in Boston.[27] The British traditionally did not campaign during the winter season, and with the culture of the British officer class at the time, Philadelphia became an active social environment for those on the side of King George. A British officer named John André was in the thick of it.

André was the son of a middle-class merchant family with a proclivity for artistic endeavors such as drawing, writing, and acting. More important, he was bright and had excellent interpersonal skills and a demeanor that made him a valuable staff officer. His ambition did not always cause him to be well liked by his peers and competitors, however. Yet when he wished, he had such an engaging personality that the Americans who eventually hanged him spoke highly of his character.[28] In November 1775, André had been captured by the Americans and placed on a parole, which enabled him to first visit Philadelphia and briefly meet the charming and attractive daughter of a leading local Tory, Margaret "Peggy" Shippen. Her father, Judge Edward Shippen, had held numerous official positions in the British colonial administration.[29] As an aide to General Howe in 1777, he renewed this acquaintance.

Attached to Howe's staff, André moved into the residence of Benjamin Franklin, then in Paris as the de facto American ambassador to the French government. His artistic talents, as well as his recognition that keeping his senior officer well entertained was career enhancing, led him to create theatrical productions and other artistic events in the city. Because the Shippen family was one of the wealthier and more prominent families, senior British officers associated socially with them on a regular basis. There is ample documentation

British major John André, General Clinton's intelligence aide and the case officer who handled Benedict Arnold. *Library of Congress*

to show that André and Peggy were socially close and probably friends but without any apparent romantic or physical interplay.[30]

During his service in North America, André developed a very low opinion of the average American, especially the colonial military.[31] He also demonstrated the standard British officer's distaste for those considered disloyal to king and country. When he departed Philadelphia in June 1778, like his fellow officers, he took everything of value possible from the house where he had stayed. Because it had been Franklin's home, he may well have taken extra pleasure in shipping off Franklin's scientific instruments, personal papers, and records in addition to the household furniture.[32] His low opinion of his enemies could explain some of the sloppiness in his actions later when contacting Arnold. In the intelligence game, as in most of life, underestimating your competition is not a good idea.

Once appointed military governor of Philadelphia, Arnold began various

A 1778 portrait of Margaret "Peggy" Shippen, drawn by John André. She was from a prominent loyalist family, and André was a close social acquaintance of Peggy's when the British occupied Philadelphia. She later married Benedict Arnold and assisted him in his treachery. *Yale University Art Gallery*

commercial activities involving his position that were ethically questionable if not illegal. For payment he provided certain merchants with special rights to import goods and conduct certain commercial activities. He also involved himself in purchasing deals of commercial goods formerly owned by Tories who had left with the British, which were not open to competitive bidding. Finally, he used military logistical resources—wagons and horses—to move nongovernment property for his own financial benefit.[33]

While in Philadelphia, Arnold also maintained a standard of living characterized as lavish and well above his military income.[34] His types of commercial activities were not uncommon among many American political and military leaders during the war, as some biographers of Arnold note. However, the scope of his activities and their transparency made them public knowledge. Arnold's new cash flow was manifested in social activities that included the wealthy Tory families that remained in the city.[35]

These activities included the lovely Peggy Shippen. Arnold met her shortly after his arrival and was immediately taken with her beauty and personality. By the winter of 1778, she was Arnold's public escort to all social events. Her family eventually destroyed all her correspondence with Arnold from this period, so it is not clear exactly how she viewed his romantic overtures. But his correspondence makes it clear he held her in great affection.[36] As Arnold was, at this point, an American hero, the most powerful man in Philadelphia, not unattractive (even with a lame leg), and extremely attentive and generous in his behavior toward her, Peggy may well have returned his affection.

However, by early 1779, the Congress was looking into reports of Arnold's commercial activities, and a committee was investigating them. While Arnold was subsequently acquitted of any criminal actions, he was ordered to face yet another court-martial regarding his use of military resources for private gain.[37] He was once again furious that his honor was questioned. At the same time, he was also facing some personal financial strains because of commercial setbacks and another official review of his accounting submitted during the campaign to attack Quebec. He sought Washington's assistance regarding the court-martial and was greatly offended when the general did not take an active role to support him.[38]

On April 8, 1779, Arnold married Peggy. As man and wife they must have had a great deal to talk about, because Arnold in early May, with Peggy's approval, decided to offer his services to the British. There is strong evidence to conclude that she actively encouraged her husband to take this step, based on her own Tory orientation and the ungrateful manner both believed Arnold was being treated by his American political enemies.[39]

From a counterintelligence perspective, Arnold took actions after his marriage that both financially and socially should have aroused interest if not suspicion. He began to sell off his real property, both land and houses.[40] While his debts could explain such actions, considering the value that real property held in terms of one's social status within colonial America, his actions could also be viewed as an act of separating himself from the American side. But while his actions were public knowledge, they aroused little official notice because a centralized counterintelligence structure did not exist in either the army or the Congress.

While documents make it clear that the British had developed a list of American officers who they hoped could be motivated to rejoin the king's service, Arnold was not considered a potential defector in early 1779.[41] Thus any suspicion that he may have been enticed to become a traitor by British actions is misplaced. Clinton made this clear in a letter to his sisters of October 4, 1780. He stated that Arnold had approached him without any effort on the part of the British.[42]

One common trait among exposed spies is to claim that their spouse was not involved in their spying activities and indeed was unaware of them. But counterintelligence investigations more often than not find that the spouse was aware and in most cases abetted the activities. One notorious example of spousal complicity from the 1990s was Aldrich Ames's wife, Maria del Rosario Casas Ames, who pled guilty to espionage along with her husband. In the specific case of Peggy, there is no question of her knowledge of Arnold's plotting—only the degree to which she encouraged Arnold to make his decision.

Both Arnold and his wife knew a Philadelphia merchant named Joseph Stansbury. He had been a city official when Howe occupied Philadelphia but took an oath of loyalty to the American cause when he remained in the city after it reverted to American control. Peggy knew him from her family's Tory circles, and Arnold had, at least, met him when he purchased some household furnishings from him a year earlier. There is evidence that he was one of the British's stay-behind agents who were to report on American activities from inside the city or support that collection effort in some manner.[43]

Arnold asked Stansbury to travel to New York City, seek a meeting with Sir Henry Clinton, the British commander in chief, and offer to him the services of a senior American military officer. Stansbury was not to reveal Arnold's identity to anyone, including Clinton, at this initial phase of negotiations.

Stansbury agreed and immediately went to New York. His first contact was with the Reverend Jonathan Odell, an Anglican priest employed as the chaplain to a loyalist militia unit encamped on Staten Island. Odell was a member of a British intelligence network working for William Franklin.[44]

Franklin was the illegitimate son of Benjamin Franklin and had been the royal governor of New Jersey, then involved in creating an organizational structure for Tories in the colonies willing to assist the British. As a royal governor, Franklin had experience in intelligence activities and had acted as a communication channel for Congress member Joseph Galloway to pass information on the Continental Congress to London.[45] As part of his organizing of the loyalist elements, Franklin was working to establish agent networks and their supporting elements such as couriers and safe houses.

On May 10, a little over a month after Arnold's marriage to Peggy, Stansbury was introduced to Franklin by Odell and then to John André, Clinton's recently appointed intelligence officer. Ignoring Arnold's instructions that his identity was to remain secret, Stansbury named him as the senior military officer who was willing to cooperate. André was, understandably, excited at the prospect of such a well-placed potential intelligence source. After he told Clinton about Arnold, André instructed Stansbury to tell Arnold that he would be generously rewarded. André then provided a list of activities for Arnold to report on: to provide American and French planning documents, to identify American agents working in British-controlled areas, to provide an order of battle for the American forces, and to try to influence others toward the British side.[46]

These requirements, while broad in nature, reflect the classic intelligence approach to vetting and focusing a new reporting source: They are general enough to not identify the intelligence service's current collection abilities and gaps, but the responses would assist in identifying Arnold's areas of access useful for future specific requirements. At this point André had a potentially significant opportunity, but the volunteer's true intent and sincere willingness to report as directed was unknown. The next phase of the operation was to test and verify Arnold's capability and willingness to satisfy British requirements.

André also began to establish the support capabilities necessary for an agent operation. He suggested security measures for communications: Arnold's code name was "Monk," and the correspondence was to be in invisible ink and in code based on what is known as a book code. This well-known type of code, used by the British in many of their intelligence operations, was keyed to a specific edition of a book. André suggested a common book of the times, Blackstone's

Commentaries on the Laws of England. In addition to these security measures, André planned to use an unwitting cutout to receive the correspondence and forward it without knowing it contained invisible writing. This individual was to be a girlfriend of Peggy's who was in social correspondence with André. Stansbury would continue to be the courier of the innocent-looking correspondence, passing it to Odell who would develop and decode the message for André. As another communication method, André suggested that if Arnold needed to send a message directly through Stansbury, he phrase the cover letter in commercial terms. Arnold was to sign that letter as "Gustavus"—later changed to "John Moore"—and address it to "John Anderson," a New York City merchant.[47]

Stansbury returned to Philadelphia the evening of May 11 and provided Arnold with André's response. On May 21, Arnold and Peggy provided their response, deciding to use a different book as the key code, the twenty-first edition of *Bailey's Dictionary*, as Arnold found *Commentaries on the Laws of England* too cumbersome to work with. Arnold also decided to add yet another layer of security by adding one to all the numbers in the invisible message. For example, page 123 would be 234, line 27 would be 38, and word 12 would be 23.[48] While he thought in a disciplined clandestine manner regarding the security of his reporting, Arnold was less skilled in use of the invisible ink. When Odell attempted to develop this letter, he found the invisible ink had run together and was unreadable.[49]

This must have been quite frustrating for André, as Arnold's response to his offer and any useful information he provided based on André's previously transmitted requirements would have been very helpful in the vetting process of his potential new agent. Perhaps André could also have considered the poor use of the invisible ink a ploy to stimulate more correspondence from him that might provide the Americans with additional information on his intelligence requirements. At this point, André only knew that an American senior military commander, viewed as a hero within Continental Army ranks, had volunteered his services—and the motivation seemed to be financial. He had no proof of Arnold's sincerity and had to harbor some suspicion that this could be a double agent or disinformation operation by Washington.

In a letter a few days later, Arnold wrote to emphasize his concern about adequate compensation for his efforts and provided the information that Washington planned to move up the Hudson Valley for a summer campaign. He stated he would not forward any documents but would provide summaries of them based upon his reading and conversations regarding them. Arnold also specifically relayed Peggy's regards to André.[50]

André was probably pleased at the response and the information but again a bit suspicious of the refusal to provide documents. Documents are an excellent way of vetting intelligence provided and also verifying the access the spy claims. Summaries of plans are useful but much easier to phrase in a manner intended for misinforming or influencing the enemy. Also, summaries are, of course, less accurate in specific detail.

As he began his negotiations with the British, Arnold wrote an emotional letter to Washington that included this sentence: "The interest I have in the welfare and happiness of my country, which I have ever evinced when in my power, will, I hope, always overcome my personal resentment for any injury I can possibly receive from individuals."[51] Obviously, his personal interests had already overcome his interest in his country.

While some historians suggest this statement represented the internal conflict Arnold felt regarding his loyalties, an intelligence officer might well view it simply as a demonstration of the hypocrisy that is characteristic of the ego-driven spy—a trait that must be carefully monitored when dealing with such an individual. Considering the information that the British had about Arnold's ego at the start of the negotiations, this was another factor André had to consider in his efforts to bring Arnold into the British camp

In mid-June, Arnold wrote again to André, this time through an old commercial contact in New York City, merchant Edward Antill. He reported on American troop strength, locations, and planned movements. He also again pushed hard on the issue of his compensation. André replied later that month in somewhat vague and stern language. Arnold didn't appreciate André's tone and in reply argued for guaranteed compensation of £10,000 for his services, regardless of what he was able to accomplish for the British. He also provided Stansbury with intelligence for André regarding detailed planning for the campaign against Detroit, details of General Gates's forces in Rhode Island, and other useful order-of-battle information.[52] But Stansbury found Arnold's behavior suspicious. He had difficulties meeting with Arnold, who claimed his military responsibilities were too demanding to make time for a meeting. Stansbury also wondered why it had taken Arnold so long to respond to André's last letter. He shared his concerns with André.[53]

An experienced intelligence officer knows that when it takes an agent longer than the anticipated time to respond to requirements, one reason might be the time it takes for the agent to have the material approved, and perhaps manipulated, by his actual controlling service. In suspect double-agent operations, a standard counterintelligence ploy is to create a situation where the agent must respond quickly and then compare the intelligence reported with his previous reporting to determine if the content seems different. Arnold's delay in responding, as well as Stansbury's concerns regarding Arnold's tone and behavior, were additional troubling issues for André as he attempted to determine Arnold's true intentions.

By late July, it was public knowledge that Arnold was under investigation for using army property for personal gain, and this created another concern for André to consider in his negotiations: Would Arnold, if judged guilty of those charges, ever have another command of value to the British? At this point both Arnold and André were frustrated—Arnold with the lack of a British commitment to his compensation demands and André with counterintelligence concerns about Arnold's true allegiance and military future. Negotiations became stagnant, and both participants focused their efforts on other, more pressing matters.

Throughout the fall and spring, Arnold continued to face charges—or insults to his character as he saw them—based upon his previous handling of government funds. Finally, on April 6, 1780, Washington made his decision known regarding Arnold's use of army resources in Philadelphia. He issued an official, and therefore public, reprimand of Arnold. In reality, Arnold got off quite easy considering the facts, and Washington sent him a personal letter stating he would provide opportunities for Arnold to regain his public reputation.[54]

During this same period, Arnold's financial troubles reached their peak. His personal debts were great, and he was unable to sell his properties or commercial goods to settle them. He had not been repaid the funds he claimed from the Canadian campaign and had not received his salary as an army officer for several years. On April 22, the Congress Treasury Board reported that Arnold owed the government some $70,000.[55] These circumstances convinced Arnold that it was time to restart his negotiations with the British.

In May, he met with former general Philip Schuyler, his old army friend and political ally, who was now a New York delegate to the Congress. Schuyler agreed to suggest to Washington that Arnold be given command of West Point, the key defensive position on the Hudson River.[56] Later that month, Arnold sent Stansbury to New York City with the message that he would work with the British. However, his message also included his set of terms: £10,000 and independent command of a loyalist battalion, with the rank of brigadier general. Arnold also reported he had rejoined Washington's headquarters and insisted on a personal meeting with a senior British officer to finalize all the details of his cooperation.

When Stansbury arrived in New York City, both Clinton and André were in South Carolina, where British forces were defeating the Southern Army. He delivered Arnold's message to Maj. Gen. Wilhelm von Knyphausen, the Hessian general left in command of the city. Knyphausen told Stansbury he would brief Clinton on the information from Arnold and gave Stansbury instructions and a ring to take back to Arnold. The ring was to be a recognition signal: The British officer sent to him would be carrying a duplicate ring.[57]

Arnold was pleased with Knyphausen's response and in return sent the British information on Washington's plans for a joint American-French land and sea attack on Quebec, which Washington had shared widely with his officers. Unknown to Arnold, that information was part of a deception plan, which Washington had designed to draw British forces out of New York City with the hope the city might then be vulnerable to attack. Washington was well aware that by allowing news of the plan to be widely disseminated within the American army, the British would learn of it.[58] However, there is no evidence that he suspected Arnold of being a British agent. Clinton accepted Arnold's information as accurate, primarily because it supported his personal belief of Washington's intentions and because he probably had similar reporting from other British sources. Ironically, this false information, honestly reported by Arnold, was one of the key reasons that caused the British to believe that Arnold was sincere in his desire to work with them.

Now that he felt accepted by the British, Arnold's reporting became more frequent. On June 15, he reported he would soon have command of West Point and, based upon an inspection tour of the location, provided details of the garrison. The next day, he provided a comprehensive description of the weaknesses of the defenses and suggested a plan of attack for British forces.[59]

Upon their return to New York from the South in mid-June, Clinton and André were told of Arnold's recent reporting. While Clinton was taken with the intelligence regarding the joint campaign against Quebec, he did not take the time to respond to Arnold's request for formal confirmation of their agreement. He did, however, write to William Eden, the British undersecretary of state and a senior official with intelligence responsibilities, about the opportunity that Arnold's position and access offered.[60] Meanwhile, André was attempting to verify Arnold's reporting and had Tory agents follow him as he conducted personal business.[61] On July 7, Arnold had Stansbury carry the message that he wanted a response to his month-old correspondence and included the information that the joint campaign had been a ruse that he unwittingly had passed along. He also included other current military information.[62]

Frustrated by no response from the British, in mid-July Arnold sent a message to Clinton through Samuel Wallis, a Philadelphia Quaker he knew to be of Tory sympathies. Since he had received no replies to his recent messages sent via Stansbury, he was not confident that Stansbury had delivered them. This message, encoded based on a book suggested to him in the Knyphausen communication, made a clear offer to surrender West Point for £20,000. Again he asked for a personal meeting with a senior British officer and warned that if no reply to his offer was received, he would break off all communication. He also requested that Wallis be given £1,000 as a sign of goodwill toward the £20,000.[63] As Wallis was another stay-behind agent working for British intelligence in Philadelphia, André and Stansbury were soon aware of the message.[64]

At the end of July, for the first time in about a year, André responded to Arnold in a guarded message. He made no specific commitments but suggested an interest in the Hudson River forts and that he might be the officer sent to meet Arnold. A second message, encoded with the Knyphausen book code, was also sent to Arnold, agreeing to the £20,000 price for West Point. But because of difficulties getting those messages through American lines at a time of increased military activities, Arnold left to take command at West Point before he had his answer. Nevertheless, through letters to his wife, Arnold continued to report intelligence on Washington's plans and intentions, which Peggy was supposed to pass to Clinton via Stansbury. Finally, on August 25, Peggy was able to get word to Arnold that the British had agreed to his offer. Now both Arnold and the British were on the same page.[65]

When Arnold notified the British that he had command of West Point, he was premature. Washington first wanted Arnold to command the left wing of the Continental Army. This was a clear indication that Washington continued to have great confidence in Arnold's military skills, bravery, and loyalty. When Arnold turned down the offer, complaining that his war injury no longer made him fit for a combat command, Washington believed Arnold's spirit has been worn down by both his physical injury and the stress of his public battles over his reputation. It was not until the start of August that Washington agreed to give him command of West Point, and he increased Arnold's command authority to include all American forces from Albany to the British defensive lines outside New York City.[66]

On his way to take command of West Point, Arnold stopped at the home of Squire Joshua Hett Smith, an individual who managed to make both sides believe he supported them and ran an intelligence network of equal opportunity, depending upon payment.[67] He was in charge of the American agents reporting in the area. Arnold found Smith pleased to ingratiate himself with the new area commander, and Arnold saw Smith as someone who might be helpful in his future dealing with the British.

In August and September, Arnold carefully did as much as he could to weaken the defensive capabilities of the West Point defenses by moving men about, allowing units to be transferred for other duties, ignoring maintenance issues, and playing fast and loose with his provisions. He openly sold portions of the troops' provisions to private merchants for personal profit, explaining to an aide that he did so to compensate himself for expenses not reimbursed to him by the Congress.[68] He also questioned his local commanders regarding their intelligence networks and agents but was only partially successful in obtaining this information.[69] Arnold saw such information as personally useful, because he could inform the British of the identities of American agents as André had requested in his initial requirements and he could ensure that none of these agents were in a position to learn of his secret dealings with British intelligence.

With knowledge of British acceptance of his terms, Arnold became reckless. He attempted to send a letter to André, using André's commercial alias of "John Anderson," under the guise of a commercial correspondence, the text of which would indicate to André that he and Arnold were in agreement. For the courier, Arnold chose William Heron, a civilian who wished to conduct some personal business in New York. Heron was an associate of Gen. Samuel Parsons, who commanded elements of the Connecticut Line of the Continental Army in the West Point area. While Heron accepted the letter, as he needed Arnold's signature on his pass to get through American lines, he did not deliver it to any British official. Instead, he brought it to Parsons. Unknown to Arnold, Heron was a double agent, working for both the British and the Americans when it profited him. Parsons, perhaps not the brightest of the American commanders, did not view the letter as suspicious.[70]

On September 3, Arnold wrote another letter to "John Anderson," in encrypted form, and had a wife visiting her British prisoner-of-war husband carry it to British lines. In it he made clear his agreement to work for the British and that he wished to meet André at the American outpost at South Salem, the headquarters of Col. Elisha Sheldon. In an attempt to develop a cover-for-action story that would explain his meeting with André, Arnold had his aide prepare this coded letter under the guise that it was part of a plan to establish an American collection capability in New York City. The letter was addressed to Odell's alias, James Osborne.

Days earlier, Arnold had written Sheldon to tell him to expect a visit from an American agent coming through British lines. Arnold wanted André to meet him in civilian clothes to make the meeting seem more innocent. So when Sheldon received a letter from John Anderson on September 8, he assumed it came from the civilian agent previously mentioned by Arnold. Arnold then confirmed to Sheldon that Anderson was the agent. He further instructed Sheldon to protect the agent upon his arrival until Arnold could meet with him. He also stated that Sheldon could tell his superior, Parsons, of the planned meeting.[71]

However, as so often happens in even the best-planned intelligence operations, outside events managed to cause the meeting to be aborted. British patrol boats, seeing the American boat carrying Arnold, opened fire on it—after all, there was a war going on. André had not, either because of oversight or because he wished to keep the planned meeting as secret as possible, advised the Hudson River naval authorities to expect and ignore American boat traffic in that area on that date.[72] The September 11 meeting therefore did not take place, and Arnold had to set in process a hasty alternative meeting plan that would eventually lead to André's capture and Arnold's hurried desertion to the British.

On September 15, Arnold sent another message to André that explained why he had not appeared on the 11th and suggested a new date to meet, the 20th of September.[73] Earlier that day, Arnold received word from Washington that he would be in the area on his way to meet with French commanders to plan joint operations. Arnold said in his letter that Washington would be at King's Ferry next Sunday evening. This information would have allowed the British to capture Washington and many of his key staff officers if they could move quickly.[74]

In light of the professional and personal support Washington had extended to Arnold for several years, his eagerness to turn Washington over to the British is yet another indication of his personal ethics, or rather the lack thereof, and the degree of his commitment now to the British cause. Had Washington been captured by the British, how he would be treated was far from clear. Would he be considered a prisoner of war because of his military stature or a traitor to Britain? If the former, his treatment would not be too harsh, but if the political situation in Britain cast him as one of the leading traitors, then death would probably have been the result. Throughout the history of intelligence, the ego-driven spy has not turned out to be a very loyal friend to anyone except himself or herself.

At the meeting with Washington, Arnold provided a misleading briefing on the West Point fortifications and garrison, avoiding information on their actual weaknesses. He sent a more accurate and complete report earlier that day to André.[75] The next day, Arnold received a letter from a Tory officer asking for a meeting under a flag of truce. In this letter was a reference to Odell's alias so that Arnold would understand the true reason for the meeting. He had his aide prepare a response but included a private letter to André before the packet was sealed. The meeting on September 20 was confirmed.[76] However, once again the war got in the way. André traveled from New York City up the Hudson on the HMS *Vulture*, a British sloop of war. American troops near the meeting point took the opportunity to fire at the ship, causing it to anchor farther down the river, and the meeting did not take place.

Arnold then decided to use Squire Smith as his unwitting agent by sending him to the ship with a pass for John Anderson, the supposed American civilian agent, who just happened to be on a British naval vessel in the uniform of a British officer.[77] Finally, on September 21, Arnold and André met, and Arnold gave him six documents describing the West Point fortifications for planning a British attack.[78] There is no record of what was discussed at this meeting. After Arnold's defection, in an October 8 letter to Clinton, he only saw fit to state what financial compensation André had agreed to at the meeting.[79] But before André could return to the *Vulture*, a local American commander, concerned about Tory forces in the area and fearing the ship was supporting their efforts, ordered American artillery moved to the riverbank to drive off the ship. The ship had to move downstream, leaving André stranded.[80]

André's only remaining option was to travel by land, first through American lines with a pass from Arnold, then through the infamous neutral ground, and then into British lines.[81] The neutral ground was a dangerous and lawless place where irregular forces of both sides operated to settle personal and business scores and to rob and kill for their own purposes under the guise of the war. The supposed Tories were called "cowboys," and the Americans were known as "skinners." In addition to the pass, Arnold had Smith function as André's guide and travel companion. He also suggested that André hide the documents he had provided in his boots.[82] Arnold then returned to his headquarters to await the British assault.

Smith advised André that Arnold thought it best for him to travel in a civilian disguise, so André removed his officer's coat and put on an old coat of Smith's.[83] At this point, André had ignored Clinton's orders regarding how he was to operate during his mission: He had not stayed in neutral territory and was not in the uniform of a British officer.[84] Clinton had set these rules to protect André from being considered a spy in the event he was captured. André, perhaps caught up in the excitement of the intelligence operation, sealed his fate by not thinking through the consequences of ignoring Clinton's instructions.

A depiction of Benedict Arnold convincing Maj. John André to hide plans of the West Point defenses in his boots. This tradecraft mistake cost André his life. *Library of Congress*

This is not an uncommon behavioral characteristic, especially among inexperienced field intelligence officers. The sheer excitement of an important operation can overcome the rational concerns and operational discipline required for a professionally conducted activity.

Smith and André rode through American lines on September 22 with little difficulty. On the morning of the 23rd, Smith informed André that he was only a couple of miles from British lines and sent him on alone into the neutral ground. Actually, André was almost fifteen miles from the nearest British outposts.[85] Later that day, Arnold received a dispatch from Colonel John Jameson at North Castle stating that a John Anderson had been arrested with documents describing the fortifications at West Point. Jameson stated that he had forwarded the captured documents to Washington but had sent Anderson to Arnold. But Anderson had not come with the messenger.

The plot had fallen apart, and Arnold had to move quickly to save himself. Within the hour he also received word that Washington and his party would soon arrive for a brief visit. Arnold told his wife to burn his papers and stall for time while he got his horse and informed his aides that he was riding to West Point and would return within the hour. Instead, he rode to his boat and at pistol point forced his crew to row him downriver to the *Vulture*.[86]

Prior to going to Arnold's headquarters, Washington conducted his own inspection of the West Point fortifications and was shocked at the disarray and deterioration of the defensive lines.[87] As Washington arrived at the headquarters, the messenger with André's documents caught up with him, and he immediately recognized that Arnold had been cooperating with the British. Washington sent several of his aides to try to capture Arnold. Then, according to one researcher, Washington briefly broke down in tears as he absorbed the full impact of Arnold's treachery.[88] But he quickly recovered and began to deal with a hysterical Peggy, who wished Washington to believe that she was innocent of the conspiracy.[89] Two days later, from the *Vulture*, Arnold sent a letter to Washington attempting to explain his actions. In it Arnold claimed he had always acted out of love of country and also managed, once again, to note the ingratitude he had received from "my country."[90]

It is quite common among ego-driven spies to contend that their actions were really meant to assist their country. But their further explanations of their actions seldom logically support that claim.

Arnold did make a point of stating that his aides and Smith were unaware of his actions and thus innocent of involvement in them.[91] Some may view that statement as an honorable gesture, but a more plausible explanation may well be that protecting Smith was in Arnold's interest. He had no intention of ending his active role with the British against the Americans, and Smith could be of future use. Washington believed Arnold's aides were innocent but did have Smith arrested. When cleared of being a part of the conspiracy, Smith fled to New York City, then to Britain. He returned to America after the war and, having lost most of his wealth, died in obscurity in New York in 1818.[92]

As to the fate of poor André, on the morning of the 23rd (after Smith's departure), he was captured by a group of skinners just inside the neutral ground. After André mistook them for Tories and identified himself as a British officer, they searched him for valuables and found the documents concerning West Point. While André attempted to bribe them handsomely to turn him over to British authorities, they decided a safer action would be to get a reward from the local American commander.[93] They took him to the militia command post at North Castle, where Colonel Jameson then dispatched him to Arnold's headquarters. Had André made it to Arnold's protection, there would have been some chance that the plot might still have been saved.

However, just at the right time in history a bright and experienced intelligence officer entered into the action. Maj. Benjamin Tallmadge arrived at the post and learned of the recent capture of John Anderson. Ten days earlier, Arnold had written to Tallmadge identifying Anderson as an agent and requested protection for him.[94] However, when Tallmadge learned Anderson had been carrying plans of the West Point defenses, his counterintelligence instincts were aroused. He convinced Jameson to send a rider to retrieve Anderson and have him sent to South Salem, far enough inland to preclude any British attempt to rescue him.[95]

Washington quickly ordered a court-martial for André, headed by Gen. Nathanael Greene, at Orangetown, New Jersey. On September 29, André was found guilty of being a spy and condemned to death. Clinton had learned of André's capture three days before and began efforts to have him exchanged as a military officer. André claimed in his defense that Arnold had forced him to wear a disguise and carry the documents. He explained he was a British officer acting as such when captured. Alexander Hamilton, then a member of Washington's staff, secretly communicated with Clinton on September 30 in a letter using disguised handwriting. The letter indicated that André could be exchanged but only for Arnold. There is no documented proof that Washington was aware of this offer or that he approved of it, although his desire to get his hands on Arnold was obvious.[96]

Of course, trading Arnold for André was something that Clinton, regardless of his personal and professional feelings, could not do. Turning a spy who has sought protection based upon his intelligence activities back over to his country's authorities is against one of the most basic rules in the intelligence profession because of its obvious impact on motivating anyone else to cooperate with your side.

André was hanged on October 2, 1780. Soon thereafter, the British government honored his services by providing funds and other rewards to his family members. The king had a monument erected in his honor in Westminster Abbey.[97] There is also a report that after the war, when Arnold and Peggy were living in London, they happened upon the monument while visiting the church.[98]

With André's death ended the most promising British intelligence operation of the war. It is doubtful that the loss of West Point would have ended American armed resistance, and the British would still have had to continue to conduct military operations against American forces with forces far inadequate to the task. Yet West Point's loss could well have forced a peace agreement more favorable to Britain than eventually resulted.

Why did it fail? The key reasons were André's poor judgment and his lack of basic intelligence professionalism. Blame also rested with Clinton, who had overall responsibility for the operation. André was only twenty-nine years old at his death and had been involved in intelligence only a short time. And his involvement had been primarily as a staff officer and operations manager, not a field operative. At the start of the operation, when Arnold volunteered, André was slow to test and validate Arnold's identity and his capabilities. Had he used the well-established British network functioning in Philadelphia for comprehensive communications with Arnold, he could have developed a better understanding of Arnold's motivations and thus how to use him most effectively. Instead, Arnold's ego was not given the attention he wanted. Had André been more experienced, he would have attempted to work out a plan with Arnold for his long-term penetration of the American command, with a subtle plan permitting the capture of West Point without the need for his defection to the British and thus the loss of his access. Arnold's motivation was ego and compensation, both of which could easily have been used to manipulate him effectively by a more experienced case officer.

Instead, André and Clinton failed to demonstrate any urgency in an operation that they both recognized had strategic potential for the British cause. By the time Arnold felt he had the agreement he wanted with the British, he was running the operation on his own terms. He used ad hoc couriers, created cover stories without the knowledge of the British, and set the meeting sites and conditions. André found himself in the role of complying with his own agent's instructions. That is not how to run an intelligence operation. When the agent runs the operation, his or her objectives set the priorities, and all too often these priorities have little to do with conducting a sound and secure intelligence operation. It is the intelligence officer who must have control over both the actions of the agent and the planning of the overall conduct of the operation. André had neither. But his previous association with Peggy had gotten him involved at the start, and his personal relationship with Clinton had kept him involved.

André simply was the wrong man to handle the job, although others were readily available who probably could have pulled it off successfully. William Franklin and Robert Rogers immediately come to mind, and several other experienced Tories operating networks were also available. However, as can be the case in all social and professional structures, personal relations trumped experience and competence, and a potential strategic intelligence success became a failure.

After his defection, Arnold found that personal and professional politics were as prevalent in the well-established British military structure as in the newly developing American one. While officially treated with some respect, on a personal and social basis the results were mixed and in many cases downright hostile. His arrogance and aggressiveness were immediately evidenced in his military activities for the British. He led an independent command and performed both bravely and brutally. After the war he moved to England, then to Canada, and then back to England. His commercial ventures never quite succeeded, and he continued to feel undervalued and unappreciated by his British benefactors.[99]

Arnold learned that individuals viewed as traitors or defectors are seldom really welcomed by their new friends once their usefulness is over. The intelligence officers who recruit and run these agents do so out of some sense of patriotic and professional loyalty to their country and service. Thus the perceived motivation of the agent or defector plays a role in how well he or she is accepted. The individual seen as working for moral or ethical reasons is often better received than those seen as motivated purely by ego or financial gain. Because Arnold's motivation was obvious—and his behavior in the service of the British only reinforced this—it is not surprising that like many others who have defected since, he never found satisfaction in his decision to sell out his friends and country.

CHAPTER 9

AMERICAN INTELLIGENCE ACTIVITIES REACH MATURITY

[margin note: - central location, bay facilitates transport]

The New York City area was an excellent location for the primary British base of operations in the American colonies. Its port offered facilities for the Royal Navy, which could ensure resupply of both men and equipment from Canada and Great Britain for the British army. Also, the navy could use the port as a base to patrol the American coastal areas. This gave the British military superior lines of communication for the deployment of troops, logistics, and command-and-control functions.

Washington, however, had to deal with troop movements and logistics on interior land roads, most in poor shape and vulnerable to weather conditions, making their use difficult and slow. To manage this weakness in his military capabilities, Washington needed timely intelligence on British plans and intentions so that he could anticipate rather than react to their actions. To accomplish this, he needed a comprehensive intelligence reporting network around New York. *[margin note: had to make up for poor roads w/ speedy intelligence]*

[margin note: Even balance?] As a commercial center in its own right, New York City had its share of citizens loyal to the king, as well as local farmers willing to sell their products for British currency. However, a significant population of the area was committed to independence. The city, like Boston, had been a hotbed of anti-British political activities with a large and active Sons of Liberty chapter. Some of these patriots living under British military occupation were willing and able to provide the American army with intelligence, often quite timely and accurate in detail, on British actions, plans, and intentions.

As Washington settled into winter quarters in January 1777, he planned
how to structure his intelligence operations against the British in New York
City. About that time, Nathaniel Sackett, a previously mentioned senior counterintelligence officer working with John Jay on the New York State Committee and Commission for Detecting and Defeating Conspiracies, was
recommended to Washington as someone who might help him. On February
3, Sackett met with Washington at his Morristown headquarters to discuss
intelligence operations in the New York area. The next day, Washington agreed
to pay Sackett $50 a month and provide $500 as operational expenses for his
collection activities.[1]

By March, Sackett was sending agents into the city under various commercial guises such as involvement in the poultry business. While there are few
documents describing Sackett's intelligence accomplishments, one of his operations is known in some detail. In late March 1777, he sent a woman married
to a known Tory into the city. Her cover for action was to complain to British
authorities regarding the American forces' seizure of her personal property. Her
story was true and readily verifiable. Her mission was to provide observational
reporting on British activities in the city, and she was able to report that they
were constructing flat-bottom boats to be used in a campaign against Philadelphia. She reported back to Sackett in early April.

On April 7, Sackett wrote to Washington providing her details of British preparations to attack Philadelphia. Washington reacted immediately. On
April 10, he sent Gen. Thomas Mifflin to Philadelphia to begin establishing a
stay-behind intelligence capability in anticipation of the British taking control
of the city.[2] However, Sackett's intelligence efforts ended shortly thereafter, and
he was paid $500 to close out his services. The reasons for Sackett's termina-
tion are not clearly documented, but comments in Washington's letter to him
of April 8 seem to indicate that issues of the overall accuracy and timeliness of
his reporting were involved.[3]

Many other sources run by local Continental Army commanders, as well
as by militia officers from New York, New Jersey, and Connecticut, were also
reporting tactical observations on British activities in the New York area. Some
of their most valuable agents were functioning as double agents. Washington
used them, as he did throughout the war, both for intelligence on British activities and to pass along disinformation, or sometimes true information, to manipulate British planning. Particularly valuable were those double agents used
by the British as couriers between New York City and other British-controlled
areas. Washington achieved a significant advantage by having the ability to

read British communications without their knowledge, but he was careful in his use of these valuable agents. He only used them as disinformation channels when the strategic situation justified the risk of exposing them should the British learn of their duplicity. *double agent*

One such individual, Elijah Hunter, was a prolific source of Clinton's plans and intentions because he was a trusted courier carrying such information to senior British commanders in Canada. By the summer of 1779, Hunter, working for New York's royal governor William Tryon, was not only acting as a courier but also charged with reporting intelligence on American military activities he observed during his travels. During this period, the British seized several fortified points on the Hudson River, including Stony Point, and seemed to be threatening West Point, the most strategic American position on the river. Washington arranged for Hunter to report to Clinton a mixture of true and false information regarding the Continental Army's strength. His objective was to keep Clinton from making more aggressive moves up the Hudson Valley. To give Hunter's reporting some accuracy, Washington had Hunter report the exact locations of the American army's four major supply facilities outside the city.[4] This intelligence could be validated by the British through their own intelligence reporting, but the facilities were located in areas where the British were unable to seize them. This was a classic example of "feed material" being provided to double agents to enhance their reporting credentials while doing no harm to the controlling entity. *"build-up", not really important*

It is worth noting another American intelligence collector who operated from inside the city, because of the unusual circumstances involving his activities. Continental Army lieutenant Lewis J. Costigin was sent by Washington in January 1777 to report on British activities in the area of New Brunswick, New Jersey, after the Battle of Trenton. He had been a merchant in New Brunswick and thus knew both the area and whom he could trust. He was captured by the British, apparently in uniform, or enough thereof to claim to be a soldier, and was processed as a prisoner of war and sent to New York City.[5] There, as an officer, Costigin was placed under parole, which gave him freedom to move about the city as long as he did not try to escape. *significant tactic*

He was formally exchanged for a British officer on September 18, 1778, but instead of returning to the army, he stayed in the city. Continuing to wear his uniform, he continued his daily walks about the city, speaking with various residents, including British officers and officials whom he had known for the past twenty months.[6] Now, however, he was legally and ethically free to assist the American cause by reporting what he learned. Why the British

— human error? *fortunate- allowed intelli*

authorities permitted him to remain has never been documented, but anyone who has dealt with a bureaucracy would understand that this kind of mistake happens. Most probably, he had become such a standard part of the scene in New York that his presence was simply considered the norm—a great cover for action.

Costigin spent some four months reporting from inside the city, using the mark "Z" to sign his reports, before he finally rejoined the army on January 17, 1779. Washington's papers contained three reports that can be sourced to Costigin, dated December 7, 16, and 19, 1778. These reports provided details of the movements and activities of senior British officers, British troop movements to the Florida region, details of military shipping, and information on British army food rations and supply issues.[7] Details of how he managed to send his reports outside the city are unclear, but it is documented that he spent his own funds on these intelligence activities. And after he submitted his accountings, he waited several years until the government reimbursed him.[8] Anyone who has ever filed a government expense report can relate to that.

While these singleton agents provided useful intelligence, Washington needed comprehensive and consistent reporting to compensate for his other military disadvantages. He began the planning for this network, to be known as the Culper Ring, in mid-1778. The name of the ring is believed to have been chosen by Washington based upon an area in Virginia where he had done surveying work early in his life—Culpeper, Virginia. He ordered Brig. Gen. Charles Scott to establish this network. However, when Scott left the service in November of that year, Washington turned to a junior officer, Maj. Benjamin Tallmadge, to act as the case officer for the ring. Tallmadge had been involved in the plan from its inception and met with Washington as early as August 25, for what was probably the first planning session for the ring.[9]

agency, not individuals needs consistency for accurate intel collection

There are indications that Tallmadge had earlier that month worked with Connecticut authorities to get Abraham Woodhull, who was in jail because of his trade with the British in New York City in agricultural products, released and subsequently recruited as the principal agent for the ring.[10] Tallmadge's cover for action to be in the area necessary to manage the ring and receive its reporting was his position as an officer in the Continental Army's Second Light Dragoons, stationed along the Connecticut shore across Long Island Sound from Long Island.

While Tallmadge functioned as the managing case officer for the ring, Washington was its senior intelligence officer, as well as its primary customer. Documents demonstrated Washington was personally involved in directing its activities and provided sound advice regarding its operations when he thought

Maj. Benjamin Tallmadge was one of Washington's senior intelligence officers and the case officer for the Culper Ring in New York City. *Library of Congress*

as an intelligence officer. He also provided some less professional advice when he wore his military hat as the primary customer.

One of his earliest messages to Tallmadge regarding the ring stressed the compartmentation required for the operational security of the network. On November 20, 1778, he wrote to Tallmadge: "You will be pleased to observe the strictest silence with respect to C——, as you are to be the only person intrusted with the knowledge or conveyance of his letters."[11] Washington recognized that it took time to develop a reporting network even if the need for intelligence was immediate. He gave Tallmadge and Woodhull the time necessary to spot, recruit, and vet ring personnel before he sought to strengthen the ring's internal structure by developing parallel reporting capabilities within its organization. Washington waited almost a year, until June 13, 1779, before agreeing to the recruitment of a second individual who could share with Woodhull some of the responsibilities of principal agent.[12] Having two individuals share these responsibilities was both a sound operational and personnel decision. Woodhull had become nervous over his frequent trips into and out of the city, and this frequent travel made him more visible to British authorities. Woodhull responded several days later that he had identified such a person, Robert Townsend.

Then, in early July 1779, Washington drafted a message of instruction to his principal agents. The letter provided clear guidance on their roles and the ring's prioritization of its collection targets. It ended with a strong admonition regarding the requirement for disciplined operational security. This letter of instruction gave the ring its general organizational plan for operating but was not so specific as to take away the initiative that field operators must have to handle daily realities of collection network activities.[13] The letter once again demonstrated that Washington had a solid understanding of his role as the senior intelligence officer.

Another example of his sound guidance involved a recommendation made by Woodhull regarding Townsend's commercial activities in the city. Woodhull advised that he wanted Townsend to stop spending his time on his commercial activities in order to have more time for his ring responsibilities. Washington, writing to Tallmadge on September 24, 1779, made it clear that he did not agree. Writing from the perspective of an intelligence officer who understood the requirement for an agent to have both cover for status and cover for action, Washington explained that Townsend's business activities provided "greater security to himself and greater advantage to us, under cover of his usual business, than if he were to dedicate himself wholly to the giving of information."[14] This, of course, proved to be true. While the cover duties did take some time away from his ring activities, in reality much of this time overlapped with his development of sources, elicitation from contacts, and observational collection about the city. Most important, it provided a logical reason for his activities.

Unfortunately, there were also times when the pressures of Washington's military role caused him to forget or ignore his intelligence experience and demand efforts by the ring that could harm its security. For example, in February 1780, he made it clear that while the intelligence being produced was valuable, he wanted to receive it on a more timely basis. Townsend, wishing to follow orders, decided to use a young cousin as a courier to speed up the delivery time. Described later in this chapter, that ended up as a comedy of errors but could easily have been a disaster for the entire ring.

Washington felt a similar frustration a few months later and wrote a May 19 letter to Tallmadge stating that in view of the ring reporting taking so long to get to him, its value was so little that it should be shut down.[15] Woodhull took this criticism personally, and as Townsend had just stated his intent to reduce his efforts for the network, Tallmadge was faced with the real possibility of the ring's demise. However, by midsummer Washington was expecting the arrival of a French fleet and badly needed to know British reactions to its arrival. He ordered Tallmadge to get the network active again.[16] And by late August, it was. This type of pressure from intelligence customers, and the impact it can have on case officers attempting to keep their agents productive and happy, has always created a strain in intelligence organizations.

The Culper Ring was the best-documented intelligence collection network run by the American side during the Revolutionary War. Records of its activities, often identifying members by a code number, a code name, initials, or infrequently a true name, can be found in the papers of several army officers involved in managing the network's activities.[17] These records provide detailed descriptions of the ring's methodology, collection access, support mechanisms, successes in collection, and insights into the management and personality issues of running the collection network.

While Tallmadge, using the alias of "John Bolton" in his correspondence with the network,[18] was the case officer for the ring, two principal agents conducted its clandestine activities. The first, Woodhull, using the alias "Samuel Culper Sr.," had by late November demonstrated reporting capabilities across a wide geographical area of New York City and its environs, including Long Island. In a report sent to Washington on November 23, Woodhull provided details of British defenses around Long Island and stated that the British had intercepted coded dispatches bound for France from French admiral Charles Hector, comte d'Estaing.[19] Woodhull's previous commercial activities with the British in New York City provided cover for action for his movements about the area.

On February 26, 1779, he sent a lengthy report describing British troop dispositions in the city and on Long Island, information on new troop reinforcements, news of British naval movements, and observations on the future plans and intentions of General Clinton.[20] In the early months of the year, he also recruited other members into the ring.

However, in early June, Woodhull narrowly missed being captured by the Queen's Rangers, a Tory unit, after having been denounced by a Tory prisoner of war who had just returned from prison in Connecticut.[21] The rangers raided his home in Setauket, Long Island, and physically abused his father. Luckily for Woodhull, he was able to travel to New York City and hide there until the raid was over. But the incident caused him to seriously consider the personal risks involved in his intelligence activities. It was at this time that Woodhull advised Tallmadge that he had recruited another trusted individual to assist him because the British were now suspicious of him.[22] When he agreed to a second principal agent, Washington also made it clear that he did not wish to know the person's true identity or that of others involved in the ring's activities. From the end of June 1779 onward, Tallmadge would be directing two principle agents: Woodhull and Townsend, who would use the alias "Samuel Culper Jr.," the fictitious son of Culper Sr.[23]

Townsend was from the Oyster Bay area of Long Island and may have been involved with the Sons of Liberty back in the early 1770s. However, he was a Quaker and considered to be neutral in the political struggle and thus willing and able to trade with the British. By June 1779, he was involved in a business in New York City selling dry goods and groceries in a partnership with Henry Oakman. The company of Oakman & Townsend was a supplier to both British military and civilian authorities. His business provided opportunities for both source identification and cultivation and social elicitation of intelligence from his various contacts. He even joined a Tory militia group in 1780 to further publicly demonstrate his pro-British loyalties. He was also a silent partner in a coffee shop with the well-known Tory journalist James Rivington, the editor of the anti-American newspaper the *Royal Gazette*. At some point in their relationship, Townsend apparently even recruited Rivington as a reporting source.[24] There has been speculation that Townsend, to additionally build his cover as pro-British, wrote articles for the newspaper. The coffee shop, however, was frequented by senior British officers and provided a casual social setting perfect for elicitation of intelligence on British activities. As his father continued to live in Oyster Bay, family business gave him the perfect excuse for frequent travel out of the city to courier reports for Tallmadge and onward to Washington.[25]

Both Woodhull and Townsend engaged in their dangerous activities out of

James Rivington, a well-known Tory newspaper publisher in New York City, became an American spy as part of the Culper Ring. *Library of Congress*

a sincere belief in the cause of American independence. However, Townsend was somewhat more pragmatic in his view of the business aspect of his activities. He fully expected to be reimbursed on a timely basis for his expenses and was often disappointed. Woodhull, however, was more idealistic and understanding about delays in repayment.[26]

The tradecraft used by the ring was quite professional, but its organizational composition was incestuous, as many of its members were interrelated by family or marriage. Many of the ring's members had support duties in addition to collection responsibilities. Some functioned as couriers, carrying the reporting out of the city or across the Long Island Sound to Tallmadge. Others provided safe houses for agents where family relations could be used to explain the continuing personal contacts with others traveling into and out of the city. Several agents owned businesses in the city with contracts with the British army or that provided services desired by British officers. These venues offered opportunities for social development of relationships with the British authorities and created an exploitable environment for elicitation of their future plans and intentions. The commercial dealings themselves were equally valuable in identifying future British movements based upon the types of orders placed for provisions and equipment, reasons provided for particular delivery dates, and casual details provided regarding the purposes of the orders.[27]

Communications is always the weakest security link in the intelligence collection and reporting process—it connects the clandestine collector to the much more readily identifiable intelligence officer managing the activity. And for the Culper Ring to get its reporting from the collectors to Tallmadge on the Connecticut shore was often the most dangerous, and time-consuming, task of the network. British forces conducted security checkpoints at their outer defensive lines, and Tory sympathizers and militia units patrolled the neutral ground between British- and American-controlled areas. While the couriers usually had legitimate reasons for their travel between lines, the messages they carried could easily expose them if read in their true context. And although various hiding places on the person of the courier or in his personal or business goods could be fashioned, the information itself had to be protected from exposure even if the messenger was captured.

Intelligence reporting by human sources, regardless of how written, must by its very nature tell a great deal about where it came from and thus who could have collected it. For example, the numerical size of a British unit would only be known by certain individuals from that unit or others higher in the command structure. Thus a counterintelligence effort attempting to identify how the enemy knew such information could focus on those people and those with whom they gossip about such details. In a report involving numerous British units' strength, individuals with such collective knowledge became even fewer and thus easier to investigate. The same issue exists in observational reporting of fortifications or unit activities. Individuals with access to such information—those just passing through the area or those with regular business in the area—would be under suspicion. And if the reporting addressed more than one area or unit, cross-referencing of individuals with access to both areas and units would hasten the process of identifying the probable source of the reporting.

The records of the ring indicate that the cover stories utilized by the couriers carrying the written reports were usually adequate to avoid extensive searches by British forces. Less official units, both Tory and bandits operating in the neutral ground between the opposing armies, often cared more about the valuables being carried than the purpose of the trips. In these cases, the concealment of the reports had to be carefully thought out. Carrying the reporting inside one's apparel, as did Nathan Hale and Major André, offered scant protection from a search seeking any item of potential value. In a letter in early October 1779, Woodhull reported to Tallmadge that he had been stopped outside British lines by a group of men. There he was forced to submit to a complete search. However, he had hidden the reporting he was carrying in a concealed portion of his horse's saddle, and it was not discovered.[28]

Tallmadge, well aware of the counterintelligence threat posed by the ring's communication system, established several methods to hide the text and content of the intelligence reports as they traveled from the collectors to him. He issued both principal agents a chemical liquid writing substance then referred to as "stain." This invisible ink would dry into the paper and remain hidden until a separate chemical substance was used to develop it back into readable text.[29] Several types of liquids were used by both sides for this purpose during the war, with Washington's favorite type invented by Sir James Jay, the brother of John Jay.[30] It was always in short supply, and at one point Woodhull managed to spill his entire supply accidentally. In a letter from Tallmadge to Washington dated April 21, 1779, Tallmadge explained that Woodhull was writing his report in his room in the city when suddenly two individuals burst through the door. Knowing that British officers were also quartered in the building, in his haste to hide his writings he spilled his vial of stain. As it turned out, the intruders were only two young women attempting to play a trick on him.[31] But the damage was done, and his supply of the liquid gone. There are also documented incidents of ring reporting lost because of smearing of the ink or other mistakes in its use and its developing.

In addition to hiding the text, Tallmadge also had the ring use several forms of encoding in their reporting. One was a series of numbers to represent individuals, locations, and common terms in order to disguise the specific meaning of the reporting content. For example, each of the members of the ring was identified by a specific three-number code, as were places such as New York City and Long Island.[32] However, the unencoded portions of the text would often make the true meaning of the message quite easy. Thus it depended upon the discipline of the writer not to allow the open text to provide any references that could be used to identify the encoded words.

To further enhance communication security in the summer of 1779, Tallmadge began to use a much more secure type of code—a book code. Tallmadge used a popular dictionary of the time as his key, *Entick's Dictionary*. While this was a much more secure code than the number-substitution method, it also involved more time to compose and to decode. This was probably the reason that it was seldom actually used in ring correspondence.

Tallmadge also addressed the issue of how to disguise the invisible writing, with some very specific suggestions on the subject from Washington.[33] The approach used was based upon common sense, as is true of most tradecraft, in that placing something in the open is much less suspicious than attempting to hide it. So, rather than have a piece of paper with nothing on it stuck in a coat lining, Tallmadge instructed the ring to have the reporting written on material that could readily be explained if questioned by the British. The ring used blank pages and margin spaces in pamphlets and books, spaces between lines in social or business correspondence, and in several cases inserted pages of reporting into larger packages of blank paper being transported for sale or business use. However, regardless of how well the reporting was disguised, the couriers still had to have the skill and courage to carry it through British lines in the face of often harsh questioning. The travel alone was usually dangerous, and the ring was fortunate to have well-motivated and dedicated individuals willing to take these risks.

Long Island Sound was part of the neutral ground that surrounded much of the British-controlled portions of the New York City and Long Island areas. British naval craft, Tory militia boat crews, and plunder-motivated privateers clashed daily with New York and Connecticut State Navy boats, local militia units, and Continental Army boat crews. Arguably the movement of the reporting across this waterway was the most physically dangerous part of the communication's path. The group responsible for the task of transporting the ring's reporting across the sound was Continental Army lieutenant Caleb Brewster's boat unit. He picked up the reporting on the Long Island shore and took it to Fairfield, Connecticut, where Tallmadge's dragoons carried it to him and then onward to Washington. Brewster was a very aggressive and motivated individual, constantly seeking action with the enemy. Prior to the establishment of the Culper Ring, he had volunteered to Washington to provide intelligence of British naval movements on the sound. But with the start of the ring's reporting, his primary mission became to transport its reports. That said, he always found a way to use his small fleet of whaleboats offensively against the British and their Tory counterparts. Under orders from Tallmadge, he began his sound courier duties in November 1778.[34]

By early the next year, Brewster had also established his own small group of sources reporting on British and Tory activities in the sound to protect his own unit's activities. His boat unit could not be considered clandestine as its existence was well known to the British, but until late 1781, when British spies reported on his courier activities, Brewster was able to hide the fact that his primary responsibility was transporting intelligence from New York City.[35] He usually relied upon his knowledge of the sound's navigational conditions and his crew's sailing and fighting abilities to safeguard the reports. However, there is evidence that the reporting was placed in a weighted glass bottle that, being tied to the boat, could be let loose and sunk if danger indicated it might be captured by the enemy.

While he engaged in several battles with the enemy during the time he was supporting the Culper Ring, only once did he engage in a fight that involved a courier mission. He reported to Tallmadge on August 18, 1780, that while he waited for Woodhull to arrive with reporting, he was attacked by pro-British boatmen and had to kill two of them.[36] While Brewster's boats were manned with numerous crews, only two of his men can be identified, Joshua Davis[37] and Jonathan Pinner.[38] Davis often acted as Brewster's deputy in command, but little else is known about either of them.

As noted earlier, the danger to the ring of Woodhull acting as the only courier between the city and Brewster quickly became apparent. Initially, he used both his agricultural business with the city and his relatives residing there to justify his frequent travel.[39] However, even with these plausible cover stories, his frequent travel did invite British suspicion.

Around mid-December 1778, Tallmadge recruited another Setauket resident, Jonas Hawkins, to act as a courier between Woodhull and Brewster. Hawkins had grown up in the town and was well known to Brewster and Woodhull, as well as Tallmadge, who vouched for his loyalty to Washington. Hawkins traveled to the city, discreetly met Woodhull and eventually Townsend as his role in reporting grew, received the consolidated reporting, and then traveled back to Setauket. There he passed the reports to Brewster. However, Hawkins was also quite concerned about his own security, and as the British enforced stricter questioning and searches of travelers entering and leaving the city, he became less willing to assist the ring. For a brief period he and another courier, Austin Roe, shared the duties.[40] But by September 1779, Hawkins stopped working with the ring out of concern for his safety.[41]

Roe began assisting the ring in early 1779, and his courier activities overlapped with those of both Hawkins and Woodhull for several months. The use of three individuals was a significant security enhancement, as cover stories for travel into and out of the city could be better documented when less frequent. Roe was another Setauket resident and operated a tavern located close to Woodhull's property. His loyalty to the patriot cause was vouched for by the other Setauket members of the ring, and he was a frequent courier from about April 1779 until June 1781.[42] In an arrangement established before he joined the ring, Roe used portions of a meadow owned by Woodhull as a grazing site for his cattle. This enabled Roe to utilize a dead drop in the field for the reporting from the city. Roe, under the guise of attending to his cattle, left reports in a box hidden in the meadow's underbrush, and Woodhull, also under the guise of attending to his cattle grazing there, retrieved them sometime after Roe had left the area. While Roe performed his courier duties well, he and Woodhull had some type of personality conflict, which occasionally rose to the surface.[43] There are few details regarding the cause of Woodhull's dislike of Roe and no indication that it impacted on the ring's operations.

However, in human operations, in addition to the tradecraft and operational discipline and security issues, the case officer and the principal agent(s) must also ensure that personality conflicts do not create issues dangerous to the operation. In this case, Woodhull's dislike of Roe could have resulted in his refusal to report sensitive information through him or even prompted him to stop his collection activities, as he later did out of concern for his personal security. So, one can suspect that Tallmadge and Woodhull both had to take steps to see that this issue did not adversely affect the mission.

Another part of the ring's communication plan involved informing Brewster when to travel across the sound to pick up a report and where to land. A local Setauket housewife, Anna "Nancy" Strong, capably handled this role through a series of signals using her laundry drying line. From his base in Fairfield, with the assistance of a telescope, Brewster watched the laundry that Strong put up to dry. The prearranged signals were communicated through the items and number on the line. For example, when a report was ready to be picked up, a black petticoat was hung out. At the same time, the number of handkerchiefs also would indicate at which cove or inlet Brewster was to land to await the report.[44] While Tory reporting from Connecticut identified that a woman was involved in signaling Brewster regarding his travel to Long Island, the British never learned her identity.[45]

One other name is mentioned in the ring's communication activity but for only one mission, which, through a series of mistaken identities, required Washington's personal intervention to protect the individual and the report he was carrying. This individual was James Townsend, a young cousin of Robert's. As noted earlier, at one point Washington, while pleased with the ring's reporting, was critical of the time delay involved in getting the reports to his headquarters. When he was instructed to reduce this delay, Townsend's desire to please Washington came at the expense of good tradecraft. He decided to use his inexperienced, and apparently immature, young cousin James as a courier.

On March 22, 1780, James Townsend passed through British lines successfully but then encountered individuals he thought were Tories. He engaged them in conversation that indicated he was also of a pro-British loyalty. As it turned out, they were patriots and were now certain that they had captured a British spy attempting to enter American territory. (This was the same mistake made by Nathan Hale and Maj. John André.) James was searched, and his belongings were sent to Washington's headquarters. As was his practice, Robert Townsend had used stain to write his report, and Washington recognized the telltale characteristics of its use between the lines of a lengthy poem James had been carrying.

While Washington received that report sooner than by the normal city-to-Setauket-to-Fairfield-to-headquarters route, it was not without subsequent problems. He had to spend many hours arranging appropriate cover stories to get James released without compromising the ring's operations.[46]

In addition to various couriers, the ring also had support assets operating at least two safe houses in the city, both functioning as boarding houses. In both cases British soldiers were also billeted in the house, providing both an opportunity for collection activities and lending some measure of legitimacy to their operation. These sites were used for meetings with sources and as locations for preparation of intelligence reports. The better-documented safe house was run by Amos and Mary Underhill. At various times both Woodhull and Townsend resided there while in the city. Mary was Woodhull's sister, which provided him with a natural reason for staying there when in the city.[47] Townsend had business dealings with the Underhill family, which explained his presence. The second safe house was run by Jacob Seaman, who was married to a daughter of a Tory officer involved in counterintelligence activities in the city.[48] Townsend stayed there on occasion.

While several of the ring's collection agents have been identified, the two best known were Rivington and an Irish tailor named Hercules Mulligan. Rivington, as previously noted, was an English-born Tory publisher with long-standing pro-British ties. His *Royal Gazette* was highly popular with the British and Tory population in the city. (He first arrived in the American colonies in 1760, and ended up in New York City.) His public support for British government policies caused the New York Sons of Liberty to ransack and destroy his newspaper office, printing equipment, and residence in 1775, forcing him to flee back to England. He returned in 1777 with an appointment as the king's printer and published his *Gazette*. In addition to his newspaper and coffee shop enterprise, he ran a bookstore, which also was an excellent location to overhear information of value or to practice elicitation in a relaxed and comfortable social setting.

Ring documents did not provide many examples of intelligence that could be directly sourced from Rivington. In fact, when he made his greatest intelligence contribution in 1781, he provided the material to an American officer not connected to the ring.

Rivington's date of recruitment to the American cause is of significant importance because his access to senior British and Tory officials would have enabled him to provide Washington with timely and valuable intelligence. While opinions abound regarding when he did agree to work for the American cause, to date, no documentary evidence has been found to provide a clear answer. The private papers of George Washington Parke Custis, Martha Washington's grandson, discussed Rivington working for the patriots as early as 1776, yet he did not return to America until the next year. These papers also stated that he provided intelligence of significant value based upon his relationships with Sir William Howe and Sir Henry Clinton.[49] If it was true that he was reporting while Howe was still in America, this would mean he was a spy about a year before Townsend joined the ring. If this was true, then Washington's instructions regarding Townsend's public association with Rivington, as well as his clear instructions that Townsend not give up his commercial activities, would have to be considered in a different context. From an intelligence network perspective, in such a scenario Townsend's connection to Rivington was created to enhance an already existing well-placed reporting agent. But this can only be speculation as Washington, as usual, was very careful in not documenting sources and methods information in his official documents.[50]

Yet another possibility exists, based upon New York delegate Gouverneur Morris's advisement to the Continental Congress on October 24, 1778, that he had received a request from a New York City resident who could produce intelligence of value in return for living safely in the city after the British departed.[51] This volunteer could have been Rivington, but there is not adequate documentation to identify this volunteer.

Based upon available information it appears that Townsend was the individual who assessed Rivington's needs, developed the personal rapport required to engage him in a dangerous clandestine relationship, and recruited him into Washington's service. One writer with an intelligence background has noted that the partnership between Townsend and Rivington in the coffee shop might have also indicated the start of their intelligence relationship.[52] In any event, their partnership provided their association a natural cover for action. While the date of Rivington's recruitment is unknown, his motivation for cooperation seems quite obvious: money to support his lifestyle and a desire to continue to live in New York City after the British had departed. And like the good businessman he was, Rivington was faithful to his commitment.

The tailor Hercules Mulligan was able to function as an American spy in British-occupied New York City thanks to human error, either in record keeping or British counterintelligence sloppiness. His past activities as a member of the New York City Sons of Liberty and the Committee of Correspondence and Observation were well known in the city. Indeed, when the British first occupied New York City, Mulligan was briefly arrested because of his connection to these organizations.[53] He was the son of Irish immigrants and had arrived in America with his parents and brother Hugh at the age of six. He and Hugh built a profitable and socially respectable life in New York City.

As was true of the vast majority of Irishmen of that time, little love existed within his family for the British government. As a youth he embraced the cause of seeking freedom from the mother country. Also by chance, his passion for the American cause was well known personally by Alexander Hamilton, one of Washington's aides. Hamilton had boarded in the Mulligan household while a student at King's College (now Columbia University) years earlier.[54] Hamilton is believed to have suggested to Washington that Mulligan, by then a successful tailor with a clientele composed of British officers and Tory gentlemen, would be willing to engage in intelligence activities. There are several differences of opinion among researchers regarding when Mulligan began his reporting, but apparently it was between the spring of 1777 and the summer of 1779.[55]

Documentation indicates that Mulligan did work within the ring on occasion, but it also seems apparent that he ran his collection operations and reporting channels separate from the ring. In fact, in a letter from Tallmadge to Washington on May 8, 1780, Tallmadge noted that he did not know what Mulligan was doing and asked Washington for any information on the subject that might affect his intelligence activities.[56] Mulligan had the classic Irish gift of a smooth tongue and a glib personality, as well as the brains and cunning that are so often overlooked in the Irish, especially by the British. His most dangerous moment occurred after Benedict Arnold defected to the British. While seeking a position with the British military, Arnold accused Mulligan of being a spy for Washington and briefly had him placed under arrest. While Arnold had suspicions regarding Mulligan based upon what he had learned of American collection activities in the city while commanding West Point, he had no actual proof. And Mulligan was soon released.[57]

Mulligan's collection methods were observation and elicitation, based upon professional and social association with his clients. In addition to his business contacts, he had married a niece of a Royal Navy admiral, which gave him social access to senior British military circles. As a tailor to individuals of social, official, and military importance, Mulligan listened to his clients' gossip while he fitted clothes and showed fabric. He also was clever enough to make comments, further drawing out and filling in details of the gossip. His observational reporting was the result of his natural reason to travel about the city conducting his business. Also, subtle queries regarding dates and reasons for completion of clothing provided additional context for bits of information he collected. Finally, like many in the city, Mulligan had British officers quartered in his home and used this opportunity to socially elicit information useful to Washington.

His brother Hugh was also a valuable collector. Hugh was a senior partner in a well-respected import and export business, also involved in financing various enterprises. The firm, known as Kortwright & Company, had a great deal of business with the British military, as well as other wealthy and well-connected Tory merchants in the city. Hugh's access, his mobility within the city and in British military facilities, and his social and professional relationships produced information complementing that of Hercules.[58]

Little is known of the specifics of Hercules's reporting other than that two of his reports concerned British plans to capture Washington while he was traveling close to the city.[59] Documented comments and Washington's personal visit to Mulligan's shop and purchase of clothing from him clearly indicated he had been very productive and valuable to Washington. Apparently he did know Woodhull and may have used him as a courier to get his reports out of the city. It is known that he often used his African American servant Cato as a courier to get his reporting across British lines. Cato was successful for some time, and his status as an African American made him appear quite nonthreatening to British sentries. However, on one mission, which became his last, Cato did come under suspicion and was severely beaten in an attempt to get him to confess his true purpose in traveling to and from the city. Even after the savage beating, he did not compromise his mission and was thrown into jail. Mulligan was soon able to get him released through the influence of his powerful contacts, but Cato's usefulness as a courier was finished.[60]

Finally, before other issues regarding the ring are addressed, a few comments are necessary regarding another agent, who has been the subject of interest to several historians over the years. This individual is identified in a ring document only by Tallmadge's code number 355, which stands for "Lady." Within the vernacular of the time and the context of her residing in the New York City area, one could surmise that Lady, if a collector, was a female of a certain social class and that her access to British and Tory officials with intelligence of value was based upon her ability to socially interact with them. However, 335 is mentioned only once in ring correspondence, in a coded letter to Washington. Within the context of this message, it appears that 335 represents part of a plan for couriering reports from the city to Washington and in this case probably refers to Anna Strong.[61]

Yet a romantic myth does exist about 335 thanks to Morton Pennypacker, a New York historian who began researching and writing about the Culper Ring in the 1920s. Most of his research was well done and remains valid and valued to this day. However, in the late 1940s, he somehow developed a complex story about 335. Pennypacker believed she had a child with Robert Townsend (aka Samuel Culper Jr.), was exposed as a spy, arrested by the British, and subsequently died on a British prison ship in New York Harbor. The child, named Robert Townsend Jr., survived and even served a term in the New York state legislature. It was not until the mid-1990s that researchers discredited the story. The child who grew up to be Robert Townsend Jr. the politician was indeed the illegitimate child of Robert Townsend but from an affair with his housekeeper. The child was not born until after the war was over.[62] Quite possibly, between his intelligence activities and his personal security concerns, he was too busy during the war for an affair.

As is true in all intelligence operations, mistakes, accidents, human errors, and events unrelated to the operation popped up to pose potential counterintelligence problems and a great deal of personal stress for all those involved. This was certainly true of the Culper Ring. For example, periodic changes in the degree of attention paid to individuals passing through British lines constantly caused concern for both principal agents and the other couriers. And more direct counterintelligence issues also arose. For example, in July 1779, Tallmadge's unit was surprised by a British raiding party, and his baggage was captured. Included in his belongings was intelligence correspondence from Washington identifying George Higday in New York City as someone who could be of some service to the ring. The British quickly arrested Higday, and in a letter to Sir Henry Clinton he admitted meeting Washington and agreeing to assist but stated he never had the chance to do so.[63] Nothing further is known of his fate, but Clinton was quite a humane individual in his official dealings, and Higday probably got off lightly. Tallmadge received an appropriate reprimand from Washington and thereafter was much more careful in what information he retained in his belongings.

Perhaps the most worrisome counterintelligence threat to the ring was Arnold's defection to the British in September 1780. As West Point commander he had made efforts to learn the identities of American agents in the New York City area but was not very successful, thanks to the operational security discipline of Tallmadge and other military officers conducting operations there. However, Washington had shared some sensitive information with Arnold based upon his West Point assignment that caused Arnold to suspect the identities of some sources. Woodhull and Townsend did not know if they had been identified to Arnold and were greatly concerned for their well-being when Arnold arrived in the city. The only individual Arnold felt he could identify was Mulligan, and that seemed to be as an individual rather than as part of any collection network.

However, Tallmadge wrote to the principal agents to assure them that Arnold was not aware of their identities.[64] In a mid-October letter, Townsend responded that he was happy Arnold did not know his identity and also expressed regret at the death of Major André, whom he stated he had known socially.[65] The months of October and November saw little reporting from the ring because of concerns about the security situation in the city.

In December, some reporting was provided, but Townsend continued to have concerns for his safety and preferred to report only verbally to Woodhull. By June 1781, Woodhull had stopped reporting entirely because of concerns his new wife had for his own safety. It wasn't until April 1782 that he resumed his reporting, and within several weeks Woodhull was able to report that the

British were preparing for the end of armed conflict on both land and sea.[66] On August 2, Washington was officially informed of the British government's acceptance of American independence by Sir Guy Carleton, the new British military commander in chief. However, even with cession of armed hostilities, Washington instructed Tallmadge to continue to report on British activities in the city. The last report from Townsend was in mid-September 1782, and Woodhull's last communication, an accounting of his operational expenses, was dated July 5, 1783.[67] Working with Brewster, Tallmadge sent several individual agents into the city for observational reporting from the summer of 1781 through the end of the conflict to supplement the sparse reporting from the ring.[68] The days when the ring represented a valuable intelligence network to Washington had ended.

That the ring was a valuable source of intelligence for Washington cannot be debated. His appreciation of its information during the war was well documented, even though in a letter to Tallmadge on September 11, 1783, after the conflict ended, he did question whether the ring had been worth the funds expended on it.[69] To put his comment in perspective, Washington was by nature a rather frugal individual and as a gentleman of the times probably did not view spies, even his own, as being of the highest character. Also, intelligence agents, like infantrymen, are seldom as appreciated as much after the conflict as in the heat of it. In terms of intelligence funds actually expended, Washington's final accounting indicated that about one quarter of his total intelligence budget went to finance the ring's activities.

Three intelligence reports—one of a counterintelligence nature, one regarding British counterfeiting planning, and one regarding troop movements to Rhode Island—are indicative of the value of the ring's reporting to the American cause. The first, from Townsend and dated July 15, 1779, named Christopher Duychenik as a British agent then attempting to pass as a patriot.[70] Duychenik was identified as working for former New York royal governor William Tryon, at that time a major general in a Tory military unit involved in brutal raids along the Connecticut coastline. The report, to which Woodhull added some comments and details, provided some background on Duychenik and that he was reporting through David Mathews, the former Tory mayor of New York City.[71] What this report demonstrated was that the ring had access to internal information on the Tory intelligence system being run by William Franklin, the illegitimate son of Benjamin Franklin, and the former royal governor of New Jersey. Franklin's intelligence network among Tories and their sympathizers, in which Tryon was involved, worked closely with Clinton's military intelligence organization, first through Major André and then after his death through his replacement, Oliver DeLancey.[72]

Penetration of the enemy's intelligence organization is, for obvious reasons, one of the highest priorities of any intelligence service. That the ring accomplished this demonstrates the significant value of the reporting it could generate. Townsend was adamant that this intelligence be closely protected because its exposure would put him at risk. This indicated that the source was one of his recruited agents rather than one of Woodhull's. While the report's source is not known, a review of which of his agents had this type of access further demonstrated the degree to which the ring had access to secret and sensitive British information.

Rivington immediately comes to mind based upon his association with senior British and Tory leaders. However, the source could also have been Jacob Seaman. He had access through his wife to her father, the Tory intelligence officer. And Townsend himself could even have been the source based upon his association with Tory leaders in the city. Yet another possibility existed in the access of the merchant William T. Robinson, a wealthy and socially prominent figure within New York Tory circles. His reporting was passed along to the ring with the assistance of Joseph Lawrence of Bayside, Long Island, who was married to a member of the Townsend family.[73] Finally, another member of the Woodhull family and the ring, Nathan Woodhull, who may have been in contact with Townsend as well as Abraham Woodhull, was an officer in a Tory militia unit and could have had access to this information.[74]

The second report had to do with British attempts to lessen the value of Continental Congress monetary script by counterfeiting those notes and thus making it even more difficult for the Congress and army to obtain supplies. British efforts in this field were constant throughout the war. However, usually the print quality, design, and the paper stock used by the British did not exactly match that of the Continental notes, and careful examination could reveal the British notes as forgeries. However, in a report to Tallmadge on November 29, 1779, Townsend stated that the British had procured paper stock that matched exactly what the Congress was using.[75] Recognizing the damage this could cause to a currency already held in low repute among American merchants and farmers, Washington advised the Congress of the situation in a December 7 letter.[76] The Congress decided in March 1780 to recall all of its currency, with the ring's warning of improved British counterfeiting capabilities being one of the deciding factors.[77] That the ring could produce actionable economic intelligence vice just military intelligence and assist in defeating a British covert action to sabotage the fragile American economy demonstrated the wide scope of access enjoyed by the network's collectors.

The third report concerned intelligence that caused Washington to consider an attack on New York City but then decided instead to initiate a deception operation to change Clinton's plans to send a British force against the newly arrived French forces at Newport, Rhode Island. A ring report authored by Townsend in mid-July 1780 was forwarded by Woodhull to Tallmadge on July 20. The original report has been lost, but Woodhull's accompanying message stated that the ring had learned that Clinton was sending eight thousand British troops and twelve warships to Newport to attack the French.[78] Washington's headquarters received the intelligence on July 21. The French force of 5,500 troops, under the command of Jean-Baptiste Donatien de Vimeur, comte de Rochambeau, had arrived on July 10 after a long period at sea and required some time to get organized and healthy prior to any combat.

Unknown to the Americans at the time, Clinton had learned of the planned French arrival in mid-June. His source was Arnold, who had received the information from Washington and passed it along in a letter to Major André during his negotiations leading up to his eventually hasty defection.[79] Clinton's plan was to attack the French while they were in a weakened and disorganized state. Washington, having sent a warning to the French, first considered attacking the city because its garrison was being so reduced in strength. However, in discussions with his officers, he determined that he lacked adequate supplies, particularly artillery and ammunitions, to succeed in such an attack. Instead, Washington decided his best course of action would be to protect the French forces by deceiving the British into believing that he was planning to attack the city with a strength of twelve thousand men. He used a variety of methods to allow the British to believe they had discovered his plan to attack, including having an agent, whom the British believed to be a Tory, bring to a British outpost a bag of American courier documents he supposedly found on the road.[80] Clinton was apparently convinced that the danger was real and recalled his troops to protect the city. As these French forces were so vital in the American victory at Yorktown, protecting them from significant casualties that could have resulted from a British attack was the correct strategic decision. While attacking, and even capturing, the city for a brief period would have been a significant military achievement, with no naval capabilities to stand up to the Royal Navy the Americans could not have defended it against a British counterattack. The value of the ring's reporting in protecting the French forces must be considered to have been of strategic value to the American cause.

Most other intelligence collection activities outside the city during this period of the ring's activities was observational and of a tactical nature. However, the American surprise attack on Stony Point in July 1779 offers an example of how Washington and his subordinate commanders used aggressive and dangerous covert collection activities in their combat operations. On June 1, 1779, British troops seized this strong defensive position on the western side of the Hudson River that protected the crossing at King's Ferry. It was also part of an outer defensive ring protecting the strategically important West Point fortifications. Washington initially feared this attack might be some prelude to a British movement up the Hudson Valley, but thanks to his New York City reporting agents he soon learned no such operation was in preparation.

On July 1, 1779, he instructed Brig. Gen. "Mad Anthony" Wayne to develop the intelligence necessary on the British strength there to permit an attack.[81] A few days later, Washington added some additional advice: "Single men in the night will be more likely to ascertain facts than the best glasses in the day."[82] Wayne began his intelligence collection by having several officers reconnoiter the British positions and terrain, including a highly skilled engineering officer, Col. Rufus Putnam.[83] In addition, he decided to send an experienced intelligence officer, Capt. Allen McLane, into the British camp for a close-up look at their positions and troop dispositions. McLane entered the camp by accompanying the mother of an American who had recently deserted to the British at Stony Point. Under a flag of truce, the mother was permitted to visit with her son. McLane reported that the point was lightly garrisoned and provided details of its defensive weak points and its security procedures.[84] Wayne combined McLane's report with information from the reconnaissance efforts and developed a plan for a night attack using only the bayonet to ensure surprise. On the night of July 15–16, in a stunning victory thanks to his extensive knowledge of the enemy's disposition, Wayne captured Stony Point with only minor casualties. He took several hundred enemy prisoners and then destroyed the fortifications prior to withdrawing.

And Washington was able to get Clinton's frustrated reaction to the battle in a July 29 report from Townsend.[85]

CHAPTER 10

NATHANAEL GREENE AND INTELLIGENCE IN THE SOUTHERN CAMPAIGN

American intelligence activities in the South during the Revolutionary War have not received a great deal of attention compared to those in the northern and middle colonies.[1] And for the first three years of the war, the important fighting took place outside that region. However, with the defeat of Major General Burgoyne at Saratoga in October 1777, British strategy began to shift to the South. The British government believed that a majority of the people in the southern colonies were loyalists and could be motivated to join regular British army forces in creating a British government structure there. The British plan was to send a strong military force there to seize control of the major population areas, while Tories in the countryside would assist in bringing those areas under British control.[2]

By early 1780, British general Sir Henry Clinton, moving from his New York City base, had a sizeable force slowly trapping American general Benjamin Lincoln in a siege at Charleston, South Carolina. On May 12, 1780, Lincoln surrendered some five thousand troops to Clinton. This serious blow to the American Southern Army caused the Congress to instruct Washington to send several thousand troops to the Carolinas, further reducing the strength of his already weakened army.[3] The Continental Congress also decided to send Gen. Horatio Gates, who had commanded at Saratoga, to command what was left of the Southern Army. Gates demonstrated his lack of military skills rather quickly and was soundly defeated by Gen. Lord Cornwallis at the battle of

Camden, South Carolina, in August of 1780, surrendering an additional 4,100 American troops to the British.

With the second southern military crisis of the year, Congress accepted Washington's recommendation that Gen. Nathanael Greene take command there. The multivolume collection *The Papers of General Nathanael Greene* provides a valuable source from which to study his intelligence collection activities as the commander of the Continental Army in the southern theater.[4] His military exploits are well documented by historians, and his use of the tactics of mobile warfare during his southern campaign is highly respected among military strategists. It is doubtful that Mao Tse-tung read of Greene's campaign while structuring his protracted warfare strategy that resulted in the communist victory in China after World War II. He did, however, give some credit to Sun Tzu, the author of the Chinese military treatise *The Art of War*, which at the time was considered the greatest of Chinese texts on military strategy and tactics. It is equally doubtful that Greene even knew of Sun Tzu. Yet Greene's and Mao's strategic approaches and tactical implementations were remarkably similar and successful.[5]

Information regarding Greene's intelligence activities is seldom discussed in most Revolutionary War histories and narratives. Even in his own writings, he is often vague in his references to intelligence collection and its use. While this is not unusual even today in writings by military and civilian leaders, it is particularly characteristic of those involved in insurgency conflicts for practical as well as security reasons. Political, personal, and commercial loyalties in the colonial South, all linked by family and community ties, were even more complex than in the more populated northern colonies. Exposure of individuals involved in espionage against the British could bring immediate harm to that individual. But of equal importance after the conflict ended, these individuals might have to live among colleagues and peers whose actual loyalties, or personal equities, had been with the Crown. In addition to these pragmatic factors, Greene's personal and professional relationship with Washington, who was a mentor to him, also played a role in his careful discretion regarding exposure of intelligence activities. He worked closely with Washington and was well aware of the commander in chief's views on secrecy in intelligence operations.

Still, a careful review of Greene's correspondence, placed within the context of the military situations, provides some interesting insights into his dealings with his senior intelligence officers and their sources and methods of intelligence collection—from the perspective of the overall military commander. For

Engraving of Gen.
Nathanael Greene by
Johnson, Fry & Co.,
1862. Washington sent
Greene to take command
in the South in 1780
to salvage a disastrous
situation in the wake
of two major defeats at
Charleston and Camden.
*Rhode Island Historical
Society*

example, his appreciation of the value of intelligence to a field commander—as
well as his knowledge of the requirement for, and methodology of, operational
security in a collection operation—was made clear by his letter to Col. Francis
"Swamp Fox" Marion on December 4, 1780. It was written upon his taking
command of the Southern Army. Marion, one of his militia commanders, was
constantly engaged with the British forces, and Greene expected him to be a
timely source of intelligence on British activities:

> Spies are the Eyes of an Army, and without them a General is always
> groping in the dark and can neither secure himself nor annoy his
> Enemy: at present I am badly off for Intelligence. It is of the high-
> est importance that I get the earliest Information of any Reinforce-
> ments, which may arrive at Charlestown or leave the Town to join Lord
> Cornwallis. I wish you therefore to fix some Plan for procuring such
> information and for conveying it to me with all possible Dispatch. The
> Spy should be taught to be particular in his Enquires and to get the
> names of the Corps, Strength and Commanding Officer's name, Place

from whence they came and where they are going. It will be best to fix
upon some Body in Town to do this, and have a Runner between you
and him, to give you the Intelligence as a Person cannot make these
Enquires without being suspected who lives out of Town. The utmost
secrecy will be necessary in this Business. Whatever Sums of money are
advanced for these Purposes shall be repaid.[6]

By the end of the war, after he had the opportunity to reflect on both his
collection of intelligence and the uses to which he put it, Greene's description
of its importance became even stronger. In a February 4, 1785, letter to Benjamin Guerard, governor of South Carolina, he stated that "intelligence to an
Army is like the soul to the body[,] it directs all its motions."[7]

During the southern campaign, a war of mobility where Greene's Continentals were numerically weaker than his enemy, timely and accurate intelligence was the key to his army's survival. The vast majority of the intelligence
collected by Greene was enemy order-of-battle information: identification of
British and Tory units, their strength, and the details of the fortifications they
defended. He also had priority interest in the enemy's routes of march and
logistical arrangements. These types of intelligence are best collected through
personal observation by individuals within or close to enemy lines. Also important because of his constant weakness in troop strength was foreknowledge of
enemy intentions: intelligence regarding British plans and tactical objectives.
This type of information was much more difficult to obtain, as it required
access to individuals knowledgeable of British planning or the interception of
orders as they were being disseminated for implementation. While Greene's
successes in this type of operation were numerous, they were significantly less
frequent than his order-of-battle collection activities.

However, in a letter to the governor of South Carolina after the British
evacuated Charleston, their last stronghold in the southern colonies, Greene
emphasized that he had collected intelligence of immediate use in combat,
and used it effectively: "I have been obliged to employ a number of characters
to furnish me with the earliest intelligence of the Enemy's intentions. From
which, I have in most cases been able to counteract their designs."[8]

The earliest record of Greene's involvement in intelligence collection involved a report to the deputy governor of Rhode Island, Nicholas Cooke, on
July 17, 1775. As commander of the Rhode Island troops at Boston, he advised Cooke that John Roulstone, who recently departed Boston, had reported
that the British casualties from the battle of Bunker Hill were fifteen hundred

killed, wounded, or missing. Roulstone also said that eight British ships carry-ing sixteen hundred troops had recently arrived, bringing British strength in the city to about nine thousand. Half the troops were in the town and the rest at Bunker Hill. Greene concluded his report by noting the British had adjusted their defensive positions on the hill, and he prophetically added that "there are some traitors among us."[9]

On August 9, Greene again reported to Cooke that another Boston resident told him that since April 19, British casualties, from both combat and sickness, totaled about twenty-five hundred, and that British troop morale was poor.[10]

Greene's concern about traitors would prove to be true a few weeks later when he became involved in the counterintelligence investigation of the first American traitor, Dr. Benjamin Church. As discussed earlier, in the summer of 1775, Church had entrusted his mistress to deliver an encoded letter to the British containing information on American forces. When she sought the assis-tance of a former friend in Newport in delivering the letter, that individual be-came suspicious. After several days of consideration, he brought it to Greene's attention, as the senior Rhode Island military officer. Greene then passed it on to Washington and was a member of the council of officers that charged Church with corresponding with the enemy.

During 1776, as the Continental Army moved from Boston to the New York City area, Greene continued to gather tactical intelligence. In March, he identified Joshua Bently as one of his informants in Boston and ordered his troops to provide assistance and protection to Bently as required.[11] On August 4, he advised Washington that another informant, a Mr. Skinner, had provided a list of principal Tories in the New York City area.[12] And in November, he reported to Washington that a Staten Island agent, Justice Mercereau (probably Joshua Mersereau), had reported the movement of ten thousand British troops from New York to South Carolina. Mercereau also reported that American prisoners of war in the city were suffering under poor conditions.[13]

Greene's role in and knowledge of the most significant intelligence success of that year, Washington's attack on Trenton, is not mentioned in his correspon-dence. However, as a senior army commander, as well as a close confident of Washington's, he was aware of the planned attack as early as December 21.[14] If indeed he was not aware of the identity of Washington's sources of intelligence, he at least recognized that the detailed information on Hessian positions must have come from observation inside the enemy camp.[15] Considering Washing-ton's personal and professional discipline regarding compartmentation of his intelligence sources, it is most probable he did withhold identification of his source even from his most senior officers.

Throughout the next year, Greene engaged in periodic intelligence activities as the army fought in and around New York City. On February 20, he reported to Washington that colonels Joseph Reed and John Cox had employed new agents to collect intelligence.[16] And later in the spring, he reported intelligence on enemy activities in the area of New Brunswick, New Jersey, and on British movements toward Philadelphia from an agent and the interrogation of a deserter from the British Seventy-First Highlander Regiment.[17] Contemplating his combat experiences that year, on November 5 he expressed his view on the importance of intelligence to one of his senior intelligence officers, Maj. John Clark: "Intelligence is the life of every thing in a war."[18]

Once Washington asked Greene to become quartermaster of the army in early 1778, his involvement in intelligence was significantly reduced. However, in June 1780, near the end of that assignment, there was correspondence that indicated his involvement once again in intelligence activities. On June 22, he informed Washington that a spy, just returned from Elizabeth, New Jersey, had reported that British general Henry Clinton, having recently returned from Charleston to New York City with reinforcements, was about to move his forces to block any American movement up the Hudson River Valley. However, Greene was aware that Clinton had not yet moved his troops. He questioned the accuracy of the reporting and wondered if the agent had been turned against the American cause by the British.[19] Subsequently, Clinton did feint a move toward the Hudson Highlands but then returned his forces to the city for the remainder of the year.

Later that year, in September when Greene was back in a combat command, he sent Washington intelligence on British fleet and troop movements from New York City to Rhode Island and Virginia. However, the sources of this information were not disclosed.[20]

Once Greene assumed command of the Southern Army, his papers began to provide numerous references to intelligence-collection activities, and from them can be identified his primary military intelligence officers and some of their agents. Also, there are references to various intelligence methods, security considerations, and collection-support requirements that clearly indicated he had a solid knowledge of what is now called intelligence tradecraft. For example, Greene understood well the requirement for source protection of both his agents and their information. In his communication plans for his agents, he used simple code names—often a single identifying letter—for each source.[21]

As the British used similar methods to protect their communications, Greene also employed individuals adept at breaking codes and ciphers in captured enemy correspondence.[22]

Communication security between Greene and Col. Henry "Light-Horse Harry" Lee was the topic of correspondence twice in April 1781. In the first few days of the month, the use of code for reporting intelligence was discussed.[23] Later that month, Greene told Lee that a letter sent to him might have fallen into enemy hands. Because of a staff officer forgetting to bring the cipher book, the letter had been prepared in plain text, as opposed to enciphered. Greene lamented the damage that might have resulted from the information not having been enciphered.[24]

While counterintelligence activities were not discussed as often as were intelligence-collection operations, both defensive and offensive counterintelligence activities were mentioned in Greene's papers. Defensively, two clear warnings regarding British intelligence-collection operations were documented. On August 18, 1781, Lee identified a Mr. Moore as a British agent reporting on the activities and movements of Greene's army. He said that Moore used two of his slaves to gather intelligence for him.[25] Later that year, Greene advised Lee of another potential counterintelligence threat, citing the need to protect the local inhabitants from British plundering of their slaves. His concern was that the British would get "their best intelligence" from these slaves, depending upon how well they were subsequently treated by the British.[26]

Only one offensive counterintelligence operation, apparently a classic double-agent ploy, is mentioned in Greene's correspondence. As double-agent operations are considered the most sensitive type of counterintelligence activities, it is surprising that an individual, John McQueen, was mentioned by name. Whether this was a true name is not clear, and no additional details of the operation were provided.[27]

Greene discussed various agent-management issues as well. One constant issue was the lack of adequate funds to support his forces, and this would have included funds for his intelligence efforts as well.[28] In December 1780, he twice wrote to Thomas Jefferson, governor of Virginia, lamenting his lack of funds and the difficulties this caused for his intelligence operations. As late as June 9, 1781, Greene complained, "Not a shilling of money have I had since I came to this department not even to get intelligence with."[29] Three days later, Robert Morris, the superintendent of finance for the Continental Congress, offered him five hundred guineas for intelligence activities. However, throughout his command of the Southern Army, Greene was constantly plagued by a lack of funds, not only for intelligence activities but also for his military operations. Neither the Congress nor colonial governors provided a reliable source of funds for his conduct of the war.[30]

Greene arrived at Charlotte, North Carolina, on December 2, 1780, and found an army that was understrength, poorly equipped, low in morale, and with a history of poor leadership and military defeats. In addition to the requirements for reinforcements, supplies, and training, he identified a priority need for intelligence on the enemy as essential to his future success on the battlefield. It was at this point in his correspondence that frequent references began to appear regarding intelligence activities. A picture emerged of numerous well-run agent operations, with instructions and guidance to his field intelligence-collection officers and careful attention to a variety of intelligence-collection methods. While traditional military reconnaissance under his chief scout, Capt. C. K. Chitty, played a key role in his intelligence mix, his writings also described several other types of intelligence activities. These included principal agents running networks of local informants, organized procedures for debriefing and manipulating British deserters, comprehensive interrogation of prisoners of war, structured questioning of civilians crossing over from enemy lines, interception of enemy communications, and specific requirements for human spy missions into the enemy's camp.

Greene used his senior military officers as his primary intelligence-collection managers in the field. These officers ran the collection networks, as well as consolidated information from scouting units, prisoners of war, and debriefings of those coming from enemy lines, both civilians and deserters. The field commanders most often mentioned in regard to intelligence activities were Col. John Laurens, Brig. Gen. Francis Marion, Capt. William Wilmot, Brig. Gen. Thomas Sumter, Col. Henry Lee, and Col. Thaddeus Kościuszko, who assumed Laurens's responsibilities upon his death. In addition, his correspondence identified over twenty-five other army and militia officers involved in intelligence collection during his command of the Southern Army.

Colonel Laurens, the son of Continental Congress leader Henry Laurens, had joined Washington's staff as an aide-de-camp in August 1777. He was active in the campaign around New York City prior to being sent to Paris in December 1780 to work with the Paris Commission in the implementation of its efforts in support of the Revolution. He returned to the army in time to take part in the surrender of Cornwallis at Yorktown and then joined Greene in early December 1781. He was soon given command of the light troops in Greene's Southern Army. This post placed him nearest to enemy lines, where he could direct intelligence operations for Greene.[31] He operated along the Ashley River, west of Charleston. While aggressive in his collection activities, making him both a productive and timely provider of intelligence to the army, his behavior was often "rash and impetuous."[32] On August 27, 1782, he was killed in action while participating in a rather meaningless action at Combahee Ferry, in a manner that reflected his behavioral traits.

With the plans and intentions of the British forces in Charleston as his primary collection requirement, Laurens developed several sources with access to information from the city. One of his first agents, Roger Parker Saunders, was a planter from St. Paul's Parish in the Edisto River area with extensive social and business contacts in the city. He had been recruited by Colonel Lee in early December 1781 and tasked with both reporting and creating an informant network in Charleston.[33] The only member of that network identified in correspondence, and then vaguely so, was the "gentleman." By late that month, Saunders had begun reporting on British troop movements and dispositions using a slave, identified as William, as the courier carrying the intelligence from him to Laurens. As noted before, the public status of slaves in that period usually made their actions of little importance to local authorities, and this was particularly true in the South.

However, William's reports to Laurens were not always accurate.[34] Regardless, Saunders's loyalty did not fall under suspicion, perhaps because he seems to have served in the South Carolina First Regiment of the Continental Army until at least 1778. Ten years later, he was also a representative at the South Carolina state convention that approved the United States Constitution.

Yet other reports received through William, such as one in January 1782 regarding British troops' movements from Charleston to James Island, where cattle were kept to supply British forces, were accurate and valuable.[35] Suspicions relating to the cause of inaccurate information reported by William were never resolved. It was possible that Saunders was mistaken in his reporting or may have mistakenly provided William with false details. It is also possible that William misunderstood some of the details. And the possibility that British deception was involved, either in Saunders's reporting or in William's actions, also have to be considered. Such situations, precisely because humans are involved, are a normal part of the intelligence business and the primary reason that counterintelligence is a discipline fraught with great frustration.

Thomas Farr was another productive agent handled by Laurens. He was a merchant with commercial dealings in Charleston but resided outside British lines on his Hickory Hill plantation in St. Andrew's Parish near the Ashley River ferry. He was also involved in the colony's politics, having been in its legislature and had even served as its speaker. Farr was engaged in trade with Charleston merchants who assisted the British forces, and this was illegal as far as the American authorities were concerned. However, he used these business dealings to acquire intelligence on British activities and plans, which would be known to the merchants who supplied the logistical support required for these actions. He began his reporting in early January 1782.[36]

His initial reporting was composed of information concerning troop movements by British and German forces out of the city and food shortages within the city's garrison. However, his early efforts were somewhat obvious and aroused some British suspicion. In late February, Laurens reported to Greene that Farr had received an anonymous letter warning him that the British were watching his activities.[37] While no mention is made in Greene's correspondence regarding improvements in Farr's operational security or better instructions regarding his collection behavior, apparently appropriate actions were taken. Farr's reporting in the subsequent months proved quite valuable. His intelligence provided details of the movement of specific British and Hessian units and supporting artillery from Charleston to reinforce the defenses at James Island. He also told Laurens of several individuals he believed to be British agents reporting on Greene's activities: John McQueen, who had previously volunteered information to Greene, a mulatto servant of McQueen's, and a merchant named Robert William Powell.[38] Farr's identification of McQueen, who was in fact a double agent working for Greene, demonstrated that Greene's tight control over his intelligence activities was effective. Not only Farr, but also Laurens was unaware of McQueen's true loyalty.

In midsummer 1782, at a time when Greene's intelligence priorities focused on British planning to evacuate their forces from St. Augustine, Savannah, and Charleston, Farr reported the arrival of transport ships at Charleston. To acquire more specific details of evacuation plans, Farr sent a trusted contact, Archibald McKay, into the city. McKay was able to learn that twenty-seven transport ships were currently in the harbor. He further learned from British officers that the British commander, Gen. Alexander Leslie, planned for the ships to first evacuate the troops at St. Augustine and Savannah and bring them to Charleston. Then the Charleston garrison would load onto the ships for the final evacuation. He also reported information on plans for the garrison's embarkation, as well as identified which troops would function as a rear guard to protect the garrison's loading onto the ships.[39]

Farr's last recorded report forwarded to Greene, dated September 9, 1782, informed him that his wife had visited Charleston the day before. She had observed several ships being loaded with equipment, indicating the garrison's withdrawal. He also reported information from another source that the eastern side of the city was virtually undefended and that most of the artillery had been removed from the defensive lines around the city.[40]

Farr's motivation for providing information and accepting the serious risk to himself from the British was seemingly clear, based upon his involvement in South Carolina colonial politics. However, an incident in the spring of 1780, as Clinton laid siege to Charleston, probably also influenced his decision to take an active role against the British. He and his son were captured by British troops and during their confinement were humiliated by being forced to do menial work in public view.[41]

The agent least trusted by Laurens was Eliza Clitherall, the wife of loyalist physician Dr. James Clitherall. The Clitheralls resided in Charleston, and their political orientation and social standing provided natural access to British senior officers in social environments. Her motive in assisting the American side was purely self-interest as opposed to ideology, and this influenced how a passionate patriot such as Laurens viewed her activities.

In April 1782, Mrs. Clitherall offered to provide information on the British in return for assistance in transporting various goods through the American lines surrounding Charleston. For long-term cooperation she wanted a pardon for her husband and the removal of their country estates from the American confiscation list.[42] Documents indicated she was not a very active or productive collector and reported for only a few months, with her final report received in late August. Her information was often vague and on one occasion consisted only of a copy of the *Charleston Royal Gazette* newspaper. It quickly became clear to Laurens that she would do as little as possible in return for her compensation.

Clitherall's most comprehensive report was submitted in early August and provided intelligence on the situation of the British and French fleets after their recent engagement in the West Indies, on the withdrawal of the British from the Quarter House (a strongpoint on the outskirts of Charleston), and on the arrival of the British fleet from Savannah and its debarkation of troops.[43] A few days later, Laurens forwarded another report from her to Greene but described it as insignificant. In total, her brief reporting efforts' only value was to confirm information provided by other sources.[44] Nevertheless, Greene maintained Laurens's agreement, and in 1784, the South Carolina legislature pardoned her husband and returned their confiscated estates based upon her intelligence activities for the Southern Army.

Another of Laurens's agents, Andrew Williamson, also cooperated out of a desire to ensure that local authorities would not punish him once the British departed. However, his motivations were far more complicated than those of Mrs. Clitherall. Williamson had been a general in the South Carolina militia, and in June 1780, shortly after Lincoln's surrender to Clinton, he had ordered his command to disband, effectively terminating any significant American resistance to the British in the colony. He has often been referred to as the "Benedict Arnold of the South."

However, there is some debate regarding his reasons for ending his resistance to the British forces and whether he did it because his militia forces were leaving to the degree that further resistance would have been ineffectual, if not suicidal. What is clear is that after he decided to end this participation in the armed conflict, Williamson decided to assume an equally dangerous role as an intelligence collector for the patriots. The controversy regarding his true loyalties and motives has never been settled.

After returning to his Whitehall plantation, located just west of the town of Ninety Six, Williamson was captured by a band of patriots who considered him a traitor. However, he managed to escape to Charleston. Greene's correspondence offered no details regarding how Williamson began reporting on British activities, but it is clear that he considered Williamson both a reliable and productive source. In fact, his praise for Williamson's efforts would seem to indicate significant intelligence was received from him.

Greene's papers provided only a general time frame: early spring of 1782, for the start of Williamson's reporting.[45] On June 24, he said that he wanted Greene's help in stopping the South Carolina legislature from seizing his properties. He also hinted that others were aware of his intelligence collection for the patriots.[46] In July and August, Laurens forwarded several reports from him to Greene. These reports related to Greene's priority requirement for details and timing of the British evacuation of Charleston. Williamson reported that the British would not have adequate transportation to evacuate the town until additional transport ships arrived from New York City and the West Indies. He confirmed other agents' information on the removal of artillery and munitions from the town. He also provided details of British positions at the outpost at Shubrick's Plantation, about three miles from Charleston, and said that he would travel to James Island to collect intelligence on British forces there.[47]

Once again, Greene kept his part of the agreement and in December 1782 requested John Mathews, the governor of South Carolina, to remove all penalties pending against Williamson. He cited Williamson's contributions to the patriots' cause in glowing terms: "He has faithfully served the Army; and has given generally the best information we have had, being much in the confidence with the enemy and a man of sense and observation."[48] After the war, the legislature did restore his property and estates with only a slight penalty.

In addition to the four agents mentioned above, Greene's papers noted several other sources reporting on events in Charleston. But only one is described in sufficient detail to judge the value of the intelligence. Edmund Petrie, a Charleston merchant, seemed to have ready access to British general Leslie. While Petrie publicly appeared as a Tory, he may have secretly been a patriot and used his public image as a means of access for intelligence purposes. However, there were also indications that, as a sound businessman, Petrie sensed the British were not going to win, and he subsequently decided to protect his future through cooperation with Greene. Once again, the true motivation of an agent was uncertain or was unclear from information in official records. During the period of June through August 1782, Petrie's reporting both corroborated and complemented Williamson's information and that of other sources regarding British plans for evacuating the town.[49]

Upon Laurens's death, Colonel Kościuszko assumed responsibility for directing his intelligence network. Kościuszko, a Polish nobleman, had arrived in America in the summer of 1776 to join the American cause. He was an engineering officer, and his talents were both needed and subsequently highly respected by Washington. He was eventually sent to assist Greene in reconstituting the Southern Army. Demonstrating his sense of operational security, one of his first steps in managing the network was to eliminate true name identification of sources when forwarding reporting. He used only initials; for example, Williamson became "W" and Petrie became "P."[50]

Williamson continued to report on British troop deployments and fortifications on James Island and provided another individual, Prince, a "Negro" who had access around the island and could observe British activities.[51] Petrie also continued his collection activities in and around Charleston, often using Prince as a courier for his reporting.[52]

In a message to Greene on September 19, 1782, Kościuszko discussed an operational issue with the courier arrangement for another of Petrie's sources, "James." He wanted to change his courier from Prince to a Mr. Clark.[53] While seemingly a small matter, an issue such as this must be carefully planned in order for the natural, seemingly innocent contact between the collector and courier and between the courier and the final recipient of the intelligence to have plausible explanation to all observers, especially the British. Later in

September, Petrie provided a counterintelligence lead, reporting that a major in the American camp, not further identified, was writing a person in Charleston describing activities at the camp.[54]

Petrie's last documented report was in mid-November. He reported that the British were pulling in their outposts around Charleston, and rumors were that troops would soon start loading onto ships in the harbor.[55] As he did with Williamson, Greene made it a point to inform the South Carolina governor of Petrie's role as an intelligence collector. In mid-December, he wrote Mathews, stating that Petrie had served as an intelligence agent "with great fidelity" until the British left Charleston, and he asked the South Carolina legislature to remove Petrie's name from the list of loyalists whose property was to be seized.[56] This was done the following spring.

Another of Greene's senior intelligence officers, Francis Marion, monitored British activities at Charleston from the north. Marion was a South Carolina militia officer and a renowned veteran of the Cherokee War. He had served bravely in its third campaign, which forced the Indians to end the conflict in 1761. While he is recognized in history for his skillful use of guerrilla tactics against the British, it is often overlooked that his military successes depended upon having sound intelligence on enemy plans and actions. Rather than recruit agents in British-occupied areas, he focused upon traditional military intelligence-collection methods: reconnaissance, scouting, interception of enemy communications, and debriefings of prisoners and others coming from British lines. Another probable reason for his lack of agents in British areas was his constant lack of financial resources—he had no funds to pay them with. In response to Greene's orders to emphasize intelligence collection through agents or informants, Marion responded that he would try to do as directed "but shall meet with great Difficulty, as nothing but Gold or Silver passes here, and I am Destitute of Either."[57]

From late December 1780 through the following January, Marion provided accurate and timely intelligence prior to the Battle of Cowpens on the movements of General Leslie's forces from Charleston to the Camden area and onward to join Lord Cornwallis.[58] During the same period, he intercepted a letter from an officer of the Sixty-Fourth Regiment to Leslie. This letter provided details that identified and confirmed Leslie's location as of late December. It also identified the location of the forces under Cornwallis.[59] This information was of significant value to Greene and subsequently more important to Gen. Daniel Morgan as he prepared to meet British troops commanded by Lt. Col. Banastre Tarleton at Cowpens on January 17, 1781. In his report to Greene on his victory, Morgan noted that the intelligence had provided him with knowledge of the movements of the British prior to the battle.[60]

Marion's debriefing activities proved particularly valuable during the July-to-December period of 1781. At this time both sides anticipated that hostilities would cease in the near future and that military control of territory would be a key negotiating issue in the final peace settlement. Therefore, Greene sought to maneuver his forces to block British attempts to expand their areas of control outside of Charleston. In July, Marion debriefed prisoners from Lord Francis Rawdon's command and learned the strength and composition of his forces, details on the physical condition of the soldiers, and that he planned to move up the Congaree River within a few days.[61] Other prisoner debriefings also provided useful intelligence on Col. Alexander Stewart's forces involved in offensive operations to protect the outer defenses of Charleston. In mid-August, Marion provided Greene with general information on the size of Stewart's forces, which corroborated intelligence obtained by Colonel Lee.

In late November, Marion captured a prisoner who provided specific numbers for Stewart's troops stationed at Monck's Corner. The prisoner was an orderly sergeant who stated that there were 2,121 men in the command—1,193 fit for duty, 695 in the hospital, and 233 sick at the camp.[62] During the same period, Marion also debriefed town residents passing through his lines and was able to report conditions inside of Charleston. By analyzing Marion's intelligence along with the information being provided by Laurens's collection network, Greene created an accurate picture of British capabilities regarding which areas they might be able to hold for negotiation value and, more important, which the British would not be able to defend against his army.

Another intelligence officer working for Greene was Capt. William Wilmot of the Second Maryland Regiment, stationed near John's Island, south of Charleston. His reporting, from the spring of 1782 until his death in battle on the 15th of November of that year, focused on British troop movements and their positions. His reporting was detailed and comprehensive. For example, in April he reported on a British fleet arriving in Charleston, describing the ships and citing the exact number.[63] Less than two weeks later, he provided intelligence identifying the units that had embarked on the ships and their strengths, as well as the units and their strengths posted at various British outposts surrounding the city, including the strategically important James Island. He also informed Greene that General Leslie had moved his headquarters into Charleston. These details indicated that he had agents operating for him in addition to the reconnaissance missions he was conducting. In fact, in this report he noted that he was trying to recruit a captain in the British service.[64] This individual, according to Wilmot, wanted a pardon from the South Carolina government in return for providing current and future intelligence on British activities.

This captain was never mentioned again, but Greene's papers subsequently indicated that Wilmot used the title captain to mask the identity of a very important and well-placed new agent. In his report Wilmot also mentioned that Col. Edward Fenwick, a South Carolina loyalist militia officer, as well as a company commander in the South Carolina Light Dragoons, who was stationed at James Island, had recently spoken with him under a flag of truce. Fenwick mentioned that fifteen hundred troops had sailed with British general Charles O'Hara for Jamaica. This statement is most interesting. In a May 8, 1782, letter that Greene sent to Wilmot, he advised Wilmot to be most careful to restrict knowledge of his intelligence activities, especially the identities of his agents, to as few people as possible.[65]

While no specific examples of intelligence sourced to Fenwick were found in Greene's papers, the identity of the captain became apparent in a serious breach of operational security several months later when Greene wrote the following formal certificate:

To Whom It May Concern
Headquarters (Ashley Hill, S.C.) August 14th 1782
Copy of a Certificate given to Col. Edward Fenwick
With the British Army

This may Certify that Colonel Fenwick in the British Army has agreed to send me intelligence from time to time of all the Military operations of the Enemy which they may concert to the Prejudice of the United States or any part thereof, and that he agrees to run every risque necessary to give the earliest intelligence for saving the States harmless. I do further certify that he has been in this employ for some Months past and that on all occasions has served with fidelity and ability. He then said Fenwick is to keep with the British Army until the close of the war and give intelligence from time to time as forsaid. Upon performing this duty faithfully I do promise to use all my influence with the State of South Carolina to restore him to all his fortunes and the rights and priviledges of a Citizen. And if the State of South Carolina should refuse to restore him for whose particular benefit he engaged in this

service I do promise and engage to recommend his case to Congress for
such compensation as they may think his services claim.

> Given at Headquarters August 14th 1782
> Nath Greene[66]

Why did Greene, usually so careful in his protection of sources and methods, write a certificate that named a valuable source and also placed him at
great personal risk should the British, or a British agent, learn of it? The answer
seems to lie in the personality of the agent, which always tends to be an issue
in how the operation is actually run. An agent who either knows or believes his
access to be important can demand many things from his intelligence handler.
Often, such demands fly in the face of sound operational security and professional handling practices, but keeping the agent motivated and active is the
only way to ensure continued reporting. From what information is available
on Fenwick, it appears that he insisted upon the certificate because self-interest
was his key motivation. He does not appear to have been particularly committed to either the American or British cause. The certificate was for his personal
protection after the war, and he considered this more important than protecting his ability to collect intelligence for the American cause.

Wilmot used the illegal, but active, trade between the American-controlled
countryside and the British in Charleston as cover for action for most of his
intelligence agents. This trade provided excellent justification for travel in and
out of the city and was a personally profitable enterprise for the individuals involved, thus ensuring their motivation to meet his collection requirements. In
the months before his death, he supplied very accurate and timely intelligence
on British plans to transport troops from the city to various destinations.[67] No
doubt Fenwick's access as a senior officer in the British command played a key
role in the confidence Wilmot expressed to Greene regarding his capabilities.
He even moved his headquarters to a location opposite Charleston so he could
get his intelligence to Greene within two hours of its reception.[68]

Thanks to Wilmot, Laurens, and Marion, Greene had comprehensive and
timely intelligence on the activities of the British in and around Charleston
until they evacuated the city in December 1782. Since Greene did not have
adequate troops to force the British out militarily, yet needed to keep up some
pressure on them, his intelligence activities enabled him to effectively use those
forces he had.

Gen. Thomas Sumter, a veteran combat officer of the French and Indian
War, was yet another productive intelligence officer for Greene. Known by the

nickname "The Gamecock" for his aggressive and disciplined military style, he commanded a South Carolina militia regiment. His professional relationship with Greene was often strained because of issues of status and command authority. As a general officer in the South Carolina Militia, he did not consider himself to be under the command of the Continental Army and often refused to respond to Greene's requests for military assistance. However, he did provide Greene with valuable intelligence during the first half of 1781. This was the period when British forces suffered serious setbacks at the battles at Cowpens and Guilford Courthouse, as well as supply issues that forced their retreat from the Carolina countryside.

Just prior to the engagement at Cowpens, Sumter provided Greene with a comprehensive report on the strength and location of British forces in the area. He reported that General Leslie had twelve hundred men at Camden, Cornwallis's troops were at McCallister's Plantation, a hundred men were at the Congaree River under a Major Maxwell constructing a fort, and about a thousand other enemy soldiers were in the area combined as one element. He added that an unknown number of British troops had departed Camden and crossed the Santee River at Nelson's Ferry.[69] As with the intelligence provided by Marion, this information proved valuable at the Battle of Cowpens.

Throughout the spring, Sumter continued to report on British movements. Of particular value was a report in early May alerting Greene that Cornwallis was headed north out of the Carolinas.[70] Sumter then focused his collection efforts on the British garrison at Ninety Six and the movements of Lord Rawdon's command. His final report documented in Greene's papers, submitted in early July, stated that British forces were moving to reinforce the garrison at Ninety Six.[71] This intelligence was of particular value to Greene, as he was in the process of planning siege operations against several of the British positions, including Ninety Six.

Col. Henry Lee was the final senior intelligence officer whose activities were well documented by Greene. Lee joined Washington's army in April 1777 and quickly developed a reputation as an excellent cavalry officer. When Greene was put in charge of the Southern Army, Lee accompanied him to his new command. There he led a combined force of infantry and cavalry known as Lee's Legion. By early 1781, Lee provided Greene with a steady flow of intelligence that continued through early 1782. (Serious health issues forced Lee to leave the army that summer.) Correspondence between Greene and Lee touched not only on intelligence reporting but also on counterintelligence, communication security, and the ever-present difficulties of financing intelligence operations.

Like Sumter's, Lee's reports focused on Lord Rawdon's forces, British strength at Ninety Six and Fort Granby, and the situation at Colonel Stewart's camp at Thompson Plantation near McCord's Ferry. His reporting came from several sources, including prisoner interrogations,[72] debriefings of British deserters,[73] reconnaissance by his troops, and agent operations.[74] Between the reporting of Lee and Sumter, Greene was able to corroborate and validate not only British positions, but also the reliability and accuracy of his various sources. As the British pulled back to defend Charleston, Lee followed them and continued his reporting. One significant report, obtained from a prisoner of war, provided information on the size of the British garrison on John's Island and that recent reinforcements from New York consisted of only three hundred men, mostly new recruits.[75] A January 1782 report stated that no additional British reinforcements were expected unless Gen. Sir Henry Clinton decided to send his entire army.[76]

With the British evacuation of Charleston, Greene's activities shifted from combat operations to repositioning his forces in order to maintain law and order while local civil authorities reestablished a governing structure. At this point his intelligence networks ceased to be of value and were disbanded. However, Greene did not forget to honor his obligations to his former agents and in appropriate cases documented their activities in support of the American cause to state authorities.

Greene's use of intelligence to fight a war against a superior enemy force, in which tactical defeats weakened the victors to the point that they eventually led to strategic victories, represented one of his great talents as a commander. He tended to use his intelligence in a defensive manner, to avoid major combat while inflicting frustrating small assaults on less-well-defended British positions. Yet, by the time the British were evacuating Charleston, his collection capabilities were so comprehensive that in early October 1782 he provided Washington and Secretary of War Benjamin Lincoln with the entire British order of battle in Charleston and also indicated where these troops were to be sent upon departing the city.[77]

CHAPTER 11

YORKTOWN AND THE ENDGAME

After the British losses sustained at the Battle of Cowpens and the Battle of Guilford Courthouse in the early months of 1781, Cornwallis no longer had adequate forces to hold the Carolinas against Greene's Southern Army. He moved his forces into Virginia in late April to link up with other British forces there. Soon after his arrival, he received a request from his commander, General Clinton in New York City, to send three thousand of his troops back to the city to bolster its defenses. This request, and subsequent decisions that created confusion between the two officers, were in response to Washington's most important and comprehensive strategic deception operation of the war: convincing General Clinton that American and French forces intended to attack New York City. This, in turn, made Clinton uncertain as to the degree he could reinforce and support Cornwallis's forces in Virginia.

This confusion enabled the Continental Army, with strong French support, to defeat the British at Yorktown. The Battle of Yorktown, acknowledged as the victory that forced the British to end the conflict, was a battle where intelligence information, both strategic out of New York City and tactical from within Yorktown's defenses, combined with Washington's strategic deception activities, were key elements in the military result.

In mid-December 1780, Benedict Arnold—by then a brigadier general in the British Army and eager to punish his former countrymen—was sent to Portsmouth, Virginia, on the Elizabeth River across from Norfolk. His mission was to wreak havoc on the local militia forces, with the hope of drawing some

The young, inexperienced French nobleman Marquis de Lafayette came to America to fight the British and ended up a skillful soldier and personal favorite of George Washington. *Library of Congress*

American forces away from Cornwallis's troops farther south. There was also some slight British hope that he could create an area under British control where Virginia loyalists could rally to the king's cause.[1] It was believed within British government and military circles—and with some validity—that significant numbers of the population in the southern colonies would support the king if given the physical security to do so by the presence of British troops. Cornwallis had found that his forces in the Carolinas had not been large enough to create such an environment. Clinton believed Arnold might do so in Virginia.

However, Arnold's tactics and aggressiveness in his military operations did not win the hearts and minds of the locals. He took great personal enjoyment in punishing his former side, and he tended to define the enemy as anyone not openly supportive of the king.[2] By January 1781, he had expanded his activities into the Richmond area, causing Washington to send Lafayette south with a small force in an attempt to counter his activities. Washington had originally hoped for a joint American-French action involving a French fleet from New England, but the French were slow in sailing and upon arrival met a British fleet at the mouth of the Chesapeake Bay, where they were defeated and forced back to Newport. Thus Lafayette's force and local militia units were the only American troops facing Arnold in early 1781.

By late March, the British had reinforced Arnold's force with some two and a half thousand additional troops under Maj. Gen. William Phillips, who had assumed command of all the British forces in Virginia. In April, Arnold conducted a successful raid at Petersburg, sacking the city and soundly defeating local militia units opposing him. His next objective was the city of Richmond, but Lafayette's troops moved in position to shield the city, and Arnold returned to Petersburg. Within a few weeks, in late May, Cornwallis arrived at Petersburg with his worn-out army. He had left North Carolina for Virginia on his own initiative rather than under Clinton's orders. When Clinton learned of Cornwallis's movement, correspondence between them became quite tense by the standards of official communication then, and as the military situation in Virginia developed, orders and planning between them became confused. After the Battle of Yorktown, both men authored written defenses of their conduct, placing blame on the other for the decisions that led to the defeat.[3]

Upon assuming command of the British forces in Virginia, which now consisted of Arnold's original force and Phillips's reinforcements, Cornwallis had a total of approximately seven thousand troops at his disposal. This was about double the number Lafayette commanded. Cornwallis eventually decided to concentrate all his forces at Yorktown, which was a good choice for a defensive position, as it protected a harbor that could shelter Royal Navy ships. Cornwallis anticipated using Yorktown as his base of operations, with Clinton providing supplies and reinforcements as required.[4] However, Clinton had his own concerns about the security of the main British base in New York City.[5] He was aware of the joint American-French forces' movements and concerned that their objective was to capture New York City. This concern, which Washington had been encouraging for over a year, provided Washington with the opportunity to affect the strategic balance of forces in Virginia.

Many histories of the war cite evidence through documents and correspondence that Washington's preferred target was indeed New York City and that the French army's commander, Rochambeau, was responsible for forcing Washington to bypass the city and move into Virginia. He allegedly did this by urging the commander of a large French fleet to sail to the Chesapeake Bay rather than to the New York City area.[6] According to this scenario, at a joint American-French planning meeting on May 22, 1781, Washington proposed an attack on New York City. He felt comfortable to do so because the combined allied forces outnumbered Clinton's garrison's strength. Under his plan the allied ground forces were to concentrate at a point above the city, near White Plains, in anticipation of the French naval assault.[7] However, in early June, Rochambeau sent a personal note to the French fleet's commander, Adm. François Joseph Paul de Grasse, comte de Grasse, suggesting that he sail not to New York City but instead to the Virginia area.[8] Rochambeau had serious doubts that the joint forces could take the city after all the years the British had spent building fortifications protecting it. De Grasse took his French colleague's advice, and Washington only learned of the destination change many weeks later. In August, he was advised the French fleet could only remain along the American coast until mid-October. This information forced him to decide that British forces in Virginia offered the best target for an allied attack. On August 19, the majority of American and French troops began marching southward, leaving behind a small force to protect the Hudson Valley. To support this scenario, Washington's entry of August 14, 1781, in his official diary is often cited:

> Received dispatches from the Count de Barras [Jacques-Melchior Saint-Laurent] announcing the intended departure of the Count de Grasse from cape François with between 25 and 29 Sail of the line and 3200 land Troops on the 3rd Instant for Chesapeak bay. . . . He should be under a necessity from particular engagements with the Spaniards to be in the West Indies by the Middle of October. . . . Matters having now come to a crisis and a decisive plan to be determined on, I was obliged . . . to give up all idea of attacking New York, and instead thereof to remove the French Troops and a detachment from the American Army to the Head of the Elk to be transported to Virginia for the purpose of co-operating with the force from the West Indies against the Troops in that State.[9]

On September 5, at the Battle of the Capes at the mouth of the Chesapeake, French admiral de Grasse's fleet met and forced a smaller British naval force under Adm. Sir Thomas Graves back to New York. This effectively sealed off the British land forces from naval resupply. This naval action was the key tactical victory of the Yorktown campaign. By September 28, the allied American and French forces had surrounded Yorktown.

Based on confusing correspondence with Clinton, as well as communication delays, Cornwallis still believed that Clinton would send additional reinforcements. In a poor tactical decision, Cornwallis evacuated his outer perimeter defenses to concentrate his forces within the city's defensive lines. With the aid of French engineers and heavy artillery, which the French fleet had brought from Rhode Island, Washington adopted traditional siege warfare. He began construction of trench lines moving closer and closer to the town's defenses. On October 19, the British were forced to surrender. The only missing part of this victory was a very personal one to the American commanders: Arnold was not captured with the other British soldiers.

This military defeat effectively ended the British government's effort to regain control of its American colonies. There simply was no more domestic political support for the war. When Lord North, the British prime minister, was informed of the defeat, he supposedly cried out, "It is all over."[10] And it was, even though minor armed engagements over control of certain areas for negotiation purposes were yet to come.

However, what is seldom mentioned in the narrative of the Yorktown campaign is the strategic deception plan that Washington implemented successfully for almost a year to encourage Clinton to believe New York City was his military objective. It never was. The August 14, 1781, diary entry was yet another example of his security awareness in protecting his active intelligence agents and activities from exposure. Seven years later in a letter to a noted scholar seeking the true details behind the Yorktown campaign—well after the need to protect the secrecy of his plan—Washington stated clearly that New York City had not been his objective and that earlier documents so stating were designed to deceive his own army as well as Clinton:

> It was determined by me (nearly twelve months beforehand) at all hazards to give out and cause it to be believed by the highest military as well as civil Officers that New York was the destined place of attack, for the important purpose of inducing the Eastern and Middle States to make greater exertions in furnishing specific supplies than they otherwise would have done, as well as for the interesting purpose of rendering the enemy less prepared elsewhere. . . .

I only add that it never was in contemplation to attack New York, unless the Garrison should first have been so far disgarnished to carry on the southern operations, as to render our success in the siege of that place as infallible as any future military event can ever be made.

That much trouble was taken and finesse used to misguide and bewilder Sir Henry Clinton in regard to the real object, by fictitious communications, as well as by making a deceptive provision of Ovens, Forage and Boats in his Neighborhood, is certain. Nor were less pains taken to deceive our own Army; for I had always conceived, when the imposition did not completely take place at home, it could never sufficiently succeed abroad.

Many circumstances will unavoidably be misconceived and misrepresented. Notwithstanding most of the Papers which may properly be deemed official are preserved; yet the knowledge of innumerable things, of a more delicate and secret nature, is confined to the perishable remembrance of some few of the present generation.[11]

Even at this time, Washington was careful not to provide any "sources and methods" details regarding how he deceived Clinton, with the exception of the public creation of supply areas seeming to indicate preparations for an attack on New York City. In reality, as the following analysis of his intelligence activities in support of his deception plan demonstrates, he used a well-coordinated mix of double agents, comments by senior officers in the presence of known or suspected British agents, and public actions such as troop movements and construction of support facilities to keep Clinton confused as to his real military objective.

By August 14, the date of the diary entry, Clinton was aware that the American and French forces were moving south of the city. Thus the entry, while being in a document readily accessible to senior officers, did not give the British any information of great value but did protect the fact that Clinton had been duped by reporting from individuals still useful to Washington. By late August, if Clinton had attempted to reinforce Cornwallis, he would soon have learned that the Royal Navy no longer had that capability.

Washington's deception plan, like his many others earlier in the war, was complex, and only portions of it can be identified from American and British records. However, more than enough information is available to document the lengthy and complex series of actions involved in the deception.

In early 1780, Clinton received what he considered his first creditable report that New York City would be the target of attack once the French fleet arrived. It came from a British spy in Connecticut who was trusted.[12] But it was not until early 1781 that Clinton's records reflected Washington's deception activities. In February, he was sent a report from a trusted source in Newport, Dr. John Halliburton, stating that French troops were boarding vessels to move southward and that Washington and Rochambeau were soon to hold a conference. The message was carried by a British courier named Caleb Bruen, who was actually a double agent for the Americans. By the time Bruen delivered the message to Clinton, the information regarding the troop movement had been removed.[13] Near the end of the month, Clinton was also advised that Col. Elias Dayton, well known to the British as Washington's chief intelligence officer in New Jersey, was attempting to establish new intelligence networks to collect on activities in the city.[14]

The next month another highly valued British source, "Hiram" (William Heron), reported the French would not be moving any troops for the time being. Heron's source of information was his close personal relationship with Gen. Samuel Parsons. Parsons considered Heron to be his double agent against the British, while the British considered him to be their double agent against Parsons. Heron considered himself to be working both sides for his personal advantage—holding the only correct view of his actions.[15] In his reporting to the British, Heron would pass along not only the information authorized by Parsons but also other intelligence he learned from his personal relationship with the general. In Heron's case, Washington's practice of restricting sensitive information on a need-to-know basis ensured that Heron could only report what Parsons knew, and Washington did not feel Parsons had a need to know his plans for the allied force.

In April, Washington created a situation that allowed the British to capture a courier carrying dispatches that clearly indicated that New York City was the focus of Washington's interests. He instructed the courier, named Montaigne, to take a particular route that he knew would lead to the capture of the correspondence. In the middle of the same month, General Phillips advised Clinton that from the correspondence taken from Montaigne and shared with him by Clinton, he was certain Washington would not move southward. New York City seemed the obvious target in both officers' minds.[16] On May 6, Clinton received a report that troops from Rhode Island were marching to the highlands above New York and that encampments for them had already been prepared.[17] This caused him to write Cornwallis, then the senior commander in Virginia, on May 26, urging him to send back to New York some of the troops Clinton had sent him earlier in the year.[18]

In June, Washington continued to provide Clinton with evidence of allied intentions to attack the city. A British agent, James Moody, captured American dispatches that provided details of the May 22 conference between Washington and Rochambeau. These dispatches were from Washington to generals John Sullivan and Lafayette and stated the agreement to attack New York City. Interestingly, these dispatches were not encoded, and other letters provided vague instructions regarding Tallmadge's New York City collection network and personal matters such as problems Washington was having with his wooden false teeth. These details added validity to the dispatches. Moody, who had been an agent for many years, did note that this interception was easily accomplished because of the lack of any American militia forces being in the area, which was different than in previous such missions. Clinton readily believed the authenticity of the intelligence, as it fit his established perception that his base was Washington's target.

And Washington continued to reinforce his deception. In the middle of the month, Heron also reported that the city was to be attacked, and a similar report was provided later in the month by British agent David Gray, who was another American double agent trusted by the British as both a courier for their military dispatches and as a collection source.[19]

At this point Clinton was sure the city was about to be attacked. On June 8, he wrote to Cornwallis, forwarding copies of the captured Washington correspondence. He stated that Lafayette's forces did not pose a significant threat to Cornwallis, requested that two thousand men from Cornwallis's force be sent to him, and stated that the captured correspondence made him certain New York City would be attacked.[20] Throughout the month, Clinton sent numerous dispatches to Cornwallis requesting reinforcements. By the end of the month, Cornwallis expressed concern to Clinton regarding the Yorktown base because of the possible lack of British naval superiority and therefore the lack of reinforcements.[21]

Throughout July, Washington kept Clinton supplied with intelligence that indicated an attack on New York City. In addition to a general gossip campaign within American circles, he focused his collection requirements on individuals known to be also reporting to the British on the city. For example, a New Jersey British double agent reported that Colonel Dayton had asked him for specific details of the fortifications and troop strength of the city's perimeter, focusing specifically on the bridges and road approaches. A source of British colonel Oliver DeLancey reported that the Americans intended to attack Harlem and Long Island. And yet another source reported that Colonel Dayton had let it slip that a French fleet was soon expected and would join in the attack on the city. A third source, also quoting Dayton, reported that if the allied army were to attack, its objective would be New York City. Obviously, Dayton had been both very busy and very talkative during the month. Another confirming report of the planned attack came from a British agent who sourced it to a man known to be trustworthy—David Gray, the American double agent.[22]

By August, British intelligence reporting provided increasingly conflicted views of where the enemy was and its objective. On the 2nd, Clinton was informed that some five hundred French and American troops had crossed the Hudson River and were at Tappan. A week later, a British agent who had infiltrated the allied forces reported preparations for attacking New York City.[23] By the middle of the month, Clinton also received intelligence that the French forces were moving south of the city, calling into question whether a joint attack was planned. This intelligence noted that forage and food supplies were being amassed across New Jersey for French forces and that Rochambeau's son's mistress had been sent to Trenton in order to be near her lover.

In the same period Clinton also knew that American forces were destroying barricades and other obstructions on some roads leading into the city and that French engineers were constructing large bakery ovens west of it in the Chatham, New Jersey, area. He also received reports of large encampments being surveyed opposite New York and that American units were gathering small boats along the Hudson's New Jersey shore.[24] In addition, British defensive lines were being probed, cannon were being situated, and supply dumps were being established near the city. Thus, while Clinton recognized that the enemy forces had shifted westward, their presence still posed a threat to New York. Yet it was also apparent that they could be moving southward as well, toward Cornwallis's forces in Virginia.

According to Elias Boudinot, formerly a colonel in the Continental Army but by this time a congressman from New Jersey, Washington personally involved himself in the deception plan in August. According to Boudinot, Washington sent for a former inhabitant of New York who now lived in New Jersey. This individual was known to have Tory sympathies and to have passed information on local activities to British officials in the city. Washington emphasized to the civilian that as a local resident, he could be of great help in providing information on the area around Monmouth County and New York City. He pledged the man to secrecy and by his questions made it obvious that he was interested in the British defensive posture. Boudinot was certain that by that same evening, the British in New York were fully aware of Washington's questions.[25]

Later in the month, Clinton received reports of a large concentration of allied troops at Peekskill and of an American force near Chatham, which had probed British defenses north of the city.[26] And once again, a British agent reported that Colonel Dayton let slip in a conversation that the attack on the city would come from New Jersey and Staten Island.[27] With the allied force moving westward, Clinton advised Cornwallis to keep the troops he had previously requested to reinforce the city. However, this dispatch, which stated Clinton's view that the enemy threat might be directed at Cornwallis's forces, did not reach Cornwallis.[28]

By the end of August, Clinton's intelligence indicated that the American and French forces were at Princeton and Trenton and that the supplies were stockpiled in southern New Jersey. Early in September he learned those troops were moving toward the Delaware River, and it became apparent that Cornwallis's forces in the Yorktown area were the intended objective of the American and French armies.[29] But it was too late. Clinton no longer had the capability to react by sending reinforcements to Cornwallis. The Battle of the Capes allowed the French fleet to block both reinforcements and supplies from reaching Cornwallis and closed his evacuation route. The French action also allowed Admiral de Barras to bring the French forces' supplies, as well as heavy cannon required for a siege operation, from Newport to the allied force. After shadowing the British fleet for several days, Admiral de Grasse moved to the northern part of the Chesapeake Bay and began transporting American and French forces southward to surround Cornwallis.

As the siege at Yorktown took shape, a potentially strategic piece of intelligence came into American hands. James Rivington, the New York City Tory publisher of the *Royal Gazette* and Culper Ring agent, obtained a copy of the Royal Navy's signals book.[30] This book described how the navy used its series of flags, or at night lights and rockets, to maneuver their ships in a naval engagement. Instant knowledge of how the British planned to form and use their ships in battle could give an opposing force a significant advantage in battle. How Rivington obtained the book has never been revealed. Also, while Rivington was part of the Culper Ring, the American intelligence officer who received the book from him was not directly connected to the ring.

That officer was Maj. Allen McLane, who had previously conducted intelligence activities against the British when they occupied Philadelphia. After the British evacuation, McLane was assigned to the New Jersey area to monitor British activities there. Later, he scouted the British positions at Stony Point, New York, and Paulus Hook, New Jersey. And, in late August 1781, he had just returned from the Caribbean, where at Washington's instructions he had met with the French admiral de Grasse to coordinate military operations in Virginia.[31] Some historians have reasoned that correspondence from Washington which McLane carried to this meeting, along with McLane's personal appeals, were the reasons that de Grasse agreed to the Chesapeake Bay location vice the New York City area. This seems unlikely, not just because the senior French Army commander, Rochambeau, had already suggested the bay as the destination, but also because French government correspondence had also supported that destination. Subsequently, on August 13 de Grasse sailed toward the bay, carrying with him some three thousand French troops. He arrived near Yorktown on August 26.

Why McLane was tasked with meeting Rivington to get the signals book is unknown, but at the time both Culpers were greatly concerned about their own personal security and their activities were limited. It is possible McLane was directed by Washington to meet with Rivington because of these security concerns.

In any event, in late August or early September—no specific date is known and McLane only described it as "in the fall"—he met with Rivington to obtain the book.[32] Since he had arrived in Virginia from the Caribbean on August 26, 1781, and had to travel to Long Island for the meeting, the early September period seems an appropriate time frame for the meeting. McLane's notes seem to indicate he then took the book to de Grasse. But once again no specific date was mentioned for when the French admiral received it.

In his book *Invisible Ink: Spycraft of the American Revolution*, historian John Nagy has attempted to solve the mystery regarding how McLane and Rivington arranged to meet to pass the book and has established a general time for that meeting. His theory is that personal advertisements placed in the *Royal Gazette* were used to arrange the meeting.[33] This type of clandestine communication technique, using newspaper advertisements, often in the personal sections of the paper, was well established as a tradecraft tool. In fact, it is a common clandestine communication procedure even now, although the media is often digital rather than print. However, Nagy suggests the meeting was held near the end of September or even in early October, since the advertisement offering the meeting and its location was in the September 29 edition of the paper. But McLane returned to the country in late August.[34] As Washington was constantly concerned with the speedy acquisition of intelligence, and this would certainly be the case for a document as important as the signals book, it seems doubtful he would allow a month's delay in sending McLane to meet Rivington. Because the actual dates of the book's passage to McLane, and when it was provided to the

French navy, are unknown, the book's actual use and value during the Yorktown campaign has been questioned by many historians.[35]

In addition to successfully confusing the enemy commanders regarding his military objective, Washington also caused strained relationships between the two senior British commanders. While Washington confused Clinton in New York City, Lafayette was also active both collecting on the British forces opposing him in Virginia and doing some tactical deception activities of his own. Records identified one reporting network and three American agents, two of them African American slaves, who contributed to keeping Cornwallis confused as to American capabilities and intentions.

When Cornwallis arrived at Williamsburg, Continental Army colonel James Innis, a native of Virginia, established a reporting network to monitor British activities on both the northern and southern sides of the York River. Some of his agents even entered British lines disguised as tradesmen selling provisions and goods, to obtain intelligence. While no specific details of the intelligence produced seem to exist, Innis, in a correspondence dated February 11, 1782, claimed the agents had produced good intelligence.[36]

Another agent working for Lafayette, Pvt. Charles Morgan, was used to convince Cornwallis not to move his forces northward across the James River. This kept him from escaping before the allied forces (then moving southward) could reinforce Lafayette. Morgan was a member of a New Jersey light battalion and selected by his commanding officer in response to Lafayette's request for an individual who could pose as a deserter and then gain the trust of his British interrogators. When questioned personally by Cornwallis and his colleague Col. Banastre Tarleton, Morgan managed to convince them that Lafayette had adequate boats to immediately follow the British should they cross the river. He was careful to claim that he did not know the exact number of boats Lafayette had available but only that there were enough to move the entire American force across the James River if necessary.[37]

Morgan, like Nathan Hale, undertook the dangerous mission out of patriotism. His one demand in accepting the mission was that should he be captured and hanged, Lafayette must promise he would publish in New Jersey a full disclosure that Morgan had never been a deserter but rather had undertaken a dangerous intelligence mission for the good of his country.[38]

One other interesting aspect of the mission was that after the British debriefed him, he was recruited into the British army. However, he deserted back to the Americans a few days thereafter, bringing with him several other British deserters.[39] This raises the question of how his deception mission could have been successful once he rejoined the American side and thus made his comments suspect. Yet Cornwallis did not move across the river, and Lafayette's deception objective was accomplished.

It is not totally clear why Cornwallis did not cross the river. And if Morgan's disinformation did play a role, perhaps the structure of the British army at that time offers an explanation as to why it was still accepted after his return to the American side. Intelligence collection was handled at a senior-officer level, and this included debriefings of deserters as well as British agents. However, strength reports of British units, while submitted to higher authority daily, were considered administrative details to be regarded only from an overall-strength perspective. That an individual soldier had deserted—and there were always deserters—was not of particular interest to senior commanders. Thus it is probable that once Morgan became a British soldier, his desertion was never brought to the attention of Cornwallis.

Another American agent was an African American slave, Saul Matthews, owned by Thomas Matthews, a Virginia patriot. He was permitted by his master to join the Virginia Militia. His commanding officer, Col. Josiah Parker, selected him to collect intelligence on British activities and troop strength in the Portsmouth area and particularly about Cornwallis's movements along the nearby James River. Once again, the details of his reporting have been lost, and it is unclear whether he engaged only in scouting activities or went into the British lines to collect information. However, several years later, in November 1792, his written petition describing his activities convinced the Virginia legislature to grant him his freedom for services rendered while reporting on British activities during the Yorktown campaign.[40]

During the final period of the Yorktown campaign, when Cornwallis had concentrated his forces to defend the city, another African American intelligence agent was active and successful. James Armistead, a slave owned by William Armistead of New Kent County, Virginia, proved an excellent courier and collection agent for Lafayette in the summer and fall of 1781. With his master's permission, he joined the Continental Army and was assigned to Lafayette's service in March 1781. Lafayette knew that Armistead was well known to the British from his comings and goings about the area in the service of his master. His travel gave him extensive knowledge of the local area, especially around Portsmouth. Based upon this knowledge and British acceptance of his presence as normal and unthreatening, Lafayette used him as a courier to transport intelligence collected by resident sources within British lines.[41] However, his greatest intelligence contribution involved another tactical deception plan initiated by Lafayette against Cornwallis regarding American troop strength and movements.

For this mission Armistead pretended to be a refugee running away from his master. Based upon previous British knowledge of his history of wandering between the lines of the two armies, Cornwallis decided he would make a good spy—which was true. The British recruited him and sent him back into the American lines to report on their strength and disposition. There he met with Lafayette and was given a dispatch from Lafayette to Gen. Daniel Morgan regarding the movement of certain fictitious American units. The dispatch was crumbled up and rubbed with dirt to make it appear it had been lying in the mud along the side of a road. Armistead's cover story was that he had succeeded in observing the strength of the American units in the area and while returning found the dispatch along the road. He said that because he could not read, he did not know what it said but thought it might be of interest to the British. He also reported that there had been no change in American troop disposition in the areas he visited. The British officers, who could read, believed that information in the dispatch identified new American units of which they had been unaware. Because Lafayette had personally written the dispatch, they were able to identify his handwriting, which further validated the authenticity of the document.[42]

There are some interesting postscripts to Armistead's service. After the surrender, as was social custom in eighteenth-century warfare, Lafayette invited Cornwallis to dinner. Armistead was one of the servants at that dinner. There are conflicting reports as to whether or not Cornwallis recognized his former agent, and he never mentioned it in his correspondence. Armistead also found himself in a unique situation when it came time to seek his reward for his activities during the Revolution. The Virginia Emancipation Act of 1783 allowed the granting of freedom to slaves who had rendered significant military service, but he could not qualify because his services had been in the intelligence field. It was not until 1787 that his petition for freedom, supported by Lafayette's endorsement, was granted by the Virginia Assembly. Thereafter, Armistead took Lafayette as his last name, becoming James Armistead Lafayette. Years later, he was also granted a pension for life based upon his intelligence activities during the Yorktown campaign.[43]

Once Cornwallis's defeat at Yorktown became public knowledge, the British government recognized that the conflict was effectively over except for negotiations on the terms of a formal agreement to end the war. British military activities in the colonies became defensive, and eventually Washington was notified by the British commander in New York City that his intentions were not to provoke any armed conflict. However, Indian raids along the western frontier continued, as did rumors of a new British campaign being organized in Canada. Washington was cautious and kept his New York agents busy looking for signs of hostile British intentions, but all their reporting indicated that British activities were purely defensive in nature.

In the South, the British continued to garrison Charleston, and General Greene kept his agents busy monitoring their plans. He was concerned the British would attempt to seize various strategic points in the southern colonies to use as bargaining points during formal peace negotiations. His sources did an excellent job of monitoring the enemy, and he was well informed as the British planned their evacuation from Charleston.

One other American intelligence collector, Daniel Bissell, a member of the Second Connecticut Regiment of the Continental Army, deserves mention more because of an honor given him than the value of the intelligence he provided. He is best known in American history as one of three soldiers awarded the Badge of Military Merit by order of Washington and the only one so honored for his intelligence activities.[44] Based upon this award, there has been speculation that his intelligence must have been of significant value to Washington. In the award citation, signed by Washington on May 9, 1783, at his headquarters at Newburgh, New York, Bissell is described as having "performed some important service, within the immediate knowledge of the Commander-in-Chief, in which his fidelity, perseverance and good sense . . . [are] deserving of commendation."[45]

However, research regarding what he did report in September 1782 has not identified any intelligence of particularly great value. In fact, Bissell's collection mission was a failure. In the summer of 1781, he was asked to pose as a deserter and enter New York City, observe current British activities, and then report back within a short time. Unfortunately, he had been advised by his case officer, Col. David Humphrey, a personal aide to Washington, that he could bribe New York City officials to allow him to remain in the city as a deserter. While Humphrey's information had been true in the past, it no longer was. When Bissell arrived in the city in mid-August, he found that deserters were being forced into British service. He then had to hide out, missing the boat sent to pick him up. He subsequently became ill and joined Benedict Arnold's loyalist American forces to receive treatment for his illness. Upon his recovery, it took him until late September 1782 to escape British lines and return to the American army. He was arrested as a deserter and held until Washington's headquarters learned of his return and freed him. Bissell spent a couple of days writing a report on his recent observations of British activities and the status of their fortifications.[46]

When Bissell was sent on his mission, Washington was fully engaged in his deception plan to keep Clinton focused on a possible American attack on New York City. His collection objective at that time would have been to observe what activities British forces were undertaking: Were defenses being strengthened or were troops preparing for possible departure in support of Cornwallis? Such intelligence in August 1781 would have been of significant interest to Washington. However, by the following year Washington's intelligence requirements would not have concerned whether British activities in New York indicated offensive or defensive actions. Thus Bissell's report was probably useful but not important enough to justify the seemingly special reward.

Most people in government or military service, and probably an equal number in the private sector, recognize that awards are not always given just to reward some perceived achievement. There are other reasons, such as morale boosting, inability to provide other forms of appreciation, and sometimes just the need to draw attention away from some other issue. This was probably the case with the awards to Bissell and the other two soldiers. Originally, Bissell had been promised a promotion upon the successful completion of his mission. However, by the time he finally returned to American lines, the Continental Congress had frozen promotions. Also, Washington was, typically, short of funds and unable to provide any monetary reward. Washington's inability to provide tangible rewards affected the entire army. It is possible—his noble statement regarding the award notwithstanding—that its creation had as much to do with army morale as rewarding specific acts of bravery.

A provisional agreement on November 30, 1782, brought about a cessation of armed conflict, and six months later the Continental Congress officially proclaimed the end of hostilities. By 1783, the reporting from Washington's agents in New York had become infrequent, and in July, Culper Sr. sent his last message, providing an accounting of his expenses for his intelligence activities during the war. While the American government was still young, its bureaucracy was more mature, and it would be a long time before Culper Sr. would see any government reimbursement. Those intelligence officers who followed him (and learned from history) understood that when intelligence operations are critical to national security, funds are readily available, often in generous amounts. But once the crisis is over, the willingness to spend money on intelligence activities diminishes quickly. This is true to this day.

Closer to the British evacuation of New York, Sir Guy Carleton, Clinton's

An etching of Gen. George Washington. *Library of Congress*

replacement, even began sharing intelligence from his remaining agents regarding plots to plunder the city, seize the personal property of known Tories, and settle old personal and business disputes by force.[47] Washington and Carleton worked out a procedure that allowed American forces to enter the city just as the British troops departed, to maintain public order and resident protection.

Benjamin Tallmadge requested and received permission to be among the first to enter the city so that he could ensure the safety of his agents there.[48] When Washington entered the city, he also visited at least two of his agents. According to reports from his accompanying officer, Washington had breakfast with Hercules Mulligan, ordered various clothing items from him, and permitted him to advertise as "Tailor to George Washington."[49] The general also visited James Rivington, and an aide reported that he heard the sound of gold coins being exchanged during their private conversation.[50]

In the years following the war, Washington made some efforts to personally thank many of his intelligence agents, but most simply faded back into their normal lives. After all, this was a war where neighbor against neighbor was a common situation, and while many Tories fled the country, others remained. It made common sense not to publicize secret activities. Few books or articles were written by American agents, although their subsequent petitions for Revolutionary War pensions often shed some light on their intelligence activities. Washington's discipline on operational security was shared by his senior intelligence officers, further keeping many of these activities out of public view. While some references to intelligence activities could be found in Washington's correspondence, as well as those of other senior officers, much of the details known about sources and methods in Revolutionary War intelligence came from the study of family archives and documents passed down through generations—or documents often found in old furniture and trunks in musty attics.

Oral histories taken from participants well after the conflict are yet another good source. When this information can be collated with official correspondence and documents, as well as detailed histories of events, logical conclusions can be drawn as to their validity. However, opinions can and will differ as historians have a responsibility to vet their information most carefully.

There is little doubt that today, over two hundred years after the war, details of the vast majority of American intelligence activities undertaken during the conflict still remain out of public view. Perhaps a musty New England attic or the reconstruction of an old wall in a southern colonial mansion will provide additional insights into what we do know or provide the first details of a new intelligence operation. The story is not over.

CHAPTER 12

THE AFRICAN AMERICAN ROLE IN AMERICAN INTELLIGENCE ACTIVITIES

African Americans—both slaves and freemen—played important roles in intelligence activities during the Revolutionary War. However, their exploits are not well known. There are several reasons for this. The most obvious issue is racial prejudice during that period and up through at least the civil rights era. Many of the individuals who acted either as intelligence collectors or provided support roles, such as couriers, were slaves or servants of others. Thus their masters often received the official thanks or credit for their activities. In later years, historians who were prejudiced may not have believed that the stories and contributions of African Americans were worth telling, and the contribution to American independence of those who continued to be slaves was an inconvenient truth for the dominant narrative of white Americans winning their freedom through the Revolutionary War.

Another reason that less is known about the African American role in the Revolutionary War is that many of these individuals were not literate, as teaching slaves to read and write was not a widespread practice even in the northern colonies and illegal in some colonies. Therefore, personal records of their actions, such as diaries and letters, seldom existed then or now.

Finally, the traditional practice of protecting the identity of intelligence agents to ensure they could be used successfully on future missions or would not be targets of later revenge also played a role. This is true for all spies in all eras, and it is a continual challenge for historians of intelligence to piece together the full story. However, official records do provide some identification of individuals and details of their service and on occasion note that deserved rewards were provided for services rendered. While several books have been published on African Americans' involvement in the Revolutionary period, their documentation is sometimes weak. Overall, Benjamin Quarles's *The Negro in the American Revolution* seems the best-researched secondary source to date.[1]

A case can be made that African American involvement in the Revolution's intelligence activities started as early as the Boston Massacre of March 5, 1770, and did not end until well after the surrender at Yorktown by General Cornwallis on October 19, 1781. The Boston Massacre, stimulated by the political-action campaign of the Sons of Liberty, while hardly the first bloodshed of the Revolution, was a key event in the escalation of violence in Boston leading to formal military conflicts between the patriots and the British army. One of the individuals in the mob that provoked the small British guard detachment at the Boston customhouse was Crispus Attucks, an individual of African American and Native American descent. He was one of three protesters killed at the site and is believed to have been the first to die.[2] During the final phase of the southern campaign leading to the British surrender at Yorktown, several African Americans acted as American spies, reporting on British activities and construction of their fortifications. One, the aforementioned James Armistead Lafayette, had his contributions well documented. Unlike many others, he was recognized by the government and granted his freedom and a pension for his services.[3] Gen. Nathanael Greene's papers mention "Negro" collectors and couriers operating for his intelligence nets well after the Yorktown surrender.

In 1775, when British military governor General Gage dispatched officers in civilian dress to reconnoiter roads from Boston to various locations where the patriots had military stores, it was an African American tavern maid who made a significant counterintelligence contribution by recognizing them as British officers and alerting local patriots.[4] This young woman who worked at Jonathan Brewer's tavern outside of Watertown, Massachusetts, has never been identified by name. However, her keen memory for faces and her loyalty to the patriots' cause enabled the locals to move weapons and ammunitions to more secure locations, as well as to note Tory contacts in the area to be dealt with later. And when Gage did send his forces on the fateful march into Lexington and Concord, African American patriots in the local militias responded and in one specific case played a significant tactical role in causing the retreat of the British forces.

While popular folklore tends to describe an almost spontaneous organi-

James Armistead, a slave in Virginia, was one of Lafayette's most productive spies. After successfully petitioning for emancipation after the war, he changed his name to James Armistead Lafayette. *Valentine Richmond History Center*

zation of country folk hiding behind trees and stone fences shooting at the British column in retreat, the facts are quite different. As Paul Revere and his colleagues spread the word of the British movement from Boston, a well-orga-nized system of prearranged alarms was activated throughout the countryside to rally militia units to defend their territory. This system involved a variety of methods, including the ringing of church bells, the firing of muskets, and the sounding of signal horns. And in the early hours of April 19, it was the trumpet call of Abel Benson, a nine-year-old son of a slave, that alerted the militia in Needham, the Dover area, and Dedham to the threat.[5]

During the fighting that day, numerous African American militia mem-bers, both freemen and slaves, were involved. At Lexington, the militia that faced the British was both white and black, and one of the wounded on the patriot side was Prince Estabrook, a slave, later given his freedom based upon his military service.[6] As the British continued their march toward Concord, African American militiamen Samuel Craft and Peter Salem of Newton, Cato Bordman of Cambridge, Cuff Whittenmore and Cato Wood of Arlington, and Pomp Blackman were involved in the fighting.[7]

However, it was the elderly David Lamson whose actions on that day rep-resent the most valuable military contribution by an African American pa-triot. As the British retreated from Concord in the face of a rapidly growing militia force, reinforcements from Boston were en route. This relief column included two cannon but carried with it a limited amount of ammunition in order to move quickly. Resupply wagons were to follow. When the reinforce-ments reached the retreating column, the cannon were effective in keeping the American forces at a distance where their fire was less effective.

The artillery ammunition was soon exhausted, and the patriots once again were able to pour a constant fire into the retreating British troops. Lamson, leading a small group of older militiamen, moved toward the sounds of battle and found himself positioned between the retreating British force and two supply wagons moving forward with more ammunition. After challenging the wagons and their escort to halt, and the British refusal to do so, the small band of militiamen responded with deadly accurate fire, killing the unit's two sergeants and seriously wounding the officer in charge. Now leaderless, the remaining soldiers fled toward Boston, throwing away their arms as they ran.[8] Without ammunition, the cannons became just another encumbrance to the British forces, and their retreat became increasingly disorganized and costly in terms of casualties.

At the Battle of Bunker Hill (Breed's Hill) in June 1775, once again African

American militiamen played important roles in a notable battle. Americans lost this battle in the sense of leaving the field but won in terms of both the casualties they inflicted on British forces and the psychological effect the battle had on British commanders throughout the war. Peter Salem, a veteran of the fighting at Concord, also fought in this battle. He is reported to have fired the shot that killed Royal Marines major John Pitcairn, the officer in command of the British troops at Lexington Common during this battle.[9] A local legend identifies African American militiaman Salem Poor as the soldier who shot the British commander of the Bunker Hill attacking force, Lt. Col. James Abercrombie.[10]

Estimates of the number of African Americans, freemen and slaves, who served in the Continental Army during the war vary among researchers because of the lack of accurate documentation. However, based on available evidence, a figure of five thousand seems a reasonable estimate.[11] Since the Continental Navy, as well as the various state navies, encouraged African American enlistments, it can be assumed that a large number also served in those navies. While most African Americans in American service were in integrated units, several units started out as all black, such as some companies of the First Rhode Island Regiment and the Bucks of America, a Massachusetts militia unit.

As specifically relates to African American roles in intelligence activities, my research has only been able to identify about a dozen individuals by name and not all of these by more than a first name, or the last name being that of their owner. When adequate information on their activities has been found, they are included in the appropriate chapters where their contributions can be seen in context of the dangers and value they represented.

However, there were also one-time intelligence missions that do not necessarily fit into the larger narrative. An example of this is Benjamin Dominique, who returned to American lines on July 3, 1781, after having been inside British lines at their outpost in Ninety Six, South Carolina. His debriefing provided information on the plans and intentions of the British commander, Col. John Harris Cruger, to evacuate the post before American troops under General Greene and Col. Henry Lee arrived to force a battle. Cruger planned to move his forces to Augusta and Charleston. This was valuable information that enabled Greene to avoid a battle, with the knowledge that his objective could be achieved bloodlessly.[12] Another example is an individual identified only as Quaco, a slave sold by his Rhode Island Tory master to a British officer. Subsequently, Quaco ran away, and when debriefed by American officers, he apparently provided valuable intelligence on British plans and activities in

Newport. While details of his information are wanting, its value is reflected in the fact that in January 1782, the Rhode Island General Assembly granted him freedom. His services were described as proving essential to the American cause.[13]

Greene also had numerous African American informants and couriers working inside Charleston, the key enemy command-and-control center in the southern colonies. Because by late 1781, the political loyalty of most of the population of the town was pro-British, the few remaining patriots were carefully watched by their neighbors and British military authorities. In this environment, African American agents were especially valuable because their activities were considered unalarming based upon their social status. Slaves and freemen were present there in large numbers and readily accepted—or, rather, ignored—as part of the town's daily commerce and street scene. These agents, used by Greene's principal agents Thomas Farr and Roger P. Saunders, performed a variety of functions, including collection and courier duties. However, while referred to in documents, they were not identified individually.

Yet another brief mention in documents identified a slave, described as the property of John Harleston and named Antigua, as being directed in his intelligence activities by the American governor of South Carolina, John Rutledge. While few details regarding his activities are documented, it is known that he went behind British lines to collect information and that he always accomplished his mission.[14] In March 1783, the South Carolina Assembly rewarded him his freedom based upon his intelligence activities.

On the western frontier, another African American's intelligence contributions resulted in an important military victory near what is today the city of Pittsburgh. This individual was never identified by name, but his information regarding British military plans to coordinate an attack with local Indians on the American forces at Piqua, a rural town, was of great value. His reporting to Gen. William Irvine, the commanding general of the Western Department, enabled the Americans to attack the British first, before they had completed their necessary preparations. The attack on November 10, 1782, caught the British and Indians by surprise and so undermined the Indians' confidence in British power that future cooperation was difficult. This victory virtually eliminated the British threat on the frontier for the duration of the war.[15]

Readers with a broader background in African American participation in the Revolutionary War may note the absence of any mention of the intelligence contributions of a New York slave, Pompey Lamb, to General Wayne's assault on Stony Point in July 1779. This individual has been credited with an important role in identifying British defenses and even leading a portion of the attack based upon his knowledge of that evening's sentries' password. His story was included in Washington Irving's *Life of Washington* (1859) and Benson Lossing's *The Pictorial Field: Book of the Revolution* (1852).[16] Since then it has appeared in many printed books and articles, most recently in Michael L. Lanning's *African Americans in the Revolutionary War*.[17] According to the story, Lamb gained access to the British camp at Stony Point by selling fresh fruit and vegetables to the troops. Thus he was able to observe the fortifications and troop deployments and provide Wayne with this information. Trusted by the British, he was given their nighttime password so he could sneak in with additional food to sell. He used the password to get an advance party of Americans into the base to open the gate for the main body.[18]

While this story has been popular folklore in the Stony Point area since the Revolution, independent research has been unable to identify documents or other supporting evidence. In fact, some of the details in the story stand in direct contrast with what can be documented about the attack and British activities there. Respected historian Quarles concluded that Pompey's role in the assault was questionable.[19] But the most definitive discussion of why his alleged role was unlikely is found in Don Loprieno's *The Enterprise in Contemplation: The Midnight Assault of Stony Point*.[20] However, as a metaphor, Pompey's story does represent the countless undocumented collection and reporting activities that African Americans undertook throughout the war.

The majority of African Americans at the time were considered property, not persons, and this led many whites to underestimate their intelligence and willingness to act against their masters' interests. While working around their masters, they were able to overhear or observe a great deal of intelligence. As such they represented perfect sources for passive collection and clandestine passage of intelligence information. Because most were uneducated by formal standards, little thought was given to their understanding or remembering details of conversations conducted in their presence. Yet slaves were required to perform complex functions in their work roles, based primarily on their memory of past instructions, so their ability to remember details and repeat them accurately was often excellent. As couriers carrying intelligence, being able to claim that they were carrying out tasks for their masters usually made their movements of little concern to authorities. When they were questioned about an activity, the simple reply that it was being done at the direction of the master was usually satisfactory.

The motivation of African Americans to serve the American side is a very complex issue and must be viewed on an individual basis. Neither the Americans nor the British created policies that espoused freedom with a governmental guarantee for slaves. The policies of both the American and British militaries were based on pragmatic considerations regarding enlisting African Americans into their services. Washington, as a Virginian, was initially opposed to enlisting them even though New England units did contain both free and enslaved African Americans when he took command of the army surrounding Boston. The enslaved individuals served either in place of their owners or with their owners' permission. The freemen were part of the various New England communities and served for the same reasons as their neighbors. However, as Washington's need for soldiers increased, he modified his position. In his general order of January 12, 1777, he ordered recruiters to "enlist none but freemen," and this lack of reference to race enabled free African Americans to join and serve in integrated units. Several of the southern states enacted local laws to stop African American recruitments into their army drafts, but soon manpower shortages forced them to accept all volunteers. By the end of the war African Americans were serving from all the states.

The British policy regarding African Americans was similar to that adopted by President Abraham Lincoln during the Civil War. British forces freed slaves owned by those who supported the American cause but did not free those owned by Tories. In contested areas, slaves willing to join the British service were freed, and any African Americans captured in American uniforms were sold as slaves.[21] When the British evacuated New York City at the end of the war, the British commander did transport to British territory many African Americans who had been freed by the British.

In the North and even in the South, there were African American freemen with property who may have seen personal value in the independence movement. However, for most who were slaves, the war was not about to bring them any form of freedom. In many of the documented cases of slaves who joined the American cause, the promise of freedom, usually fulfilled, played a role in their undertaking of the mission. In other cases it could have been that they were instructed by the masters to perform the activity. Yet regardless of the reason for their actions, they were undertaken at great personal risk.

At a local level there are several memorials to various African Americans who fought for American independence. For example, in the Church Hill Cemetery in Framingham, Massachusetts, Peter Salem's grave is marked by a plaque identifying him as a "soldier of the revolution." At the national level, several African Americans have appeared on postage stamps commemorating their military service, and Crispus Attucks is also featured on a stamp com-memorating the Boston Massacre. But no national monument exists in their honor. Since 1968, when the United States Congress authorized collection of nongovernmental funds to build such a memorial on the national mall in Washington, little progress has been made in creating one.

In the case of African Americans who were involved in intelligence activi-ties in support of the American cause, even fewer public tributes exist. In any event, the African Americans specifically identified in intelligence activities should be viewed as representatives of the countless others never given credit for their actions. It took ninety-five years after the death of Crispus Attucks—until the Thirteenth Amendment to the Constitution—to outlaw slavery. And it was not until President Harry S. Truman issued Executive Order 9981 in 1948 that the US military was once again fully integrated. Repayment for African Ameri-can contributions to American independence is long overdue.

CHAPTER 13

CONCLUSION

*potential thesis**

That American intelligence activities were a significant factor in defeating the British in the Revolutionary War is well documented by historical record. Secret activities with France led to the covert assistance that enabled the Continental Army to remain in the field until a formal alliance could be negotiated. Covert action, consisting of political action, propaganda, and paramilitary activities, played a significant role in convincing the French of the determination of the colonies to win their independence. Had France not been convinced of such determination, the formal alliance would not have been achieved. Thus, in obtaining first covert and then formal assistance from France, intelligence activities were vital.

Marquis - turning pt.

At the tactical level of military operations, Washington's use of intelligence at Trenton, during the British occupation of Philadelphia, and as the British attempted their southern strategy was a key ingredient in keeping his army a viable military force in the face of constant shortages of men and supplies. As in all insurgencies, Washington faced an adversary with superior forces and, at least initially, better lines of communication. His intelligence capabilities allowed him to often avoid enemy traps, take advantage of their weaknesses, and react to their plans before they were fully implemented. Greene in the South followed a similar course of action based on good intelligence capabilities.

makes up for slow speed of effecient intelligence

During this period, military victory in a battle was considered to be determined by which side controlled the battlefield after the engagement. In an insurgency situation, this measure of success is not very useful. Against the Continental Army there were many occasions, starting with the Battle of Bunker Hill, where a British victory so weakened their own forces that it adversely

Pyrrhic victory

affected subsequent attempts to capitalize on the battle. Starting with the British seizure of Philadelphia, coordinated intelligence activities allowed American commanders to obtain details of British troop strength and locations, reactions of British officers to various events, and information on their supply situation. On occasion, intelligence also provided advanced warning of British plans and movements. *✓ stratagem*

Yet the most important intelligence activity undertaken by Washington throughout the war was not collection by his agents, but his offensive use of his intelligence assets, mixed with his military deception activities, to deceive the British regarding his army's strength and his military objectives. Early in the war this protected him when both the army and its supplies were too weak to withstand a battle with a major British force. Later it enabled him to create a situation resulting in the Battle of Yorktown in a manner assuring victory.

All the above notwithstanding, intelligence is only a useful tool if used effectively. Often, this means simply exercising common sense within the context of a clear understanding of your situation. The American side was extremely fortunate to have many able individuals who knew how to use the intelligence they received. These men often were not well versed in military or intelligence affairs but had a solid understanding of their surroundings, what needed to be accomplished, and how to manage and motivate their men both on the battlefield and in the intelligence service. In the course of writing this book, I had cause to read dozens of biographies of these individuals, and it became clear that they were the real reason the Revolution succeeded.

GEORGE WASHINGTON

As a former intelligence professional, with experience as both a case officer and an operational manager during a career of thirty-plus years, I feel competent to make some judgment on George Washington's skills as both a practitioner of intelligence and a prolific user of it. He learned the business by blending his personal code of conduct with commonsense approaches to dealing with people and establishing organizational structures. These characteristics were most likely also the reason he did well in two other areas where he had no formal training: business management of his plantations and his military planning and leadership. He also had great personal discipline, and this was a key ingredient that made him successful in both his political career and his intelligence work.

micromanaged
intel. essary.

Most tradecraft is based on common sense, comprehensive planning, and a disciplined implementation of a complex plan. Thus, contrary to its public image, it is hardly exciting—although it does have its moments. With his personality traits, Washington was well suited for the role of an intelligence manager. However, he also faced a situation not unusual in that period but seldom seen in modern times: He was both the intelligence manager for the Continental Army and the chief consumer of its intelligence product. This duality of responsibilities did periodically create tensions that caused one of his roles to suffer at the expense of the other. His frustration with slow communication of intelligence, for example, caused him to seek courier shortcuts that weakened the operational security of his reporting networks. However, usually the intelligence professional side of his personality won out when his dual responsibilities came into conflict.

Washington believed in an intelligence structure with central direction and focus but decentralized implementation of these activities. He and a small secretariat of aides received, analyzed, and acted upon the intelligence collected. Within this small intelligence structure, his system was efficient and usually effective. He could readily identify information gaps and issue collection requirements to try to fill them. However, no doubt from his own experience in the field prior to and during the French and Indian War, Washington recognized that only the intelligence officer in the field knew how to get the required information. Those officers knew the local environment, what collection resources might be available, and how to craft and implement an operation to accomplish the mission. The activities of Benjamin Tallmadge, Allen McLane, John Laurens, and others demonstrated the validity of this approach. And this tends to be the managerial approach in the US intelligence community today, although the civilian and military intelligence services differ somewhat in this regard.

Washington's personal discipline also extended to his approach to the operational security of his intelligence activities. He emphasized protection of his agents and their information in his own activities and with those working for him. He understood the difficulty of establishing an agent with the access and capability to provide valuable and useful intelligence. He also recognized that if that agent was exposed or captured, there was no guarantee that similar access could ever again be established. Agents and their access are not replaceable parts in an intelligence network; rather, they are unique individuals and must be carefully and constantly protected if they are to continue to report. That he successfully instilled this discipline in his intelligence officers was demonstrated by Benedict Arnold's attempts to get local commanders, including Tallmadge, to give him the identities of their agents. Arnold generally failed in his attempt.

Washington's insistence on the need-to-know principle regarding all his intelligence operations held firm throughout the war. He maintained this discipline even within the senior levels of the army, and it proved effective. Examples of this include Arnold's passage of false information he received from Washington to General Clinton and General Parsons's inability to provide his trusted friend, William Heron, with information because he was not aware of it.

The smaller scope of Washington's intelligence concerns, when compared to the broad international scope of modern times, also gave him a significant advantage in his confidence in his field intelligence officers. He personally selected individuals such as Tallmadge and trusted their judgments and comments regarding the validity of their agents' access and reporting. In many cases, such as reportedly with John Honeyman, Washington personally selected the individual for the intelligence mission. In the case of the Culper Ring, Tallmadge knew Culper Sr. personally and recruited him specifically to create a reporting network in the New York City area. Another example was Hercules Mulligan, who reported through the Culper Ring and also independently. He was identified by one of Washington's aides, Alexander Hamilton, who vouched for Mulligan's loyalty and commitment. The advantage of being focused only on the plans, intentions, and activities of the British army also extended into the analytical aspect of Washington's small staff organization. The amount of information received was manageable for them to collate and use effectively. He did not have the problem facing intelligence analysts today where millions of pieces of information are available daily and sorting out the useful from the interesting is significantly more time-consuming and difficult.

While the Culper Ring, as well as the networks operating in and around Philadelphia during the British occupation, demonstrated Washington's professional intelligence focus, his strategic deception operation against General Clinton stands out as a particularly fine example of a complex intelligence operation. Deception operations are extremely difficult to conduct. They demand central control of all double-agent reporting, orchestrated manipulation of all suspected enemy agents, and carefully scripted indiscreet comments by senior officials. In addition, they require the command ability to orchestrate troop movements in support of the deception theme. In this case Washington's dual responsibilities worked well to his advantage.

After reviewing what Washington accomplished in his intelligence activities, in terms of both organization and productivity, I would rate him as a talented, innovative, aggressive, and quite competent intelligence manager. That is not to say he was perfect. But considering all the other responsibilities and concerns he had in fighting the British, maintaining the Continental Army, and handling the complex political relationship with the Continental Congress and the state governments, his performance was impressive. Of the three Founding Fathers of American intelligence, Washington was the most important.

BRITISH INTELLIGENCE

Another interesting, and potentially educational, aspect of the intelligence war during the Revolutionary period was the degree to which British civilian and military leaders chose to ignore intelligence in their decision making. Their intelligence capabilities were often quite good. In France they had collection networks and agents well placed to monitor American-French activities and planning. In the colonies they had a large core of Tories ready and able to report on colonial political and military activities. Therefore, it seems apparent that both ignorance and arrogance affected how the British responded to their intelligence.

To place this issue in modern terms, we would label the problem as a lack of cultural awareness regarding the American patriots. In both British governmental and military leadership, there appears to have been a complete misunderstanding about how to appeal to the hearts and minds of the rebellious colonials. The British also consistently underestimated their determination to achieve independence. Some examples follow.

By 1775, the British government was well aware of the structure and leadership, both political and military, that the American patriots had created in support of their demands for more economic freedom. For the past ten years, British officials in the colonies had been reporting on events and were quite clear that most of the most influential colonial leaders would not settle for a return to the status quo—either through political negotiations or military force. Compromise was required. And in the first years of the war, many colonists may well have been satisfied with far less than political independence. British agents, some well placed within American patriot leadership circles, sent accurate intelligence to Gen. Thomas Gage in Boston and other British officials as the armed conflict grew in size and scope. But the British government ignored this information and continued to believe that British military force could easily eliminate the radical elements and bring the majority of the colonial population back to the Crown.

Clinton's actions in keeping British forces in New York City at the expense

of reinforcing Cornwallis at Yorktown was another example of selective reading of intelligence. While Washington worked hard to keep Clinton believing
that New York was the target of the American-French joint force, Clinton also
had other intelligence agents reporting contrary information. Also, the circumstances behind some of the reports about Washington's intentions were suspicious. But Clinton was predisposed to believing that New York City was the
strategic objective and only placed his faith in reporting supporting that view
until the information disproving it became overwhelming.

The issue of decision makers allowing preconceived views to stand even
in the face of contradicting information has been with us throughout history.
American military adventures in Asia and the Near East in modern times have
suffered from this characteristic. However, there is a lesson here for intelligence
professionals. They have a particular responsibility to provide intelligence
within the context of the realities of the local culture, as do American diplomats abroad. In a modern society so swamped with information of varying
degrees of usefulness, focusing decision makers on context as well as content is
not easy—but so necessary. The British government's failure to understand a
culture different in political and economic structure and goals led to the loss of
its American colonies and eventually its empire. Modern policymakers would
do well to learn from history.

A third example was the counterintelligence failure of the British to capitalize on their complete penetration of the American Commission in Paris,
which gave the British timely details of vital American activities and diplomatic negotiations. There was a period of several months when the British
government was better informed of the status of American-French negotiations
and planned covert activities than the Continental Congress. While Benjamin
Franklin, as the senior officer at the commission, failed to enforce much in the
way of security in either personnel selection or document control, he was well
aware that British spies were targeting the commission. However, he also believed that he was smart enough not to allow the spies to get the better of him.
Intelligence officers love that attitude.

AMERICAN COUNTERINTELLIGENCE

Finally, a few words about the most controversial intelligence discipline—
counterintelligence. I believe an argument could be made that the manner in
which it was conducted during the Revolutionary War had an important and

far-reaching impact on American politics and society extending into modern times. The war was an internal civil conflict as well as a war against foreign military forces. As such, at the local levels many personal, family, and business disputes were settled by claiming that a person was working for the other side. While John Jay attempted, for a few months, to create a relatively objective and legally responsible counterintelligence process, during most of the war local groups and military units handled identifying and punishing alleged spies and traitors by whatever ugly standards they wished. Once the emotions of the conflict died down, it became apparent that unless carefully watched, the new United States government might use counterintelligence as an excuse to punish internal political enemies. And indeed, such actions were attempted with the Alien and Sedition Acts by the Federalists in 1798.

During the next period in American history requiring an active counterintelligence program, the Civil War, subjective, violent, and legally questionable governmental actions added to public distrust of this discipline. The result is a suspicion, with some historical justification, that counterintelligence is often used for political or ideological purposes rather than to protect national security. This suspicion has manifested itself in a cultural climate and legal system that make it extremely difficult to investigate, arrest, and convict individuals involved in intelligence activities for foreign entities.

In America, our culture and legal system places primary emphasis on the rights of individuals and private enterprises. The right of the government to protect itself or the country comes second. This creates a friction point when it comes to counterintelligence matters. And this issue might well have been avoided if the Continental Congress and the Continental Army had not been too busy with other activities to establish legal frameworks for counterintelligence investigations and adjudications during the Revolutionary War.

The downside is that the United States today represents one of the softest targets for intelligence collection in the world. Most intelligence and security professionals would agree with this description. Also, perhaps surprising to the general public, most intelligence and security professionals also agree that it is far more important to keep the American concept of individual rights and freedoms intact than take them away to create a more effective counterintelligence environment. Most believe the weakness of our counterintelligence environment is more than compensated for by the strengths of our political and legal systems, as well as our strong cultural commitment to individual rights and liberties.

APPENDIX

TIMELINE OF REVOLUTION-ERA EVENTS

1753

October: George Washington receives a letter from the royal governor of Virginia to deliver to the French in the Ohio Territory.

December: Washington obtains intelligence on French plans and intentions in the Ohio Territory.

1754

May: Washington attacks French troops near Fort Necessity during the French and Indian War.

July: Washington surrenders Fort Necessity to the French.

1755

July: British general Edward Braddock dies in a French attack near Fort Duquesne (Pittsburgh).

1763

February: The Treaty of Paris ends the French and Indian War.

1765

March: The British government enacts the Stamp Act in the American colonies. Chapters of the Sons of Liberty form in major colonial cities.

1766

March: The British revoke the Stamp Act.

1767

June: The British government enacts the Townshend Acts in the American colonies.

December: The first of the "Letters from a Farmer in Pennsylvania" is published in Boston.

1768

June: A riot follows British customs authorities' seizing of John Hancock's ship *Liberty* in Boston.

July: The British government decides to send two regiments to Boston to enforce order.

August: Gen. Thomas Gage sends an officer to Boston to plan for British troop deployment.

October: Additional British troops land in Boston. Gage visits Boston for evaluation of the political situation. A journal published in major colonial cities begins reporting events from throughout the colonies from the Sons of Liberty perspective.

1769

July: At Newport, Rhode Island, a mob captures and destroys the British customs vessel *Liberty*.

October: Massachusetts royal governor Thomas Hutchinson notes that the "mob" in Boston has defied the army and won.

1770

January: The Battle of Golden Hill, in which the Sons of Liberty stop British troops from tearing down their "liberty pole" in New York City.

February: Samuel Adams orchestrates a grand funeral for a child killed by a Tory defending his home from a Boston mob.

March: British troops kill several Bostonians in the "Boston Massacre."

December: The trial of British soldiers involved in the March incident ends with five acquitted and two mildly punished.

1772

February: In Rhode Island waters, the British ship *Gaspée* seizes a ship owned by Nathanael Greene.

June: John Brown of Providence, Rhode Island, leads a mob to attack the *Gaspée* and burn it.

1773

May: Samuel Adams advises the Massachusetts colonial legislature of private correspondence from royal Massachusetts officials to the British government calling for military suppression of the colony's "liberties."

December: The Sons of Liberty dump British tea into Boston Harbor to protest taxes. Similar "tea parties" are held in other colonial cities.

1774

March: The British government enacts the Boston Port Bill, closing the harbor to all commercial shipments except of food.

May: General Gage arrives in Boston as military governor.

June: Gage shuts down the Massachusetts colonial legislature.

September: The Mechanics intelligence group begins operations in Boston. The First Continental Congress meets. The Massachusetts Convention passes the Suffolk Reserves declaration and forwards it to the Continental Congress. British troops seize the Sons of Liberty arsenal in Charlestown, Massachusetts.

December: The Mechanics have sources in Gage's administration providing advance warning of British plans to seize colonial military supplies. The Sons of Liberty seize British military supplies at Portsmouth, New Hampshire, and at Newport.

1775

February: The British fail in an attempt to seize American military supplies at Salem, Massachusetts.

March: Gage orders British officers in civilian clothing to conduct a reconnaissance of the road from Boston to Concord.

April: British troops clash with American militiamen at Lexington and Concord.

May: The Second Continental Congress meets. Benedict Arnold and Ethan Allen capture Fort Ticonderoga in New York.

June: The British win the Battle of Bunker (Breed's) Hill at a huge cost in casualties. Washington takes command of the colonial troops around Boston.

July: Dr. Benjamin Church sends an encrypted letter to the British via his mistress.

August: Americans raid British gunpowder supplies in Bermuda.

September: Gen. William Howe replaces Gage as British commander in the colonies.

October: Washington receives decrypted copies of Church's letter to the British.

December: Arnold's attack on Quebec fails and his forces retreat. French agent Julien-Alexandre Archard de Bonvouloir contacts Benjamin Franklin in Philadelphia to learn American intentions toward the British government.

1776

February: Washington orders Gen. Charles Lee to begin fortifying the New York City area.

March: The British evacuate Boston.

June: The Continental Congress establishes its Committee on Spies to develop procedures for counterintelligence activities. A plot to use local residents, including members of the Continental Army, to secretly assist the British attack on New York City is exposed.

July: The Continental Congress approves the Declaration of Independence. British forces land on Staten Island. Washington obtains details of Gen. Howe's troop strength there from British deserters. Silas Deane meets the French secretary of state for foreign affairs to negotiate clandestine assistance against the British. He then meets with British spy Edward Bancroft in Paris and discusses American plans.

August: Washington gets first intelligence from a reporting agent regarding British troops on Staten Island. Washington forms Knowlton's Rangers, the first American military intelligence unit. The British commission French and Indian War hero Robert Rogers to form a loyalist unit. Hortalez & Company is established by French agent Pierre-Augustin Caron de Beaumarchais to provide covert military support for the American cause.

September: British troops cross from Long Island into Manhattan. Nathan Hale enters British lines to collect tactical intelligence. Col. Thomas Knowlton is killed in action, and his unit is destroyed. Hale's ill-fated spy mission ends with his execution. John Jay is selected to lead a committee investigating British spying in the Hudson Valley.

December: James Aitken, aka "Jack the Painter," conducts sabotage against the British naval base at Portsmouth, England. Franklin meets with the French foreign minister in Paris. The Paris Commission, America's first diplomatic post abroad, officially opens. The British government formalizes the terms of Barcroft's employment as its agent. Possessing solid intelligence, Washington captures Trenton, New Jersey, from Hessian troops.

1777

January: Washington successfully attacks Princeton, New Jersey, and orders establishment of agent networks in Philadelphia. His deception plan of his army's strength fools Howe. Aitken sets fires at the naval facility in Bristol, England. American "privateers" clandestinely supported by the French government capture their first British ships in European waters. February: Washington hires Nathaniel Sackett to establish a reporting network in the New York City area.

March: Aitken is tried and executed at Portsmouth, England.

April: The first Hortalez & Company supply ship lands at Portsmouth, New Hampshire, with military supplies and foreign officers with special talents. Washington, dissatisfied with the intelligence being provided, fires Sackett.

June: Arthur Lee's journal detailing Paris Commission activities is clandestinely copied by the British when he visits Berlin.

August: Arnold's deception plan forces a British retreat from Fort Stanwix, not allowing reinforcement of British forces moving southward from Canada. British forces begin their campaign to capture Philadelphia.

September: Washington loses the Battle of Brandywine because of poor intelligence. The British occupy Philadelphia.

October: Arnold helps defeat the British at the Battle of Saratoga.

November: Maj. John Clark reports a successful double-agent operation against the British in Philadelphia. Capt. Allen McLane establishes a network of agents surrounding Philadelphia.

December: Washington's army winters at Valley Forge. Intelligence from Philadelphia reporting agent Lydia Darragh and Majors Clark and McLane warns of British surprise attack at Whitemarsh.

1778

February: America and France sign treaties to become allies.

March: Gen. Sir Henry Clinton replaces Howe as commander of British forces in America.

April: John Paul Jones raids the English port of Whitehaven.

May: Washington orders McLane to debrief all travelers from Philadelphia. American prisoners of war who escaped from Philadelphia brief Washington on British preparations for the city's evacuation.

June: The British leave Philadelphia and march toward New York City. At the Battle of Monmouth in New Jersey, Washington successfully attacks the retreating British forces. Arnold becomes military commander of Philadelphia.

August: Washington and Benjamin Tallmadge hold their first meeting to plan the Culper Ring. Nathan Woodhull agrees to the role of principal agent, with the alias of "Samuel Culper Sr."

September: Lt. Lewis J. Costigin is exchanged for a British officer but stays in New York City and collects intelligence on British forces there.

November: Caleb Brewster accepts the job of courier for the Culper Ring, reporting across Long Island Sound.

December: British forces capture Savannah, Georgia.

1779

April: Benedict Arnold marries Peggy Shippen. Culper Sr. reports he has accidentally spilled his supply of secret ink.

May: Arnold begins his negotiations with the British.

June: Loyalist forces almost capture Culper Sr., who then recruits Robert Townsend ("Samuel Culper Jr.") to assist in running the ring.

July: With detailed intelligence on British positions, Americans under Gen. "Mad Anthony" Wayne capture Stony Point, New York. Washington provides the Culper Ring with detailed instructions on how to conduct its collection activities. Hercules Mulligan begins reporting to Washington from New York City.

October: Culper Sr. is stopped and searched while carrying intelligence from New York City, but his reporting is not found.

December: Washington's army winters at Morristown, New Jersey.

1780

April: Washington publicly reprimands Arnold for his business activities.

May: Gen. Benjamin Lincoln surrenders over five thousand troops of his Southern Army to the British at Charleston, South Carolina.

July: French troops arrive at Newport. Culper Jr. reports that the British plan to attack them there.

August: Arnold takes command of West Point. At the Battle of Camden in

South Carolina, the British defeat Gen. Horatio Gates, who surrenders over four thousand troops.

September: British major John André meets Arnold near West Point. André is captured carrying intelligence on the fort's defenses, and Arnold flees to a British ship on the Hudson River.

October: André is hanged.

December: Gen. Nathanael Greene arrives in Charlotte, North Carolina, to command and rebuild the Southern Army. Arnold, now a British general, is sent to Virginia's Tidewater area.

1781

January: In South Carolina, Gen. Daniel Morgan defeats British forces at the Battle of Cowpens.

February: First indication of Clinton receiving deception information to keep him from sending reinforcements to Gen. Charles Cornwallis in Virginia.

March: The British army's victory in North Carolina at the battle of Guilford Courthouse comes with a high casualty rate that diminishes its troop strength significantly. British forces under Gen. William Phillips join Arnold's forces in the Tidewater area. James Armistead, a slave, joins the Marquis de Lafayette's staff and becomes an intelligence agent.

May: Cornwallis moves his troops out of North Carolina into Virginia.

June: Greene's Southern Army captures Augusta, Georgia. Culper Sr. ceases all reporting out of personal security concerns.

July: Major McLane and French admiral de Grasse coordinate plans for the Yorktown campaign.

September: A French fleet chases the British fleet out of the Chesapeake Bay, isolating British forces around Yorktown. Also, McLane obtains the Royal Navy's signals book from James Rivington.

October: The British at Yorktown surrender.

1782

April: At Washington's insistence, Culper Sr. returns to an active reporting role.

August: The British military advises Washington that London will agree to American independence.

September: Culper Jr. sends his last report.

November: The British government signs the Articles of Peace with America.

December: British forces evacuate Charleston.

1783

April: Congress ratifies the preliminary peace treaty with Great Britain.

July: Culper Sr. submits his final report—his expense account.

September: The Treaty of Paris officially ends the American Revolutionary War.

November: British troops depart New York City.

December: Washington resigns as commander in chief of the American army.

NOTES

Chapter 1: George Washington Learns the Intelligence Trade

1. P. K. Rose (aka Kenneth A. Daigler), *Founding Fathers of American Intelligence*, Center for the Study of Intelligence, Central Intelligence Agency, www.cia.gov/library/center-for-the-study-of-intelligence/csi-publications/books-and-monographs/the-founding-fathers-of-american-intelligence/art-1.html.

2. Edward G. Lengel, *General George Washington: A Military Life* (New York: Random House, 2005), 369.

3. Fred Anderson, *Crucible of War: The Seven Years' War and the Fate of the Empire in British North America, 1754–1766* (New York: Knopf, 2000), 36–37.

4. King George II's letter to Dinwiddie as stated in John C. Swartz, *George Washington: The Making of a Young Leader* (Medina, OH: Harbor Bend, 1995), 39.

5. Anderson, *Crucible*, 38.

6. Dinwiddie letter to the commander of the French forces on the Ohio, Williamsburg, Virginia, October 31, 1753, as quoted in Swartz, *George Washington*, 41–42.

7. Ibid., 43.

8. John C. Fitzpatrick, ed., *The Diaries of George Washington 1748–1777*, vol. 1, 1748–1770 (Cranbury, NJ: Scholar's Bookshelf, 2005), 43–65.

9. Ibid., 46–50.

10. Ibid., 52.

11. Ibid., 55.

12. Swartz, *George Washington*, 17–26.

13. Fitzpatrick, *Diaries of George Washington*, 55.

14. Ibid., 55–56.

15. Ibid., 58–59.

16. Swartz, *George Washington*, 61–62.

17. Fitzpatrick, *Diaries of George Washington*, 87–88.

18. Ibid., 92–93.

19. Ibid., 99.

20. Anderson, *Crucible of War*, 63.

21. Ibid., 64.

22. Ibid., 64, and John Ferling, *The Ascent of George Washington: The Hidden Political Genius of an American Icon* (New York: Bloomsbury, 2009), 25.

23. Ferling, *Ascent of George Washington*, 26.

24. Lengel, *General George Washington*, 47–48.

25. Anderson, *Crucible of War*, 86–87.

26. Ibid., 95, 48 (sketch of fort).

27. Ibid., 87–91.

28. Lengel, *General George Washington*, 50–51.

29. Ibid., 51.

30. Ibid., 51.

31. Anderson, *Crucible of War*, 86.

32. Ibid., 90.

33. Ibid., 103.

34. Ibid., 95.

35. Ibid., 88–90.

36. Ibid., 97.

37. See Anderson, *Crucible of War*, chapter 9, "Disaster on the Monongahela," 94–107, and David A. Clary, *George Washington's First War: His Early Military Adventures* (New York: Simon & Schuster, 2011), 144–60, for a comprehensive description of the battle.

38. Lengel, *General George Washington*, 60–62.

39. Ibid., 64–66.

40. Clary, *Washington's First War*, 262.

41. Lengel, *General George Washington*, 79.

42. Ibid., 62.

43. Washington to Robert Hunter Morris, January 5, 1766, in *The Writings of George Washington*, vol. 1, ed. John Fitzpatrick (Washington, DC: Government Printing Office, 1931–44), 268.

Chapter 2: The United Front Campaign That Led to the American Revolution

1. Benjamin L. Carp, *Defiance of the Patriots: The Boston Tea Party and the Making of America* (New Haven, CT: Yale University Press, 2010), 31.

2. Mark Puls, *Samuel Adams: Father of the American Revolution* (New York: Palgrave Macmillan, 2006), 14.

3. From Joseph J. Ellis's review of Puls's *Samuel Adams*, on the book's jacket and at www.palgrave.com/products/title.aspx?pid=344007.

4. Joseph Ellis, *American Creation: Triumphs and Tragedies at the Founding of the Republic* (New York: Knopf, 2007), 24–25.

5. Carl Van Doren *Benjamin Franklin* (New York: Penguin, 1991), 320.

6. Stewart Beach, *Samuel Adams* (New York: Dodd, Mead, 1965), 74.

7. Thomas Fleming, *Liberty: The American Revolution* (New York: Viking, 1997), 107.

8. David Hackett Fischer, *Paul Revere's Ride* (New York and Oxford: Oxford University Press, 1994), 22.

9. Beach, *Samuel Adams*, 76.

10. Ibid., 77, and Hiller B. Zobel, *The Boston Massacre* (New York: Norton, 1970), 28–29.

11. Gary B. Nash, *The Unknown American Revolution: The Unruly Birth of Democracy and the Struggle to Create America* (New York: Viking, 2005), 49.

12. Beach, *Samuel Adams*, 74–75.

13. Ibid., 5–6, and Zobel, *Boston Massacre*, 12–15.

14. Charles Rappleye, *Sons of Providence: The Brown Brothers, the Slave Trade, and the American Revolution* (New York: Simon & Schuster, 2006), 82.

15. Zobel, *Boston Massacre*, 69.

16. Ibid., 73–74.

17. Ibid., 76.

18. Ibid., 84.

19. Ibid., 89.

20. Ibid., 91.

21. Nash, *Unknown American Revolution*, 89.

22. Zobel, *Boston Massacre*, 103.

23. Puls, *Samuel Adams*, 88–89.

24. Zobel, *Boston Massacre*, 104.

25. Ibid., 133.

26. John Adams, *Diary and Autobiography of John Adams*, vol. 1, ed. L. H. Butterfield (Cambridge, MA: Harvard University Press, 1961), 341–42.

27. Terry Golway, *Washington's Generals: Nathanael Greene and the Triumph of the American Revolution* (New York: Holt, 2005), 32–33.

28. Thomas Hutchinson, *The History of the Colony and Province of Massachusetts-Bay*, vol. 3, ed. Lawrence Shaw Mayo (Cambridge, MA: Harvard University Press, 1936), 187.

29. Zobel, *Boston Massacre*, 178.

30. Ibid., 180.

31. Ibid., 181.

32. Ibid., 181–82.

33. For a comprehensive review of this event see Zobel, *Boston Massacre*, chapter 16, 180–205.

34. Ibid., 211–12.

35. Charles Francis Adams, ed., *The Works of John Adams, Second President of the United States: With a Life of the Author*, vol. 3 (Boston: Cambridge Library Collection, 1850–56), 384.

36. Golway, *Washington's Generals*, 34.

37. Rappleye, *Sons of Providence*, 108.

38. Golway, *Washington's Generals*, 36.

39. Beach, *Samuel Adams*, 245.

40. Ibid., 244–45.

41. Ibid., 246–49.

42. Puls, *Samuel Adams*, 140.

43. In his analysis of the political dynamics of the Sons of Liberty leadership in *Defiance of the Patriots*, Benjamin L. Carp makes an interesting argument that the Boston Tea Party was actually the result of pressure on the Boston leadership to show a stronger commitment to the nonimportation agreement policy of the organization. He believes the leadership in New York City and Philadelphia felt that the Bostonians had been lax in their enforcement efforts and that to regain their "moral" leadership role in the Sons of Liberty, the Bostonians had to make a strong statement.

44. Frank J. Rafalko, ed., *A Counterintelligence Reader: American Revolution to World War II*, vol. 1 (Washington, DC: National Counterintelligence Executive, n.d.), 2.

45. G. J. A. O'Toole, *Honorable Treachery: A History of U.S. Intelligence, Espionage, and Covert Action from the American Revolution to the CIA* (New York: Atlantic Monthly, 1991), 17.

46. Alexander Rose, *Washington's Spies: The Story of America's First Spy Ring* (New York: Bantam, 2006), 225.

47. Beach, *Samuel Adams*, 256–59.

48. Ibid., 260–61.

49. Puls, *Samuel Adams*, 163–64.

50. O'Toole, *Honorable Treachery*, 11.

51. Puls, *Samuel Adams*, 167–69.

Chapter 3: The Intelligence War Begins

1. Clarence E. Carter, ed., *The Correspondence of General Thomas Gage*, vol. 2 (New York: Krause Reprint Company, 1969), 564.

2. John R. Galvin, *The Minute Men: A Compact History of the Defenders of the American Colonies, 1645–1775* (New York: Hawthorn, 1967), 90–100. While this incident is well reported in both versions, Galvin's summary provides the facts and documentation most succinctly.

3. For details of the reconnaissance to Worcester, see *The Narrative of General Gage's Spies, March, 1775: With Notes* by Jerome Carter Hosmer (Boston: Bostonian Society's Publications, 1912).

4. John E. Bakeless, *Turncoats, Traitors, and Heroes: Espionage in the American Revolution* (New York: Lippincott, 1959), 51–54, provides details of the mission to Concord.

5. Lengel, *General George Washington*, 105.

6. Fischer, *Paul Revere's Ride*, 52, 58.

7. Letter from Paul Revere to Jeremy Belknap in 1798 in *Paul Revere's Three Accounts*, ed. Edmund S. Morgan (Boston: Massachusetts Historical Society), 1968, 7.

8. For details of Thompson's intelligence activities see Bakeless, *Turncoats*, 33–36, and Allen French, *General Gage's Informers: New Material upon Lexington and Concord, Benjamin Thompson as Loyalist, and the Treachery of Benjamin Church, Jr.* (Cranbury, NJ: Scholar's Bookshelf, 2005), a reprint of the 1932 University of Michigan Press edition, 115–46.

9. Church was uncovered as a British spy through research of General Gage's intelligence reports. Gage's papers are in the Clements Library at the University of Michigan. Church's story is now quite well known and detailed in several books. The most recent is *Dr. Benjamin Church, Spy*, by John A. Nagy (Yardley, PA: Westholme, 2013). Also see Bakeless, *Turncoats*, 10–20, 25–28, and French, *General Gage's Informers*, 147–201, who did the research of Gage's papers.

10. John Grenier, *The First Way of War: American Warmaking on the Frontier* (Cambridge: Cambridge University Press, 2005), 35.

11. Charles T. Burke, "The First Traitor," Watertown Papers, 1970, 73. The Watertown Papers is a collection of historical articles held by the Watertown Free Library, Watertown, MA.

12. Jeffrey B. Walker, "The Devil Undone: The Life of Benjamin Church (1734–1778)," PhD thesis, Pennsylvania State University, 1977.

13. "Paul Revere's Ride: Personal Account," Revolutionary War and Beyond, www.revolutionary-war-and-beyond.com/paul-reveres-ride-2.html.

14. French, *General Gage's Informers*, 166–67.

15. Bakeless, *Turncoats*, 11–13.

16. An image of the actual letter, written in code, is on the Library of Congress's website at http://memory.loc.gov/cgi-gin/ampage?collId=mgw4&fileName=gwpage033.db&recNum=753. The website Colonial Williamsburg displays the contents of the letter with modern punctuation and capitalization: www.history.org/history/teaching/enewsletter/volume3/january05/primsource.cfm.

17. Bakeless, *Turncoats*, 19.

18. O'Toole, *Honorable Treachery*, 11.

19. Fischer, *Paul Revere's Ride*, 56.

20. Ibid., 58.

21. Ibid., 80.

22. Peter O. Hutchinson, ed., *Thomas Hutchinson: The Diary and Letters of His Excellency Thomas Hutchinson, Esq.*, vol. 1 (Boston: Houghton Mifflin, 1884),497–98.

23. While Fischer (*Paul Revere's Ride*, 96–97) states that Gage had no further relations with his wife after the Concord battle, Nathaniel Philbrick disagrees in his book *Bunker Hill: A City, a Siege, a Revolution* (New York: Viking, 2013), 117. He cites an interview with the current descendant of Gage and, perhaps more creditable, research done by J. L. Bell on his blog *Boston 1775* regarding their subsequent relationship (http://boston1775,blogspot.com, April 12 and 13, 2011, entry 322).

24. Jeremy Belknap, "Journal of my tour to the camp and the observations I made there, October 25, 1775," *Massachusetts Historical Society Proceedings* 4 (1860): 77–86.

25. Fischer, *Paul Revere's Ride*, 96.

26. Morgan, *Paul Revere's Three Accounts*, 7.

27. Bakeless, *Turncoats*, 86.

28. Thomas B. Allen, *Tories: Fighting for the King in America's First Civil War* (New York: HarperCollins, 2010), 30.

29. Maps of North America, 1750–89, Library of Congress.

30. Bakeless, *Turncoats*, 87.

31. Marvin Kitman, *George Washington's Expense Account* (New York: Grove, 2001), 119.

32. Bell, *Boston 1775*, March 10, 2012.

33. Lengel, *General George Washington*, 113.

34. This map is found in *George Washington's Atlas* in the map collection of Yale University's Sterling Library, New Haven, CT.

35. Barnet Schecter, *George Washington's America: A Biography through His Maps* (New York: Walker, 2010), 74–79. Efforts to document when the map came into Washington's possession are described in communications between the author and the staff of the Mount Vernon Ladies Association, which owns and operates Mount Vernon, March–April 2012.

36. Lengel, *General George Washington*, 126.

37. Rafalko, *Counterintelligence Reader*, 10–11.

Chapter 4: Covert Action in Europe Leading to the French Alliance

1. Samuel Flagg Bemis, *The Diplomacy of the American Revolution* (Bloomington: Indiana University Press, 1957), 16.

2. Ibid., 14–15.

3. Van Doren, *Benjamin Franklin*, 538–39.

4. Ibid., 539.

5. Ibid., 538.

6. Bemis, *Diplomacy*, 34.

7. Ibid., 36–40.

8. Streeter Bass, "Beaumarchais and the American Revolution," *Studies in Intelligence* 14, no. 1 (Spring 1970): 2.

9. Bemis, *Diplomacy*, 36.

10. Bass, "Beaumarchais," 5–7.

11. Charles Rappleye, *Robert Morris: Financier of the American Revolution* (New York: Simon & Schuster, 2010), 38.

12. Ibid., 53–54.

13. Ibid., 55–76.

14. Ibid., 80–81.

15. Bass, "Beaumarchais," 6.

16. Ibid.

17. Ibid., 13.

18. Ibid., 8.

19. Ibid., 11.

20. Harvey Ardman, "How George Washington Got His Gunpowder," *American Legion Magazine*, May 1975, 4.

21. Central Intelligence Agency, *Intelligence in the War of Independence* (Langley, VA: CIA Public Affairs Office, 2008), 16, available at https://www.cia.gov/library/center-for-the-study-of-intelligence/csi-publications/books-and-monographs/intelligence. To mark the two-hundredth anniversary of the raid, the government of Bermuda issued four commemorative postage stamps with scenes of the raid in October 1975.

22. Ibid.

23. Ardman, "How George Washington," 40.

24. Bemis, *Diplomacy*, 53.

25. Bass, "Beaumarchais," 9–11.

26. Bemis, *Diplomacy*, 51.

27. Ibid., 52.

28. Lengel, *General George Washington*, xxviii–xxix, and Van Doren, *Benjamin Franklin*, 578.

29. Bemis, *Diplomacy*, 17.

30. Lafayette would be involved in numerous tactical intelligence-collection efforts during the war, but his use of an African American servant to penetrate British forces at Yorktown represented a particularly significant intelligence success. Also, the Polish military engineer Col. Thaddeus Kościuszko, while serving under Gen. Nathanael Greene, took control of the intelligence networks of Col. John Laurens after his death in combat.

31. Bass, "Beaumarchais," 12–13.

32. Bemis, *Diplomacy*, 54.

33. M. J. Sydenham, "Firing His Majesty's Dockyard: Jack the Painter and the American Mission to France, 1776–1777," *History Today* 16, no. 5 (May 1966): 324–31.

34. Ibid., 326.

35. Ibid., 329.

36. Ibid.

37. Ibid., 330.

38. Ibid., 327–28.

39. Ibid., 328–29.

40. "Edward Bancroft (@ Edwd. Edwards), Estimable Spy," *Studies in Intelligence* 5, no. 1 (Winter 1961): A58. Author not identified.

41. Louis C. Kleber, "Jones Raids Britain," *History Today* 19, no. 4 (April 1969): 277–82.

42. Ibid., 277–78.

43. Ibid., 279.

44. Ibid., 280.

45. Ibid., 282.

46. Lengel, *General George Washington*, 309.

47. Bemis, *Diplomacy*, 53–54.

48. Samuel Flagg Bemis, "British Secret Service and the French–American Alliance," *American Historical Review* 29, no. 3 (April 1924): 478.

49. Van Doren, *Benjamin Franklin*, 565, 572.

50. Robert H. Patton, *Patriot Pirates: The Privateer War for Freedom and Fortune in the American Revolution* (New York: Pantheon, 2008), 173–78.

51. Ibid., 174, and Susan Mary Alsop, *Yankees at the Court: The First Americans in Paris* (Garden City, NY: Doubleday, 1982), 81.

52. Van Doren, *Benjamin Franklin*, 539.

53. Ibid., 582, and Lewis D. Einstein, *Divided Loyalties: Americans in England during the War of Independence* (London: Cabden-Sanderson, 1933), 55.

54. Van Doren, *Benjamin Franklin*, 577.

55. Ibid., 597.

56. Bakeless, *Turncoats*, 220.

57. Joel Richard Paul, *Unlikely Allies: How a Merchant, a Playwright, and a Spy Saved the American Revolution* (New York: Riverhead, 2009), 228.

58. Central Intelligence Agency, *Intelligence in the War of Independence*, 23, and Van Doren, *Benjamin Franklin*, 574–75.

59. Central Intelligence Agency, *Intelligence in the War of Independence*, 23.

60. Bemis, *Diplomacy*, 124–25, and Van Doren, *Benjamin Franklin*, 614.

61. Bemis, *Diplomacy*, 33–34.

62. Van Doren, *Benjamin Franklin*, 590–93.

63. Bemis, *Diplomacy*, 14–15.

64. *The Deane Papers: Correspondence between Silas Deane, His Brothers and Their Business and Political Associates 1771–1795, Letter of Instruction*, vol. 1, Collections of the Connecticut Historical Society, 123–26.

65. Richard W. Van Alstyne, "Great Britain, the War for Independence and the Gathering Storm in Europe, 1775–1778," *Huntington Library Quarterly* 27, no. 4 (August 1964): 328.

66. "Edward Bancroft," A57.

67. Bemis, "British Secret Service," 474.

68. For a comprehensive review of his life, see Thomas J. Schaeper, *Edward Bancroft: Scientist, Author and Spy* (New Haven, CT: Yale University Press, 2011). Schaeper makes the argument that Bancroft was not a traitor but as a British subject became an agent of the British government for a variety of personal reasons.

69. Benjamin F. Stevens, *B. F. Stevens' Facsimiles of Manuscripts in European Archives Relating to America 1773–1783, with Descriptions, Editorial Notes, Collations, References and Translations*, no. 1371 (London: Matby & Sons, 1889–95).

70. Ibid., no. 235.

71. Bemis, "British Secret Service," 491.

72. Ibid., 474.

73. Stormont Papers, dispatch of January 1, 1777, as quoted in Alsop, *Yankees at the Court*, 73.

74. "Edward Bancroft," A65.

75. Van Doren, *Benjamin Franklin*, 583–84.

76. Burton J. Hendrick, *The Lees of Virginia* (Boston: Little, Brown, 1935), 279.

77. Alsop, *Yankees at the Court*, 88.

78. Bemis, "British Secret Service," 478.

79. Sydenham, "Firing His Majesty's Dockyard," 330.

80. Stevens, *B. F. Stevens' Facsimiles*, no. 1805, 2.

81. Van Doren, *Benjamin Franklin*, 581–82.

82. Ibid., 582.

83. Ibid., 581–82, and Bemis, "British Secret Service," 479–83.

84. Van Doren, *Benjamin Franklin*, 581–82.

85. Bemis, "British Secret Service," 480–81.

86. Alsop, *Yankees at the Court*, 98.

87. Bemis, "British Secret Service," 479–80.

88. Alsop, *Yankees at the Court*, 102.

89. Ibid.

90. Rafalko, *Counterintelligence Reader*, 23.

91. Hendrick, *Lees of Virginia*, 284–85.

92. While this incident is well known, Hendrick (*Lees of Virginia*, 251–54) provides an excellent and entertaining description of the operation.

93. Bemis, "British Secret Service," 483.

94. O'Toole, *Honorable Treachery*, 32.

95. Van Doren, *Benjamin Franklin*, 569–71.

96. Ibid., 569.

97. Alben H. Smyth, editor, *The Writings of Benjamin Franklin*, vol. 1 (New York: Macmillan, 1905–7), 11.

98. Bass, "Beaumarchais," 15.

99. Richard S. Friedman, "Benjamin Franklin: Friend of a Friend," CIA: CI Online, Historical Counterintelligence, paragraph 21.

100. Hendrick, *Lees of Virginia*, 267.

101. Friedman, "Benjamin Franklin," paragraph 22.

Chapter 5: Nathan Hale and the British Occupation of New York City

1. Lengel, *General George Washington*, 129.

2. Ibid., 133.

3. Ibid., 137.

4. Bakeless, *Turncoats*, 111.

5. Ibid.

6. Ibid., 177.

7. Lengel, *General George Washington*, 141.

8. Ibid., 146.

9. Ibid., 153.

10. M. William Phelps, *Nathan Hale: The Life and Death of America's First Spy* (New York: St. Martin's, 2008), 26–27.

11. George D. Seymour, *Documentary Life of Nathan Hale: Comprising All Available Official and Private Documents Bearing on the Life of the Patriot* (Whitefish, MT: Kessinger, 2006), 39.

12. Phelps, *Nathan Hale*, 165.

13. O'Toole, *Honorable Treachery*, 21.

14. Lengel, *General George Washington*, 156.

15. Ibid., 168.

16. Mercer to Washington, July 16, 1776, and Livingston to Washington, August 21, 1776, in Peter Force, ed., *American Archives: Consisting of a collection of authentic records, state papers, debates, and letters and other notices of publick affairs, the whole forming a documentary history of the origin and progress of the North American colonies; of the causes and accomplishments of the American Revolution; and of the Constitution of government for the United States, to the final ratification thereof,* 9 vols., 5th ser., vol. 1 (Washington: Publisher not indicated, 1837–53), 369.

17. Bakeless, *Turncoats*, 111.

18. Fitzpatrick, *Writings of George Washington*, vol. 6, 18–19.

19. Bakeless, *Turncoats*, 112.

20. Phelps, *Nathan Hale*, 138–39.

21. Seymour, *Documentary Life of Nathan Hale*, 317–78.

22. Ibid., 308

23. Phelps, *Nathan Hale*, 151, 229–30.

24. Ibid., 230–33.

25. Bakeless, *Turncoats*, 113.

26. Ibid., 118, and Phelps, *Nathan Hale*, 175.

27. Phelps, *Nathan Hale*, 156.

28. Ibid., 182.

29. J. Hutson, "Nathan Hale Revisited: A Tory Account of the Arrest of the First American Spy," *Library of Congress Information Bulletin* (July/August 2003).

30. John R. Cuneo, *Robert Rogers of the Rangers* (Oxford: Oxford University Press, 1959), 265.

31. Rose, *Washington's Spies*, 27.

32. Ibid., 27–28.

33. Cuneo, *Robert Rogers*, 24.

34. Hutson, "Nathan Hale Revisited," 168–72.

35. Ibid.

36. J. Rhodehamel, ed., *The American Revolution: Writings from the War of Independence* (New York: Library of America, 2001), 229.

37. Maria Campbell and James Freeman Clarke, *Revolutionary Services and Civil Life of General William Hull Prepared from His Manuscripts* (New York: Appleton, 1848), 309.

38. Rose, *Washington's Spies*, 32.

39. Force, *American Archives*, 5th ser., vol. 3, 725.

40. H. P. Johnston, *Nathan Hale, 1776: Biography and Memorials* (New Haven, CT: Yale University Press, 1914), 108n1.

41. Steven Hempstead, "The Capture and Execution of Capt. Hale in 1776," *Missouri Republican*, January 18, 1827.

42. Lengel, *General George Washington*, chapter 9, "Retreat," 149–71.

43. Rose, *Washington's Spies*, 34.

44. Phelps, *Nathan Hale*, 174.

45. Bakeless, *Turncoats*, 122.

Chapter 6: John Jay's Efforts at Counterintelligence

1. While this book deals with American intelligence activities, many of the references also provide excellent insight into British intelligence activities against American efforts. Bakeless's *Turncoats*, Carl Van Doren's *Secret History of the American Revolution* (New York: Viking, 1941), Alsop's *Yankees at the Court*, French's *General Gage's Informers*, and of course, the Clinton Papers at the Clements Library of the University of Michigan are a few examples.

2. Fitzpatrick, *Writings of George Washington*, vol. 4, 421–23.

3. Central Intelligence Agency, *Intelligence in the War of Independence*, 11.

4. George Pellew, *John Jay*, American Statesmen Series (New York: Chelsea House, 1997), 24–25.

5. Richard B. Morris, *Witnesses at the Creation: Hamilton, Madison, Jay, and the Constitution* (New York: Holt, Rinehart & Winston, 1985), 62–63.

6. Pellew, *John Jay*, 39–40, 43.

7. Morris, *Witnesses*, 65.

8. Walter Stahr, *John Jay: Founding Father* (New York: Hambledon & London, 2005), 51.

9. Ibid., 53.

10. Ibid., 59.

11. Bakeless, *Turncoats*, 102–6, and Rafalko, *Counterintelligence Reader*, 10–11.

12. Pellew, *John Jay*, 60–61.

13. Ibid., 63.

14. Donald L. Smith, *John Jay: A Founder of a State and Nation* (New York: Teacher's College Press, Columbia University, 1968), 34–35.

15. Pellew, *John Jay*, 61.

16. Letter from Jay to Peter Van Schaack, as quoted in Pellew, *John Jay*, 69.

17. Pellew, *John Jay*, 62.

18. Stahr, *John Jay*, 72.

19. Central Intelligence Agency, *Intelligence in the War of Independence*, 20.

20. Two documents provide official accounts of Crosby's activities: "Enoch Crosby Deposition in Application for a Federal Pension, October 15, 1832," document S/10/505, National Archives, Washington, DC, and Dorothy Barch, ed., *Minutes of the Committee and First Commission for Detecting Conspiracies, 1776–78*, John Watts DePeyster Publication Fund Series, nos. 17–18, vols. 1–2 (New York: New York Historical Society, 1924–25), also available at www.archive.org/stream/minutesofcommitt571newy_djvu.txt.

A book by H. L. Barnum, *The Spy Unmasked; or Memoirs of Enoch Crosby, Alias Harvey Birch* (Harrison, NY: Harbor Hill, 1975; first published 1828), uses material from these documents but also adds artistic license to the story. Bakeless sourced most of his narrative in *Turncoats* to Barch's *Minutes of the Committee* documents.

21. "Crosby Deposition," paragraph 7.

22. Ibid., paragraphs 10 and 11.

23. Bakeless, *Turncoats*, 138.

24. Ibid.

25. Ibid., 139.

26. Ibid., 140.

27. Ibid., 141.

28. Ibid.

29. Ibid.

30. Ibid., 142.

31. Barch, *Minutes of the Committee*, vol. 2, 420.

32. "Crosby Deposition," paragraph 21.

33. Ibid.

34. Morris, *Witnesses*, 70, and Allen, *George Washington, Spymaster*, 196.

35. *Federalist Paper 64*, paragraph 7, March 5, 1788.

36. Bakeless, *Turncoats*, 151.

37. Ibid., 152.

38. Ibid., 247.

39. O'Toole, *Honorable Treachery*, 77. Wilkinson was involved in various controversies and scandals throughout his career, starting with his service in the Continental Army. An overview of his life by James E. Savage can be found online at http://history.hanover.edu/hhr/98/hhr98_1.html. Two books on his life are Andro Linklater's *An Artist in Treason: The Extraordinary Double Life of General James Wilkinson* (New York: Walker, 2009) and Keith Thompson's *Scoundrel!: The Secret Memoirs of General James Wilkinson* (Nashville, TN: NorLights, 2012).

Chapter 7: Washington Establishes His Intelligence Capabilities

1. Lengel, *General George Washington*, 170–71.

2. Bakeless, *Turncoats*, 166.

3. For details on what historian David Hackett Fischer calls "the rising of New Jersey," see his *Washington's Crossing* (Oxford: Oxford University Press, 2004), 182–205.

4. Ibid., 204, with specific sourcing documented on page 513.

5. For a comprehensive account, see the chapter "The Surprise: The Agony of Col. Rall" in Fischer's *Washington Crossing*, 234–54.

6. William S. Stryker, *The Battles of Trenton and Princeton* (Boston and New York: Houghton Mifflin, 1898.

7. Bakeless, *Turncoats*, 166–70.

8. Fischer, *Washington's Crossing*, 423.

9. Alexander Rose, "The Spy Who Never Was: The Strange Case of John Honeyman and Revolutionary War Espionage," *Studies in Intelligence* 52, no. 2 (June 2008).

10. Kenneth A. Daigler, "In Defense of John Honeyman (and George Washington)," *Studies in Intelligence* 53, no. 4 (December 2009). Also see *An Unwritten Account of a Spy of Washington* by A. V. D. Honeyman, a reprint of an 1873 article, in *New Jersey History* 85, nos. 3 and 4 (Fall/Winter 1967), 219–24.

11. Cadwalader letter of December 31, 1776, to Washington, Papers of George Washington, Library of Congress, Washington, DC.

12. Lengel, *General George Washington*, 197.

13. O'Toole, *Honorable Treachery*, 42.

14. Bakeless, *Turncoats*, 171.

15. J. J. Boudinot, *Life of Elias Boudinot*, vol. 1 (Boston and New York: Houghton Mifflin, 1896), 72–74. Also, Frederick Bourquinn, ed., *Journal of Events in the Revolution by Elias Boudinot* (Philadelphia: H. J. Bicking, 1894), 54–53, 199.

16. Schuyler Papers, Letters and Orders, June 15–16, 1777. New York Public Library.

17. Willard Sterne Randall, *Benedict Arnold: Patriot and Traitor* (New York: Morrow, 1990), 347.

18. Details in the affidavit of Alexander's son Daniel, given in 1852 with confirmation from his mother, Alexander's wife. Pforzheimer Collection, Yale University Library, New Haven, CT.

19. Fitzpatrick, *Writings of George Washington*, vol. 7, 462.

20. O'Toole, *Honorable Treachery*, 42

21. Letter from Washington to Continental Congress, September 11, 1777, Papers of George Washington.

22. Rose, *Washington's Spies*, 46.

23. O'Toole, *Honorable Treachery*, 43.

24. What details are provided of Clark's intelligence activities can be found in his military papers at the National Archives (file S/41482) and in *The Papers of George Washington*.

25. John F. Reed, "Spy System 1777," Historic Valley Forge, www.ushistory.org/valleyforge/history/spies.html, and Rose, *Washington's Spies*, 60.

26. Reed, "Spy System 1777," 4.

27. Rose, *Washington's Spies*, 61.

28. Bernhard A. Uhlendorf, trans. and ed., *Revolution in America: Confidential Letters and Journals 1776–1784 of the Adjutant General Major Bauermeister of the Hessian Forces* (New Brunswick, NJ: Rutgers University Press, 1957), 134.

29. Reed, "Spy System 1777," 4.

30. Ibid., 6, and Bakeless, *Turncoats*, 205.

31. See John A. Nagy's introduction in his *Spies in the Continental Capital* (Yardley, PA: Westholme, 2011).

32. Bakeless, *Turncoats*, 212–14.

33. McLane's activities, but little about the identities of his sources or operations, can be found in his papers at the New York Historical Society: Allen McLane Papers, Miscellanies Manuscripts (microfilm). The Papers of George Washington at the Library of Congress also contain correspondence between McLane and Washington addressing his activities.

34. Nagy, *Spies*, 60.

35. Bakeless, *Turncoats*, 206.

36. Nagy, *Spies*, 104.

37. Lengel, *General George Washington*, 286.

38. Ibid., 287.

39. Bakeless, *Turncoats*, 210.

40. Ibid., 224.

41. Lengel, *General George Washington*, 291–92.

42. Bakeless, *Turncoats*, 206.

43. Ibid., 207.

44. Ibid., 208.

45. O'Toole, *Honorable Treachery*, 44.

46. Lengel, *General George Washington*, 300. Washington, on the field of battle, verbally and in quite harsh terms, criticized Gen. Charles Lee, whose troops were retreating in disorder.

Chapter 8: Benedict Arnold: Hero Turned Traitor

1. David Wise's book *Spy: The Inside Story of How the FBI's Robert Hanssen Betrayed America* (New York: Random House, 2002) is the most accurate account of Hanssen's story, benefiting from FBI assistance.

2. For a variation of this story, see Lengel, *General George Washington*, 344.

3. A photograph of the monument can be found on Wikipedia at http://en.wikipedia.org/wiki/Boot_monument.

4. Randall, *Benedict Arnold*, 15.

5. Anyone interested in Arnold's life has adequate material to study. Two of the best books, in my opinion, because of their comprehensive research and blending of Arnold's life into the overall context of the time, are Van Doren's *Secret History of the American Revolution* and Randall's *Benedict Arnold*. The former contains an appendix

featuring the text of correspondence between Arnold, André, and others regarding the negotiations and intelligence tradecraft involved in this operation. It also contains the text of Clinton's letters regarding Arnold and the operation. Chapter 12 of John A. Nagy's book *Invisible Ink: Spycraft of the American Revolution* (Yardley, PA: Westholme, 2010) focuses on the operation's communication plan and adds some additional perspective to it. Another perspective, stated as that of Arnold's case officer, André, is provided by Robert Amory Jr. in *John André, Case Officer* (Langley, VA: Central Intelligence Agency, Historical Review Program, 1993). Finally, see Nancy Rubin Stuart's book *Defiant Brides: The Untold Story of Two Revolutionary-Era Women and the Radical Men They Married* (Boston: Beacon, 2013) for insights into Arnold's actions from the perspective of his second wife, Margaret "Peggy" Shippen Arnold.

6. Randall, *Benedict Arnold*, 24.

7. Ibid., 42.

8. Ibid., 48–49.

9. Ibid., 82–84.

10. Ibid., 118.

11. Allen's letter of May 11, 1775, to the Albany Committee of Correspondence, printed in *Letters from the Frontier: A Sampler from Correspondence of Ethan Allen and His Family*, ed. Kevin J. Graffagnoni (Isle La Motte, VT: Allen Letters Project, 1995), 3–4.

12. Randall, *Benedict Arnold*, 91–100.

13. Ibid., 126–27.

14. Ibid., 136–37.

15. Ibid., 226.

16. Ibid., 317.

17. Fitzpatrick, *Writings of George Washington*, vol. 7, 352–53.

18. Randall, *Benedict Arnold*, 346–48.

19. Ibid., 353–54.

20. Ibid., 358–59.

21. Ibid., 359–64.

22. Ibid., 366–68.

23. Lengel, *General George Washington*, xxii.

24. Michael J. Sulick, *Spying in America: Espionage from the Revolutionary War to the Dawn of the Cold War* (Washington, DC: Georgetown University Press, 2012), 45.

25. Randall, *Benedict Arnold*, 398.

26. Ibid., 376.

27. Bakeless, *Turncoats*, 86.

28. For a comprehensive look at André's background and personality, see Randall, *Benedict Arnold*, 376–83.

29. Ibid., 378–79.

30. Ibid., 391–92.

31. Ibid., 378.

32. Ibid., 397.

33. Ibid., 412–14, and Nagy, *Spies*, 145.

34. James Thomas Flexner, *The Traitor and the Spy: Benedict Arnold and John André* (Boston and Toronto: Little, Brown, 1975), 228.

35. Randall, *Benedict Arnold*, 410–11.

36. Ibid., 423–25.

37. Ibid., 446–48.

38. Ibid., 451.

39. Ibid., 454.

40. Ibid., 452.

41. Van Doren, *Secret History*, 193–94, and Flexner, *Traitor and the Spy*, 271.

42. Van Doren, *Secret History*; see "Clinton's Narrative" in the appendix, 477–80.

43. Randall, *Benedict Arnold*, 456–57, and Allen, *Tories*, 292.

44. Van Doren, *Secret History*, 197–98, and Randall, *Benedict Arnold*, 458.

45. Bakeless, *Turncoats*, 158.

46. Van Doren, *Secret History*, appendix, "Arnold-André Correspondence," May 10, 1779, André to Stansbury, 439–40.

47. Ibid., and Nagy, *Invisible Ink*, 73.

48. Van Doren, *Secret History*, appendix, "Arnold-André Correspondence," May 1779, Stansbury to André and Arnold to André, 441–42.

49. Ibid., May 31, 1779, Odell to André, 442–43.

50. Ibid., May 1779, Arnold to André, 441–42.

51. Jared Sparks, ed., *Writings of George Washington*, vol. 6 (Boston: American Stationer's Company, 1837), 523.

52. Randall, *Benedict Arnold*, 471.

53. Ibid., 474–76.

54. Fitzpatrick, *Writings of George Washington*, vol. 18, 225.

55. Randall, *Benedict Arnold*, 497.

56. Ibid., 501–2.

57. Van Doren, *Secret History*, 458–59.

58. Randall, *Benedict Arnold*, 503–4, and Van Doren, *Secret History*, appendix, "Arnold-André Correspondence," June 7, 1780, Arnold to Beckwith, 459–60.

59. Van Doren, *Secret History*, appendix, "Arnold-André Correspondence," June 16, 1780, Arnold to Capt. George Beckwith, intelligence aide to General Knyphausen, or André, 460–61.

60. Ibid., 271.

61. Bakeless, *Turncoats*, 268, and Randall, *Benedict Arnold*, 507–8.

62. Van Doren, *Secret History*, appendix, "Arnold-André Correspondence," mid-July 1780, Arnold to André, 462–64.

63. Ibid., see photos of coded and decoded letter between 274 and 275, and text of letter of July 15, 1780, Arnold to André, 464–65.

64. Van Doren, *Secret History*, 217–18, and Nagy, *Spies*, 25.

65. Randall, *Benedict Arnold*, 509–11.

66. Ibid., 516–17.

67. Ibid., 517–18.

68. Ibid., 523.

69. Ibid., 519–20.

70. Ibid., 524–25.

71. Ibid., 527–28, and Van Doren, *Secret History*, appendix, Arnold-André Correspondence," late August to mid-September, 1780, Arnold to André, 470–72.

72. Randall, *Benedict Arnold*, 533.

73. Van Doren, *Secret History*, appendix, "Arnold-André Correspondence, September 15, 1780," Arnold to André, 472.

74. Ibid., September 15, 1780, Arnold to André, 473, and Randall, *Benedict Arnold*, 535.

75. Randall, *Benedict Arnold*, 536.

76. Ibid., 539.

77. Van Doren, *Secret History*, appendix, "Arnold-André Correspondence," September 24, 1780, Robinson to Clinton, 474–75.

78. Randall, *Benedict Arnold*, 546.

79. Ibid., 545–46.

80. Van Doren, *Secret History*, appendix, "Arnold-André Correspondence," September 24, 1780, Robinson to Clinton, 474–75.

81. Randall, *Benedict Arnold*, 548–49.

82. Winthrop H. Sargent, *Life and Career of Major John André: Adjutant-General of the British Army in America* (Boston: Ticknor & Fields, 1861), 350.

83. Randall, *Benedict Arnold*, 549.

84. Ibid., 527.

85. Ibid., 551.

86. Ibid., 555.

87. Ibid., 557.

88. Allen, *George Washington, Spymaster*, 127.

89. Van Doren, *Secret History*, 346–48.

90. Harold C. Syrett, ed., *The Papers of Alexander Hamilton*, vol. 2 (New York: Columbia University Press, 1961), 439–40.

91. Randall, *Benedict Arnold*, 560–61,

92. Van Doren, *Secret History*, 428.

93. Randall, *Benedict Arnold*, 554.

94. Sparks, *Writings of George Washington*, vol. 7, 524–25.

95. Randall, *Benedict Arnold*, 557.

96. Ibid., 566.

97. Van Doren, *Secret History*, 423.

98. Randall, *Benedict Arnold*, 594.

99. Ibid., 594–96, and Stuart, *Defiant Brides*, 136–37.

Chapter 9: American Intelligence Activities Reach Maturity

1. Bakeless, *Turncoats*, 171.
2. Ibid., 173.
3. Letter from Washington to Sackett, April 8, 1777, Papers of George Washington.
4. Bakeless, *Turncoats*, 241–43.
5. Ibid., 174–75.
6. Ibid., 175
7. Ibid., 176.
8. Ibid., 177.
9. Rose, *Washington's Spies*, 75.
10. O'Toole, *Honorable Treachery*, 46, and Rose, *Washington's Spies*, 74–75.
11. Morton Pennypacker, *General Washington's Spies on Long Island and in New York* (Cranbury, NJ: Scholar's Bookshelf, 2005), 34.
12. Ibid., 43.
13. Ibid., 49–50.
14. Ibid., 58–59.
15. Ibid., 78.
16. Ibid., 80.
17. Nagy's *Invisible Ink* provides a copy of this code in its appendix B. Pennypacker's *General Washington's Spies* also provides examples of the code on page 218.
18. Rose, *Washington's Spies*, 75.
19. Pennypacker, *General Washington's Spies*, 34–35.
20. Ibid., 37.
21. Ibid., 241–42.
22. Ibid., 44–45.
23. Rose, *Washington's Spies,* 132.
24. O'Toole, *Honorable Treachery*, 61.
25. For details of Townsend's background and personality see Rose*, Washington's Spies*, chapter 5, 125–64, and Pennypacker, *General Washington's Spies*, 102–11.
26. Rose, *Washington's Spies*, 98, 170–71.
27. A great deal of research has been done on the Culper Ring, starting with Pennypacker. His *General Washington's Spies* utilizes copies of the ring's operational correspondence to tell its story. Bakeless's *Turncoats* uses more of a narrative approach to the ring's activities. Rose's *Washington's Spies* places the story of the ring into a more personality-oriented context. In these three books, the personnel and methodology of the ring are comprehensively covered.
28. Pennypacker, *General Washington's Spies*, 62.
29. Nagy, *Invisible Ink*, 29–30.
30. Rose, *Washington's Spies*, 107–9.
31. Pennypacker, *General Washington's Spies*, 42–43.
32. Nagy, *Invisible Ink*, 139.

33. Pennypacker, *General Washington's Spies*, 58–59.

34. Ibid., 33–34.

35. Bakeless, *Turncoats*, 251.

36. Pennypacker, *General Washington's Spies*, 91.

37. Rose, *Washington's Spies*, 265.

38. Bakeless, *Turncoats*, 237.

39. Rose, *Washington's Spies*, 73.

40. Ibid., 102.

41. Ibid., 171–72.

42. Ibid., 258.

43. Ibid., 193.

44. Pennypacker, *General Washington's Spies*, 15.

45. Rose, *Washington's Spies*, 247.

46. Pennypacker, *General Washington's Spies*, 76–77.

47. Ibid., 8.

48. Ibid., 8.

49. George Washington Parke Custis, *Recollections and Private Memoirs of Washington* (Washington, DC: W. H. Moore, 1859).

50. For additional discussion of when and why Rivington joined Washington's intelligence organization, see Catherine Snell Crary, "The Tory and the Spy: The Double Life of James Rivington," *William and Mary Quarterly* 16, no. 1 (January 1959), and Kara Pierce, "A Revolutionary Masquerade: The Chronicles of James Rivington," *Binghamton University History Honor Society Journal of History*, www2.binghamton.edu.history/resources/journal-of-history.

51. *Journals of the Continental Congress, 1774–1789*, vol. 12 (Washington, DC: Government Printing Office, 1903–37), 1061.

52. O'Toole, *Honorable Treachery*, 61.

53. Ibid., 39.

54. Michael S. O'Brien, *Hercules Mulligan: Confidential Correspondent of George Washington* (New York: P. J. Kennedy, 1937), 98.

55. O'Brien believes Mulligan began reporting as early as March or April 1777, while Rose (*Washington's Spies*, 226) believes the summer of 1779 is a more realistic date.

56. Bakeless, *Turncoats*, 240–41.

57. Rose, *Washington's Spies*, 226.

58. O'Toole, *Honorable Treachery*, 39.

59. O'Brien, *Hercules Mulligan*, 99–100.

60. Linda McCarthy, "I Keep Me Ears Open," *Studies in Intelligence* 29, no. 4 (Winter 1985): 41–42.

61. Rose, *Washington's Spies*, 173.

62. Harry Macy Jr., "Robert Townsend, Jr. of New York City," *New York Genealogical and Biographical Record* 126, no. 1 (January 1995).

63. Van Doren, *Secret History*, 238.

64. Pennypacker, *General Washington's Spies*, 185.

65. Ibid., 186–87.

66. Ibid., 203–4.

67. Ibid., 206–8.

68. Rose, *Washington's Spies*, 255.

69. Ibid., 265–66.

70. Ibid., 170.

71. Pennypacker, *General Washington's Spies*, 50–51.

72. See Van Doren, *Secret History*, 235–37, and Allen, *Tories*, 298.

73. Pennypacker, *General Washington's Spies*, 10–11.

74. Rose, *Washington's Spies*, 173–74.

75. Ibid., 180.

76. Ibid., 183–84.

77. Ibid., 184.

78. Pennypacker, *General Washington's Spies*, 82–84.

79. Van Doren, *Secret History*, appendix, "Arnold-André Correspondence," no. 32, 460.

80. Bakeless, *Turncoats*, 236, and Central Intelligence Agency, *Intelligence in the War of Independence*, 22.

81. Don Loprieno, *The Enterprise in Contemplation: The Midnight Assault of Stony Point* (Westminster, MD: Heritage Books, 2009), 10–11.

82. John F. Schroeder, *Maxims of Washington* (Mount Vernon, VA: Mount Vernon Ladies Association, 1947), letter from Washington to Wayne on July 10, 1779, 122.

83. Loprieno, *Enterprise in Contemplation*, 12, 15.

84. Ibid., 12.

85. Pennypacker, *General Washington's Spies*, 52–53.

Chapter 10: Nathanael Greene and Intelligence in the Southern Campaign

1. This chapter expands on an article by the author, "Code Names, Ciphers, and Spies: General Nathanael Greene's Efforts at Espionage," in *Carologue* 20, no. 1, South Carolina Historical Society, 2004.

2. Lengel, *General George Washington*, 321.

3. Ibid., 322.

4. The primary sources for this chapter largely come from the invaluable *The Papers of General Nathanael Greene* published for the Rhode Island Historical Society by the University of North Carolina Press—thirteen volumes, covering the period from December 1766 to June 13, 1786, edited by Richard K. Showman et al., published from 1976 through 2005. Hereafter referred to as *Papers*.

5. See John Daderer, *Making Bricks without Straw: Nathanael Greene's Southern*

Campaigns and Mao Tse-Tung's Mobile War (Manhattan, KS: Sunflower University Press, 1983).

6. *Papers*, vol. 6, 520.

7. Ibid., vol. 13, 448.

8. Ibid., vol. 12, 310.

9. Ibid., vol. 1, 101–2.

10. Ibid., 105–6.

11. Ibid., 204.

12. Ibid., 276.

13. Ibid., 348.

14. Ibid., 375.

15. Theodore Thayer, *Nathanael Greene: Strategist of the American Revolution* (New York: Twayne, 1960), 137–38.

16. *Papers*, vol. 2, 24.

17. Ibid., 51, 71, 90, 94–96.

18. Ibid., 191.

19. Ibid., vol. 6, 30–32.

20. Ibid., 308–9.

21. Ibid., vol. 8, 85, 227–29. For examples of the code used, see Nagy, *Invisible Ink*, appendix L.

22. *Papers*, vol. 9, 597.

23. Ibid., vol. 8, 46–47.

24. Ibid., 133.

25. Ibid., vol. 9, 203–4.

26. Ibid., vol. 10, 13.

27. Ibid., vol. 11, 75.

28. Ibid., 423.

29. Ibid., vol. 8, 371.

30. Golway, *Washington's Generals*, 234–36.

31. Gregory De Van Massy, "A Hero's Life: John Laurens and the American Revolution" (PhD diss., University of South Carolina, 1992; UMI Dissertation Services, Ann Arbor, MI), 506.

32. William Moultrie, *Memoirs of the American Revolution*, vol. 1 (New York: David Longworth, 1802), 403–4.

33. *Papers*, vol. 10, 35.

34. Ibid., 109 –10, 122.

35. Ibid., 266.

36. Ibid., 177.

37. Ibid., 422.

38. Ibid., 495.

39. Ibid., vol. 11, 354–55.

40. Ibid., 639.

41. E. Alfred Jones, ed., "The Journal of Alexander Chesney, a South Carolina Loyalist in the Revolution and After," *Contributions in History and Political Science*, no. 7 (October 30, 1921): 119. A free copy of this article in book format is available at http://books.google.com/books/about/The_Journal_of_Alexander_Chesney. html?id=VwVPPwAACAAJ.

42. *Papers*, vol. 11, 75.

43. Ibid., 491.

44. Ibid., 516.

45. Ibid., vol. 12, 331–32.

46. Ibid., vol. 11, 368.

47. Ibid., 489–90.

48. Ibid., vol. 12, 331.

49. Ibid., vol. 11, 546, 568.

50. Miecislaus Haiman, *Kościuszko in the American Revolution* (New York: Kościuszko Foundation and the Polish Institute of Arts and Science, 1975), 132–33.

51. *Papers*, vol. 11, 680.

52. Haiman, *Kościuszko*, 133.

53. *Papers*, vol. 11, 677–78.

54. Ibid., 697–98.

55. Ibid., vol. 12, 177.

56. Ibid., 310.

57. Ibid., vol. 6, 605.

58. Ibid., vol. 7, 86–87, 135.

59. Ibid., 36.

60. Ibid., 152–55.

61. Ibid., vol. 8, 505, 513.

62. Ibid., vol. 9, 628.

63. Ibid., vol. 11, 141.

64. Ibid., 180–81.

65. Letter from Greene to Capt. William Wilmot, Manuscript Collection, Society of the Cincinnati Library, Washington, DC.

66. *Papers*, vol. 11, 545.

67. Ibid., vol. 12, 120–21.

68. Ibid., 121.

69. Ibid., vol. 7, 118.

70. Ibid., vol. 8, 204.

71. Ibid., 482–83.

72. Ibid., 443.

73. Ibid., vol. 9, 177.

74. Ibid., vol. 8, 481, 223.

75. Ibid., vol. 10, 34–35.

76. Ibid., 285.

77. Ibid., vol. 12, 20–21, 24–26.

Chapter 11: Yorktown and the Endgame

1. Van Doren, *Secret History*, 416.

2. Ibid., 418.

3. For examples of the different interpretation of their correspondence and the military situation, with some obvious subjectivity toward Clinton's perspective, see *Observations on Some Parts of the Answer of Earl Cornwallis to Sir Henry Clinton's Narrative* by Lt. Gen. Sir Henry Clinton, KB, originally published as a pamphlet in 1783 and republished by the Scholar's Bookshelf (Cranbury, NJ) in 2005. Also see the Clinton papers at the William L. Clements Library at the University of Michigan and the Cornwallis papers at the National Archives.

4. Lengel, *General George Washington*, 330–31.

5. Clinton, *Observations*, Clinton letter to Cornwallis of June 11, 1781, 109.

6. For example, see O'Toole, *Honorable Treachery*, 59 and Lengel, *General George Washington*, 332.

7. Lengel, *General George Washington*, 332.

8. Ibid., 332.

9. Fitzpatrick, *Diaries of George Washington,* vol. 2, 253–54.

10. O'Toole, *Honorable Treachery*, 63.

11. Letter from George Washington to Noah Webster, July 31, 1788, Papers of George Washington.

12. Edward F. Sayle, "Chronology of a Deception: George Washington's Deception Operations Prior to the Victory at Yorktown," *Studies in Intelligence* 25, no. 2 (Summer 1981): 2.

13. Ibid., 3.

14. Ibid., 3.

15. Bakeless, *Turncoats*, 293.

16. Sayle, "Chronology," 4.

17. Ibid.

18. Ibid.

19. Ibid., 5.

20. Ibid., 6–7.

21. Cornwallis letter to Clinton, June 30, 1781, Clinton, *Observations*, 112–13.

22. Sayle, "Chronology," 8.

23. Ibid. , 12.

24. Ibid., 13.

25. Elias Boudinot, *Journal of Historical Recollections of American Events during the Revolutionary War* (Philadelphia: Frederick Bourquin, 1894), 41–42.

26. Sayle, "Chronology," 13.

27. Ibid., 13–14.

28. Ibid., 15.

29. Ibid.

30. Allen McLane, Allen McLane Papers, vol. 2, 56, miscellaneous manuscripts (microfilm), New York Historical Society.

31. Crary, "Tory and the Spy," 68.

32. McLane, Allen McLane Papers, vol. 2, 56.

33. Nagy, *Invisible Ink,* appendix A.

34. Crary, "Tory and the Spy," 68.

35. See O'Toole, *Honorable Treachery,* 501n37.

36. Bakeless, *Turncoats,* 337.

37. Ibid., 337–38.

38. Ibid., 338.

39. Rafalko, *Counterintelligence Reader,* 10.

40. Benjamin Quarles, *The Negro in the American Revolution* (Chapel Hill, North Carolina: University of North Carolina Press), 1961, 95.

41. Rafalko, *Counterintelligence Reader,* 29.

42. Ibid.

43. Ibid.

44. Rafalko, *Counterintelligence Reader,* 29. The design for the Badge of Military Merit became that of the Purple Heart, which is awarded for being wounded or killed in combat. In Washington's general orders of August 7, 1782, it was stated that individuals could be nominated for this award for acts of unusual bravery.

45. Daniel K. Elder, *Remarkable Sergeants: Ten Vignettes of Noteworthy NCOs* (Fort Riley, KS: NCO Historical Society, 2003), 2–3.

46. Ibid., 29–31, and Bakeless, *Turncoats,* 346–58.

47. Bakeless, *Turncoats,* 358.

48. Pennypacker, *General Washington's Spies,* 281.

49. O'Brien, *Hercules Mulligan,* 49, 85.

50. Crary, "Tory and the Spy," 62.

Chapter 12: The African American Role in American Intelligence Activities

1. Benjamin Quarles, *The Negro in the American Revolution* (Chapel Hill: University of North Carolina Press, 1961).

2. Michael L. Lanning, *African Americans in the Revolutionary War* (New York: Kensington, 2000), 7.

3. Rafalko, *Counterintelligence Reader,* 29.

4. Bakeless, *Turncoats,* 40.

5. Norman Castle, ed., *The Minute Men, 1775–1975* (Southborough, MA: Yankee Colour Corporation, 1977), 208. Also see Roger Saunders, "The Midnight Ride of Abel Benson," Suite101, February 11, 2008, http://suite101.com/a/the-midnight-ride-of-abel-benson-a44331.

6. For details of Estabrook's life, see Alice M. Hinkle, *Prince Estabrook, Slave and Soldier* (Lexington, MA: Mount Pleasant Press, 2001), 36.

7. Lanning, *African Americans,* 5.

8. Fischer, *Paul Revere's Ride*, 243–44.

9. Ibid., 282.

10. Burke Davis, *Black Heroes of the American Revolution* (New York: Harcourt Brace Jovanovich, 1976), 20.

11. Lanning, *African Americans*, 177.

12. Showman et al., eds., *Papers of General Nathanael Greene*, vol. 8, 500, 511.

13. Lanning, *African Americans*, 129.

14. Quarles, *Negro in the American Revolution*, 95–96.

15. Ibid., 96–97.

16. Lanning, *African Americans*, 127–28, and Loprieno, *Enterprise in Contemplation*, 76.

17. Lanning, *African Americans*, 127–28.

18. Loprieno, *Enterprise in Contemplation*, 76–77.

19. Quarles, *Negro in the American Revolution*, xi.

20. Loprieno, *Enterprise in Contemplation*, 76–79.

21. Rose, *Washington's Spies*, 130.

GLOSSARY OF TRADECRAFT TERMS

Actionable Intelligence: Information that can be acted upon quickly to counter an adversary's actions, as opposed to information that assists in understanding an adversary's future plans and intentions.

Agent: An individual covertly employed by an intelligence organization to assist in its activities. Often further identified by his or her role in the intelligence operation.

Agent of Influence: An agent whose association with a decision maker permits that individual to influence the thinking and actions of the decision maker.

Book Code: A communication's method of sending information by using numerical numbers to represent words. A specific book is selected, and a page number, a number of a line down from the top or up from the bottom, and a number of a word starting either from the left or right margin are selected to identify a specific word, with the collection of words forming the desired communication.

Case Officer: The intelligence officer responsible, at the first management level, for an intelligence activity.

Casing: To research and observe a target to ascertain the most effective way to approach and gain access to it without arousing suspicion.

Clandestine Communication: The movement of information between agents and intelligence officers in a manner that protects it from public view. This can involve physically hiding the information, disguising it as something else, rendering it indiscernible to normal observation, and so forth.

Clandestine Operation: Activity hidden from public view.

Collection Agent: An individual with access to intelligence information through professional and/or social situations.

Compartmentation: Restricting information about an intelligence activity to only those with a "need to know," either because of their involvement in the activity or their need for the intelligence obtained. Thus different individuals may know some specific details, but not all details, regarding the activity.

Counterintelligence: The protection of an entity's sensitive information from all adversaries. In intelligence organizations this is done defensively through security practices and internal monitoring of activities and offensively by recruiting penetration agents of the adversary to identify and thwart its efforts to obtain this information.

Courier: A support agent who transports intelligence products between the collector and the case officer controlling the collector.

Cover: The ostensible, public reason for a clandestine activity. Several types of covers are utilized, depending upon the function to be performed by the intelligence officer or agent.

Cover for Access: The ostensible, public reason an intelligence officer or agent has for maintaining a professional or social relationship with an intelligence source. An example would be an agent who has business dealings with a government office.

Cover for Action: The ostensible, public reason an intelligence officer or agent has for performing a certain activity. An example would be an agent frequently visiting another residence because it was the home of a close "friend."

Cover for Status: The ostensible, public reason an intelligence officer or agent has for being in a given professional or social environment. An example would be an agent having a business or personal reason for visiting a city.

Cover Letter: A letter containing innocent content used to disguise the fact that other portions of the letter contain sensitive information. For example, a friendly letter regarding a social event that, on the back of its paper, contains intelligence information written in invisible ink.

Cover Story: The ostensible, public reason an intelligence officer or agent uses to explain some action, behavior, or personal background. This "story" often includes the "covers" described above.

Covert Action: An intelligence activity that seeks to influence the decision making of an adversary through the use of propaganda, political action, or paramilitary activities.

Cutout: An individual used, either wittingly or unwittingly, to receive and then pass along information between an intelligence agent and an intelligence officer. This individual has a logical cover story for communicating with the intelligence officer, which would not necessarily be true for the intelligence agent. This type of support agent is often connected to a mail drop.

Dead Drop: A location where an item is placed in order to separate the physical contact between the agent and the intelligence officer. For example, the agent places a report in a tin can and leaves it in underbrush at an agreed-upon site, and a few hours later the intelligence officer retrieves the can.

Deception Operation: Allowing an adversary to obtain information, which manipulates its actions to one's benefit.

Disinformation: False or manipulated information provided to an adversary through a double agent or other method to influence or disrupt its activities.

Double Agent: An individual controlled by an intelligence organization who is sent to be recruited by an adversary for the purpose of learning the activities and requirements of that adversary. That individual may also provide it with false or manipulated intelligence to influence or disrupt its activities.

Early Warning: A category of intelligence reporting that provides advance warning of an adversary's actions, allowing counteractions to be taken to reduce one's vulnerabilities.

Elicitation: The manipulation of a conversation or situation that encourages an intelligence source to provide more facts and details than originally intended. This can often be accomplished without the source recognizing the actual amount of information that has been provided.

Encode: To hide the actual meaning of a piece of data. For example, instead of writing the word "enemy," a number such as "23" or another word such as "blue" could be substituted.

Encrypt: To encode.

Feed Material: True or partially true information posing little or no threat to the controlling service that a double agent is given to provide to an adversary, with the objective of increasing the double agent's status and perceived value to the adversary.

Intelligence Manager: The senior intelligence officer responsible for an intelligence activity.

Mail Drop: An address for written communication used as a method of separating the sender from the actual intended recipient. This is often the role of a support agent whose only job is to receive the correspondence and covertly pass it along to its actual recipient. Sometimes this is referred to as an accommodation address.

Open-Source Intelligence: Information of intelligence value that is available in the public realm.

Paramilitary: Activities of a military nature clandestinely supported, and often guided to some degree, by an entity to influence the decision making of an adversary.

Penetration Agent: An individual who has direct access to an intelligence target. An example would be an individual employed at a government ministry.

Plausible Denial: A method used to deny responsibility for an action by denying knowledge of the action or claiming it was undertaken without official approval.

Propaganda: The use of information, both true and false, to affect the thinking and actions of an adversary.

Recognition Signal: An image, item, or action that an agent, from previous advisement by a known and trusted intelligence officer, recognizes as identifying an individual who can be trusted.

Safe House: A location where intelligence activity is undertaken in an environment that publicly disguises that activity under the guise of some other function. An example would be a boarding house, with actual tenants, where an intelligence officer or agent can keep a separate room to meet sources, write reports, or perform other intelligence activities.

Secret Writing: Writing invisible to the naked eye that is used to convey intelligence under the cover of correspondence, documents, and such. This usually involves two chemical compounds: one used to write the information and a second used to develop the writing.

Source: In the human intelligence sense, an individual who has direct access to information of intelligence value. This individual may be willingly passing the information or could be in a social or professional relationship that permits an intelligence officer or agent to manipulate the relationship to obtain the information.

Sources and Methods: Identifying information on who is reporting intelligence and how it is being done. This is the most sensitive information involved in intelligence operations.

Stay-Behind: An intelligence-collection capability created by having resident reporting agents live in an area under an adversary's control, with covers legitimizing their status.

Strategic Intelligence: Information having significance of value beyond a specific issue or situation.

Support Agent: An individual with primary responsibilities to support an intelligence activity in some manner, for example by providing a location for report writing, rather than personally collecting it from sources.

Tactical Intelligence: Information specific to an issue or situation.

United Front Organization: A political or social group that utilizes a general theme to attract a large membership but whose leaders have a more specific, often more radical objective, which they use the organization to attain.

BIBLIOGRAPHY

Abernethy, Thomas P. *Western Lands and the American Revolution*. New York: D. Appleton–Century, 1937.

Adams, Charles Francis, ed. *The Works of John Adams, Second President of the United States: With a Life of the Author*. Boston: Cambridge Library Collection, 1850–56.

Adams, John. *Diary and Autobiography of John Adams*, L. H. Butterfield, ed. Cambridge, MA: Harvard University Press, 1961.

Allen, Thomas B. *Tories: Fighting for the King in America's First Civil War*. New York: HarperCollins, 2010.

Allen, Thomas, G. *George Washington, Spymaster*. Washington, DC: National Geographic Society, 2004.

Alsop, Susan Mary. *Yankees at the Court: The First Americans in Paris*. Garden City, NY: Doubleday, 1982.

Amory, Robert Jr. *John André, Case Officer*. Langley, VA: Central Intelligence Agency, Historical Review Program, 1993.

Anderson, Fred. *Crucible of War: The Seven Years' War and the Fate of the Empire in British North America, 1754–1766*. New York: Knopf, 2000.

Anderson, Troyer Steele. *The Command of the Howe Brothers during the American Revolution*. Cranbury, NJ: Scholar's Bookshelf, 2005. First published 1936.

Ardman, Harvey. "How George Washington Got His Gunpowder." *American Legion Magazine*, May 1975, 4ff.

Ashcraft, Allan C. "General George Washington and the Evolution of a Military Intelligence Service during the Revolutionary War." Unpublished research project of the 837th Military Intelligence Division, Bryan, TX, 1969.

Augur, Helen. *The Secret War of Independence*. New York: Duel, Sloan & Pearce, 1955.

Bakeless, John. *Turncoats, Traitors, and Heroes: Espionage in the American Revolution*. New York: Lippincott, 1959.

Barch, Dorothy C., ed. *Minutes of the Committee and First Commission for Detecting Conspiracies, 1776–1778*. John Watts DePeyster Publication Fund Series, nos. 17–18, vols. 1–2, 1924–25. New York Historical Society.

Barch, Oscar T. *New York City during the War of Independence*. London and New York: Oxford University Press, 1931.

Barkaw, Richard. *George Washington's Westchester Gamble: The Encampment on the Hudson and the Trapping of Cornwallis*. Stroud, Gloucestershire, UK: History Press, 2011.

Barnum, H. L. *The Spy Unmasked; or Memoirs of Enoch Crosby, Alias Harvey Birch*. Harrison, NY: Harbor Hill, 1975. First published 1828.

Bass, Streeter. "Beaumarchais and the American Revolution." *Studies in Intelligence* 14, no. 1 (Spring 1970).

Beach, Stewart. *Samuel Adams*. New York: Dodd, Mead, 1965.

Belknap, Jeremy. "Journal of my tour to the camp and the observations I made there, October 25, 1775." *Massachusetts Historical Society Proceedings* 4 (1860).

Bell, J. L. *Boston 1775* (blog). http://boston1775,blogspot.com.

Bemis, S. F. "British Secret Service and the French-American Alliance." *American Historical Review* 29, no. 3, April 1924.

———. *The Diplomacy of the American Revolution*, Bloomington: Indiana University Press, 1957.

Bendiner, Elmer. *The Virgin Diplomats*. New York: Knopf, 1976.

Bidwell, Bruce W. *History of the Military Intelligence Division, Department of Army General Staff, 1775–1941*. Frederick, MD: University Publications of America, 1986.

Birnbaum, Louis. *Red Dawn at Lexington: If They Mean to Have a War, Let It Begin Here!* Boston: Houghton Mifflin, 1986.

Boudinot, Elias. *Journal of Historical Recollections of American Events during the Revolutionary War*. Philadelphia: Frederick Bourquin, 1894.

Boudinot, J. J. *Life of Elias Boudinot*, vol. 1. Boston and New York: Houghton Mifflin, 1896.

Bourquinn, Fredrick, ed. *Journal of Events in the Revolution by Elias Boudinot*. Philadelphia: H. J. Bicking, 1894.

Brown, Wallace. *The Good Americans: Loyalists in the American Revolution*. New York: Morrow, 1969.

Brumwell, Stephen. *George Washington: Gentleman Warrior*. New York: Quercus, 2012.

Burke, Charles T. "The First Traitor." Watertown Papers, 1970. A collection of historical articles held by the Watertown Free Library, Watertown, MA.

Burnett, Edmund C. "Ciphers of the Revolutionary Period." *American Historical Review* 22 (January 1917).

Butterfield, Lyman H. "Psychological Warfare in 1776: The Jefferson-Franklin Plan to Cause Hessian Defections." *Proceedings of the American Philadelphia Society*, June 1950.

Calhoon, Robert M. *The Loyalists in Revolutionary America, 1760–1781*. New York: Harcourt Brace Jovanovich, 1965.

Campbell, Maria, and James Freeman Clark. *Revolutionary Services and the Civil Life of General William Hull Prepared from His Manuscripts*. New York: Appleton, 1848.

Carp, Benjamin L. *Defiance of the Patriots: The Boston Tea Party and the Making of America*. New Haven, CT: Yale University Press, 2010.

Carter, Clarence E., ed. *The Correspondence of General Thomas Gage*. New York: Krause Reprint Company, 1969.

Castle, Norman, ed. *The Minute Men, 1775–1975*. Southborough, MA: 1977. An unpublished collection of essays of minutemen rosters, etc., from various towns surrounding Boston. Copy available at the library of the Minuteman National Historical Park, Concord, MA.

Central Intelligence Agency. *Intelligence in the War of Independence*. Langley, VA: CIA Public Affairs Office, 2008. Available at www.cia.gov/library/center-for-the-study-of-intelligence/csi-publications/books-and-monographs/intelligence.

Clancy, Herbert J. "The Activities of the British Secret Intelligence in Paris, 1776–1778." PhD thesis, Georgetown University, 1937.

Clark, John. "Letters from Major John Clark, Jr., to General Washington Written during the Occupation of Philadelphia by the British Army." *Bulletin of the Historical Society of Pennsylvania*, no. 1, 1845–47.

Clark, William B. *Ben Franklin's Privateers*. New York: Greenwood, 1956.

Clary, David A. *George Washington's First War: His Early Military Adventures*. New York: Simon & Schuster, 2011.

Clinton, Henry. *Observations on Some Parts of the Answer of Earl Cornwallis to Sir Henry Clinton's Narrative*. Cranbury, NJ: Scholar's Bookshelf, 2005. First published as a pamphlet in 1783.

Crary, Catherine Snell. "The Tory and the Spy: The Double Life of James Rivington." *William and Mary Quarterly* 16, no. 1 (1959): 61–72.

Cuneo, John R. *Robert Rogers of the Rangers*. Oxford: Oxford University Press, 1959.

Custis, George Washington Parke. *Recollections and Private Memoirs of Washington*. Washington, DC: W. H. Moore, 1859.

Daderer, John. *Making Bricks without Straw: Nathanael Greene's Southern Campaigns and Mao Tse-Tung's Mobile War*. Manhattan, KS: Sunflower University Press, 1983.

Daigler, Kenneth A. "In Defense of John Honeyman (and George Washington)." *Studies in Intelligence* 53, no. 4 (2009).

Darrach, Henry. *Lydia Darragh: One of the Heroines of the Revolution*. Philadelphia: City Historical Society of Philadelphia, 1916.

Davis, Burke. *Black Heroes of the American Revolution*. New York: Harcourt Brace Jovanovich, 1976.

Dawson, Henry B. *The Sons of Liberty in New York*. New York: Arno, 1969.

The Deane Papers: Correspondence between Silas Deane, His Brothers and Their Business and Political Associates, 1771–1795, Letter of Instruction, vol. 1. Collections of the Connecticut Historical Society.

Edger, Walter B. *Partisans and Redcoats: The Southern Conflict That Turned the Tide of the American Revolution*. New York: HarperCollins, 2003.

"Edward Bancroft (@ Edwd. Edwards), Estimable Spy." *Studies in Intelligence* 5, no. 1 (Winter 1961), www.cia.gov/library/center-for-the-study-of-intelligence/kent-csi/vol5no1/html/v05i1a07p_0001.htm.

Einstein, Lewis D. *Divided Loyalties: Americans in England during the War of Independence*. London: Cabden-Sanderson, 1933.

Ellis, Joseph. *American Creation: Triumphs and Tragedies at the Founding of the Republic*. New York: Knopf, 2007.

Ferling, John. *The Ascent of George Washington: The Hidden Political Genius of an American Icon*. New York: Bloomsbury, 2009.

Fischer, David Hackett. *Paul Revere's Ride*. New York and Oxford: Oxford University Press, 1994.

———. *Washington's Crossing*. New York and Oxford: Oxford University Press, 2004.

Fitzpatrick, John C., ed. *The Diaries of George Washington 1748–1777*. Cranbury, NJ: Scholar's Bookshelf, 2005. First published 1925.

———, ed. *The Writings of George Washington*, Washington, DC: Government Printing Office, 1931–44.

Fleming, Thomas. *Liberty: The American Revolution*. New York: Viking, 1997.

———. *Washington's Secret War: The Hidden History of Valley Forge*. New York: HarperCollins, 2005.

Flexner, James Thomas. *The Traitor and the Spy: Benedict Arnold and John André*. Boston and Toronto: Little, Brown, 1975. First published 1953.

Force, Peter, ed. *American Archives*: *Consisting of a collection of authentic records, state papers, debates, and letters and other notices of publick affairs, the whole forming a documentary history of the origin and progress of the North American colonies; of the causes and accomplishments of the American Revolution; and of the Constitution of government for the United States, to the final ratification thereof,* 9 vols. Washington, DC: Publisher not indicated, 1837–53. Available at http://dig.lib.niu.edu/amarch/index.html.

French, Allen. *General Gage's Informers : New Material upon Lexington and Concord, Benjamin Thompson as Loyalist, and the Treachery of Benjamin Church, Jr.* Cranbury, NJ: Scholar's Bookshelf, 2005. First published 1932.

Friedman, Richard S. "Benjamin Franklin: Friend of a Friend." CIA: CI Online, Historical Counterintelligence.

Galvin, John R. *The Minute Men: A Compact History of the Defenders of the American Colonies, 1645–1775.* New York: Hawthorn Books 1967.

Golway, Terry. *Washington's Generals: Nathanael Greene and the Triumph of the American Revolution.* New York: Holt, 2005.

Graffagnoni, Kevin J., ed. *Letters from the Frontier: A Sampler from Correspondence of Ethan Allen and His Family.* Isle La Motte, VT: Allen Letters Project, 1995.

Grenier, John. *The First Way of War: American Warmaking on the Frontier.* Cambridge: Cambridge University Press, 2005.

Groh, Lynn. *The Culper Spy Ring.* Philadelphia: Westminster, 1969.

Haiman, Miecislaus. *Kosciuszko in the American Revolution.* New York: Kosciuszko Foundation and the Polish Institute of Arts and Science, 1975.

Hall, Charles S. *Benjamin Tallmadge: Revolutionary Soldier and American Statesman.* New York: Columbia University Press, 1943.

Hatch, Robert M. *Major John André: A Gallant in Spy's Clothing.* Boston: Houghton Mifflin, 1986.

Hempstead, Steven. "The Capture and Execution of Capt. Hale in 1776." *Missouri Republican,* January 18, 1827.

Hendrick, Burton J. *The Lees of Virginia.* Boston: Little, Brown, 1935.

Hinkle, Alice M. *Prince Estabrook, Slave and Soldier.* Lexington, MA: Mount Pleasant Press, 2001.

Honeyman, A.V. D. "An Unwritten Account of a Spy of Washington." *New Jersey History* 85, nos. 3 and 4 (Fall/Winter 1967): 219–24.

Hosmer, Jerome Carter. *The Narrative of General Gage's Spies, March, 1775: With Notes.* Boston: Bostonian Society's Publications, 1912.

Hutchinson, Peter O., ed. *Thomas Hutchinson: The Diary and Letters of His Excellency Thomas Hutchinson, Esq.* Boston: Houghton Mifflin, 1884.

Hutchinson, Thomas. *The History of the Colony and Province of Massachusetts-Bay.* Cambridge, MA: Harvard University Press, 1936.

Hutson, J. "Nathan Hale Revisited: A Tory Account of the Arrest of the First American Spy." *Library of Congress Information Bulletin* (July/August 2003).

Johnson, H. P. *Memoirs of Colonel Benjamin Tallmadge*. New York: Gilles, 1904.

———, ed. *Nathan Hale, 1776: Biography and Memorials*. New Haven, CT: Yale University Press, 1914.

Jones, E. Alfred, ed. "The Journal of Alexander Chesney, a South Carolina Loyalist in the Revolution and After." *Contributions in History and Political Science*, no. 7 (October 30, 1921): 119.

Journals of the Continental Congress, 1774–1789. Washington, DC: Government Printing Office, 1903–37.

Kara, Pierce. "A Revolutionary Masquerade." *Binghamton University History Honor Society Journal of History*, an online journal at www2.binghamton.edu/history/resources/journal-of-history/chronicles-of-james-rivington.

Kite, Elizabeth S. *Beaumarchais and the War of American Independence*. Ithaca, NY: Cornell University Library, 2009. First published 1918.

Kitman, Marvin. *George Washington's Expense Account*. New York: Grove, 2001.

Kleber, Louis C. "Jones Raids Britain." *History Today* 19, no. 4 (April 1969).

Lambert, Robert S. *South Carolina Loyalists in the American Revolution*. Columbia: University of South Carolina Press, 1987.

Lanning, Michael L. *African Americans in the Revolutionary War*. New York: Kensington, 2000.

Lawson, John L. "The Remarkable Mystery of James Rivington, Spy." *Journalism Quarterly* 35, no. 3 (Summer 1958).

Leffman, Henry. *Notes on the Secret Service of the Revolutionary Army Operating in the Neighborhood of Philadelphia*. Philadelphia: City Historical Society of Philadelphia, 1910.

Lemaitre, Georges. *Beaumarchais*. Whitefish, MT: Kessinger, 2005. First published 1949.

Lengel, Edward G. *General George Washington: A Military Life*. New York: Random House, 2005.

Loprieno, Don. *The Enterprise in Contemplation: The Midnight Assault of Stony Point*. Westminster, MD: Heritage Books, 2009.

Macy, Harry Jr. "Robert Townsend, Jr. of New York City." *New York Genealogical and Biographical Record* 126, no. 1 (January 1995).

Massy, Gregory De Van. "A Hero's Life: John Laurens and the American Revolution." PhD diss., 1992, University of South Carolina, UMI Dissertation Services, Ann Arbor, MI.

McCarthy, Linda. "I Keep Me Ears Open." *Studies in Intelligence* 29, no. 4 (Winter 1985).

McLane, Allen. *Allen McLane Papers.* Miscellaneous manuscripts (microfilm). New York Historical Society.

Monaghan, Frank. *John Jay: Defender of Liberty.* New York: Bobbs-Merrill, 1935.

Morgan, Edmund S., ed. *Paul Revere's Three Accounts.* Boston: Massachusetts Historical Society, 1968.

Morris, Richard B., ed. *John Jay: The Making of a Revolutionary: Unpublished Papers, 1745–1780.* New York: Harper & Row, 1975.

———. *Witnesses at the Creation: Hamilton, Madison, Jay, and the Constitution.* New York: Holt, Rinehart & Winston, 1985.

Moultrie, William. *Memoirs of the American Revolution,* vol. 1. New York: David Longworth, 1802.

Mulligan, Luciel M. "Hercules Mulligan, Secret Agent." *Daughters of the American Revolution Magazine,* no. 105 (1971).

Nagy, John A. *Dr. Benjamin Church, Spy.* Yardley, PA: Westholme, 2013.

———. *Invisible Ink: Spycraft of the American Revolution.* Yardley, PA: Westholme, 2010.

———. *Spies in the Continental Capital.* Yardley, PA: Westholme, 2011.

Nash, Gary B. *The Unknown American Revolution: The Unruly Birth of Democracy and the Struggle to Create America.* New York: Viking, 2005.

O'Brien, Michael S. *Hercules Mulligan: Confidential Correspondent of George Washington.* New York: P. J. Kennedy, 1937.

O'Dea, Anna, and Samuel A. Pleasants. "The Case of John Honeyman: Mute Evidence." *New Jersey Historical Society* 84, no. 3 (July 1966); 174–81.

O'Toole, G. J. A. *Honorable Treachery: A History of U.S. Intelligence, Espionage, and Covert Action from the American Revolution to the CIA.* New York: Atlantic Monthly, 1991.

The Papers of George Washington, 1741–1799. Washington, DC: Library of Congress, ongoing.

Patton, Robert H. *Patriot Pirates: The Privateer War for Freedom and Fortune in the American Revolution.* New York: Pantheon, 2008.

Paul, Joel Richard. *Unlikely Allies: How a Merchant, a Playwright, and a Spy Saved the American Revolution.* New York: Riverhead, 2009.

Pearl, Nathalie. "Long Island's Secret Agents of General Washington during the Revolutionary War." *Nassau County Historical Journal* 7, no. 1 (1945).

Pellew, George. *John Jay.* American Statesman Series. New York: Chelsea House, 1997.

Pennypacker, Morton. *General Washington's Spies on Long Island and in New York.* Cranbury, NJ: Scholar's Bookshelf, 2005. First published 1926.

Phelps, M. William. *Nathan Hale: The Life and Death of America's First Spy*. New York: St. Martin's, 2008.

Philbrick, Nathaniel. *Bunker Hill: A City, a Siege, a Revolution*. New York: Viking, 2013.

Pickering, James H. "Enoch Crosby, Secret Agent of the Neutral Ground: His Own Story." *New York History* 47, no. 1 (January 1966).

Potts, James M. *French Covert Action in the American Revolution*. Bloomington, IN: Universe, 2005.

Puls, Mark. *Samuel Adams: Father of the American Revolution*. New York: Palgrave Macmillan, 2006.

Quarles, Benjamin. *The Negro in the American Revolution*. Chapel Hill: University of North Carolina Press, 1961.

Rafalko, Frank J., ed. *A Counterintelligence Reader: American Revolution to World War II*, vol. 1. Washington, DC: National Counterintelligence Executive, n.d.

Randall, William Sterne. *Benedict Arnold: Patriot and Traitor*. New York: Morrow, 1990.

Rappleye, Charles. *Robert Morris: Financier of the American Revolution*. New York: Simon & Schuster, 2010.

———. *Sons of Providence: The Brown Brothers, the Slave Trade, and the American Revolution*. New York: Simon & Schuster, 2006.

Reed, John F. "Spy System 1777." Historic Valley Forge, www.ushistory.org/valleyforge/history/spies.html.

Rhodehamel, John H., ed. *The American Revolution: Writings from the War of Independence*. New York: Library of America, 2001.

Rivers, John. *Figaro: The Life of Beaumarchais*. New York: Hutchinson, 1922.

Rose, Alexander. *Washington's Spies: The Story of America's First Spy Ring*. New York: Bantam, 2006.

———. "The Spy Who Never Was: The Strange Case of John Honeyman and Revolutionary War Espionage." *Studies in Intelligence* 52, no. 2 (June 2008).

Rose, P. K. (aka Kenneth A. Daigler). "Founding Fathers of American Intelligence." Center for the Study of Intelligence, Central Intelligence Agency, www.cia.gov/library/center-for-the-study-of-intelligence/csi-publications/books-and-monographs/the-founding-fathers-of-american-intelligence/art-1.html.

Sargent, Winthrop H. *Life and Career of Major John André: Adjutant-General of the British Army in America*. Boston: Ticknor & Fields, 1861.

Sayle, Edward F. "Chronology of a Deception: George Washington's Deception Operations Prior to the Victory at Yorktown." *Studies in Intelligence* 25, no. 2 (Summer 1981).

———. "The Historical Underpinnings of the U.S. Intelligence Community." *International Journal of Intelligence and CounterIntelligence* 1, no. 1 (Spring 1986).

Schaeper, Thomas J. *Edward Bancroft: Scientist, Author, Spy.* New Haven, CT: Yale University Press, 2011.

Schechter, Barnet. *George Washington's America: A Biography through His Maps.* New York: Walker, 2010.

Schroeder, John F. *Maxims of Washington.* Mount Vernon, VA: Mount Vernon Ladies Association, 1947. Schuyler Papers. New York Public Library.

Seymour, George D. *Documentary Life of Nathan Hale: Comprising All Available Official and Private Documents Bearing on the Life of the Patriot.* Whitefish, MT: Kessinger, 2006.

Showman, Richard K., Margaret Cobb, Dennis M. Conrad, Robert E. McCarthy, Joyce Boulin, Noel P. Conlon, and Nathaniel N. Shipton, eds. *The Papers of General Nathanael Greene*, vols. 1–13. Chapel Hill: University of North Carolina Press, 1976–2005.

Smith, Donald L. *John Jay: A Founder of a State and Nation.* New York: Teacher's College Press, Columbia University, 1968.

Smyth, Alben H., ed. *The Writings of Benjamin Franklin.* New York: Macmillan, 1905–7.

Sparks, Jared, ed. *Writings of George Washington*, 12 vols. Boston: American Stationer's Company, 1837.

Stahr, Walter. *John Jay: Founding Father.* New York: Hambledon & London, 2005.

Stevens, Benjamin F. *B. F. Steven's Facsimiles of Manuscripts in European Archives Relating to America 1773–1783, with Descriptions, Editorial Notes, Collations, References and Translations.* London: Matby & Sons, 1889–95.

Stone, William L. "Schuyler's Faithful Spy: An Incident in the Burgoyne Campaign." *Magazine of American History* 2 (July 1878).

Stryker, William S. *The Battles of Trenton and Princeton.* Boston and New York: Houghton Mifflin, 1898.

Stuart, Nancy Rubin. *Defiant Brides: The Untold Story of Two Revolutionary-Era Women and the Radical Men They Married.* Boston: Beacon, 2013.

Sulick, Michael J. *Spying in America: Espionage from the Revolutionary War to the Dawn of the Cold War.* Washington, DC: Georgetown University Press, 2012.

Swartz, John C. *George Washington: The Making of a Young Leader.* Medina, OH: Harbor Bend, 1995.

Sydenham, M. J. "Firing His Majesty's Dockyard: Jack the Painter and the American Mission to France, 1776–1777." *History Today* 16, no. 5 (May 1966).

Syrett, Harold C., ed. *The Papers of Alexander Hamilton*, vol. 2. New York: Columbia University Press, 1961.

Tallmadge, Benjamin. *Memoir of Colonel Benjamin Tallmadge*. New York: Arno, 1968.

Thayer, Theodore. *Nathanael Greene: Strategist of the American Revolution*. New York: Twayne, 1960.

Thompson, Edmund R., ed. *Secret New England: Spies of the American Revolution*. Kennebunk, ME: New England Chapter, Association of Former Intelligence Officers, 1991.

———. "Sleuthing the Trail of Nathan Hale." *Intelligence Quarterly* 2, no. 3 (October 1986).

Uhlendorf, Bernhard A., trans. and ed. *Revolution in America: Confidential Letters and Journals 1776–1784 of the Adjutant General Major Bauermeister of the Hessian Forces*. New Brunswick, NJ: Rutgers University Press, 1957.

Van Alstyne, Richard W. "Great Britain, the War for Independence and the Gathering Storm in Europe, 1775–1778." *Huntington Library Quarterly* 27, no. 4 (August 1964).

Van Doren, Carl. *Benjamin Franklin*. New York: Penguin, 1991. First published 1938.

———. *Secret History of the American Revolution*. New York: Viking, 1941.

Van Tyne, Claude H. "French Aid before the Alliance of 1778." *American Historical Review* 31 (1925).

Walker, Jeffrey B. "The Devil Undone: The Life of Benjamin Church (1734–1778)." PhD diss., Pennsylvania State University, 1977.

Zobel, Hiller B. *The Boston Massacre*. New York: Norton, 1970.

INDEX